September 2014

Dear Nat!

Have fun firing
up your team!

Best
Jacqueline

D0232321

FIRE UP

YOUR TEAM

50 WAYS FOR LEADERS TO CONNECT, COLLABORATE AND CREATE WITH THEIR TEAMS

JACQUELINE THROOP-ROBINSON

iUniverse LLC
Bloomington

FIRE UP YOUR TEAM
50 WAYS FOR LEADERS TO CONNECT, COLLABORATE AND CREATE WITH THEIR TEAMS

Copyright © 2013, 2014 Jacqueline Throop-Robinson.

All rights reserved. No part of this book may be used or reproduced by any means, graphic, electronic, or mechanical, including photocopying, recording, taping or by any information storage retrieval system without the written permission of the publisher except in the case of brief quotations embodied in critical articles and reviews.

Cover graphics by Casey Hooper Designs, Lori Lynch, Lissa Pattillo

iUniverse books may be ordered through booksellers or by contacting:

iUniverse LLC
1663 Liberty Drive
Bloomington, IN 47403
www.iuniverse.com
1-800-Authors (1-800-288-4677)

Because of the dynamic nature of the Internet, any web addresses or links contained in this book may have changed since publication and may no longer be valid. The views expressed in this work are solely those of the author and do not necessarily reflect the views of the publisher, and the publisher hereby disclaims any responsibility for them.

Any people depicted in stock imagery provided by Thinkstock are models, and such images are being used for illustrative purposes only. Certain stock imagery © Thinkstock.

ISBN: 978-1-4917-1597-0 (sc)
ISBN: 978-1-4917-1598-7 (hc)
ISBN: 978-1-4917-1599-4 (e)

Library of Congress Control Number: 2013921855

Printed in the United States of America.

iUniverse rev. date: 02/20/2014

This book is dedicated to my mother, Mary Irene Bourgeois Throop, and my father, Ludger Valmond Dugas Throop.

You are my unwavering guides, and I continue to learn from your wisdom.

CONTENTS

FEEDBACK AND FEEDFORWARD

PROGRESS AND FEARLESSNESS

ACKNOWLEDGMENTS

F irst and foremost, I want to acknowledge my spouse, Evan. His generous love and belief in me provide endless sustenance. I also want to recognize the support of my young children, Taylor and Jamie, who always encourage me with shouts of "Good job, Mama!"

As I wrote this book, I thought often about my first true mentor, Edward (Ted) Scott. He led by example, and his unfailing ability to see the good in people and build from strength, not from what was lacking, has been a lifelong inspiration to me. During this time, I was also mentored by my executive assistant, Kay Stevenson. She was central control for our team, keeping all the moving pieces in order and, most important, functioning as our "wise woman."

I am also indebted to David Jones, my friend and business partner, whose love, empathy and big-heartedness I treasure. As cofounder of PassionWorks! Inc., Dave has shared his work and his life with me, both in good and more difficult times. Our work researching passion has enriched how I see and experience both leadership and life.

Since 2002, I have been attending professional and personal development workshops in Vermont hosted by Robert and Rosalind Fritz. Although I have attended innumerable conferences, seminars and certifications, these remain the most influential. My work as an artist and as a business consultant, combined with my aspiration to live life consciously, found a home within Robert's work. I have done my best to explicitly recognize within the pages of this book his direct influence; however, after a decade of study, some of our ideas are undoubtedly intertwined. I would encourage all readers to discover firsthand Robert Fritz's thought leadership.

I also want to acknowledge two very special and early readers, Roger Bouthillier and Rhonda Caldwell. I am both touched and humbled by their thoughtful and insightful feedback. Also helping me in the early stages was Lissa Pattillo, whose fresh typography heavily influenced the cover design.

Before this book was born, I had an idea that if I could only hide myself away for a week, I could write this book. I approached a colleague,

Jan Fraser, and asked her if she would host a book-writing retreat. A few months later, a handful of novice writers gathered in Lake Las Vegas, in Jan's remarkable condo. Jan's hospitality, enthusiasm, positivity and willingness to share her knowledge created a container within which we all thrived. By the end of that long weekend, we had drafted our books. Jan and each person on the retreat contributed to the creation of this book.

Although clients engage me for leadership development, they inevitably teach me as well. I am blessed to have many wonderful clients, and their relationships mean the world to me. Over the last few years, two clients in particular, Wanda Richardson and Lisa Robinson, have become sources of unflagging support. Your work and love are also in these pages.

And finally, I am thankful for my editor, Susan Macaulay, who truly partnered with me, all the while caregiving for her mother debilitated by Alzheimer's. Despite the challenges she was facing at home, she remained positive, helpful and giving. Her insight and creativity were invaluable in helping me create my vision for this book.

Thank you all. I am ever so grateful.

INTRODUCTION

Welcome to *Fire Up Your Team*, a handbook to help you achieve your full leadership potential. Even if you are already a CEO, a seasoned manager or a natural-born leader, there is still untapped capacity within you—capacity you can unleash using the tools and techniques in this book. I write specifically to your inner leader and invite you to take a deep dive with me as we explore the depths of fearless people leadership.

To say leadership is a journey is a cliché, but it's true. Our leadership evolves and deepens with experience; it is an endless path of personal growth, possibility and learning. I know because I've experienced it myself and coached countless others over the past 30 years. *Fire Up Your Team* is packed full of the most valuable leadership lessons I've learned along the way.

The world has changed a great deal since I began my career several decades ago, when I was still wet behind the ears. Our global economy has become a highly complex, dynamic and interconnected system. Traditional management practices ill-equip us to navigate in its sometimes turbulent, often vast and frequently unexplored waters. The economic crisis of 2008 hammered home our collective vulnerability, and the domino effect of our mutual dependency was disconcerting to say the least. Likewise, our environmental challenges will not be overcome using traditional thinking and problem-solving techniques. The stakes are high: 7 billion people are involved, and time is running short. Today's leaders must learn innovative techniques and skills to manoeuvre successfully in this challenging new reality. The game has changed dramatically, and so have many of the rules.

Chess is commonly referenced in the business world as a metaphor for strategy. It is not unusual to see images of chessboards on marketing materials, in annual reports or in leadership-development workshops. The metaphor is part of how we currently think about strategy. Now imagine the game of chess reconfigured. Consider, for example, what might happen if the rooks and the knights were eliminated and the board was reduced in size by eight squares—one vertical row. Or what if the new game was played on three planes instead of just one? Clearly, yesterday's masters would have to relearn how to play and create new strategies from new experiences.

Old strategies are no longer relevant when a game changes. Playing on a chess *cube*, for example, would be nothing like playing on a chess *board*. And so it is in today's business environment.

Many leaders are discovering that the game they once knew, the one they played successfully and in many cases had completely mastered, has changed so much they barely recognize the rules. Best "old game" practices no longer generate the results they once did. How could they? Worse, the old approaches often create more problems than they solve.

To be successful, today's leaders must be comfortable with the notion that we need to create anew every day—new solutions, new ideas for action, new strategies. We must relinquish our attachment to old rules, old practices, old mental models and insanely detailed action plans. We must trust ourselves and our teams to navigate the turbulent and ever-shifting waters of this new world. We cannot do it alone. One person's thinking, brilliant though it may be, will never be enough to overcome the challenges at hand. We must engage those around us and invite them to collaborate to manifest a bold new global future.

Change requires us to adapt, learn and evolve. It's the essence of survival of the fittest: when our environment changes, we must adapt to survive and then thrive. Past successes do not guarantee future success, because the world and our surroundings are in a constant state of flux. We are offered new challenges and invited to respond in novel, unexpected ways. Leaders who do not understand this natural process put themselves at risk of losing credibility, losing ground and losing followers. Leaders who embrace the edge of chaos and trust in their ability to learn, adapt and thrive hold the key to the future. This kind of leadership demands we live fully in the present, in tune with the changing world, so we can be nimble and ready for what lies ahead. It requires leaders to step beyond their insecurities and fears and to calmly, confidently and unhesitatingly lead their organizations into the unknown territory of the future, one step at a time.

This book aims to better equip you to lead through a sense of play instead of through always having to know; to lead fearlessly and to dive deeply, creating new paradigms to steer through unknown terrain. To achieve all of this, we must leverage the thinking of our right brain. Right-brain thinking gives us access to our imagination and aspirations, our intuition about ideas and people. It's comfortable with ambiguity and thrives on change and uncertainty. It's orientated toward the future, not the past. It prefers collaboration to competition and play to solemnity. Our overreliance on left-brain norms and the underdevelopment of our right-brain competencies limits our effectiveness as leaders.

We all possess the wisdom, the courage and the mental capacity to lead our teams and our companies into a positive and progressive future, albeit a challenging one. We simply need to access the full range of our talents to do so.

The voice of experience

Leadership has always been important to me. My experience has shown how leadership directly affects long-term productivity and profitability. I became a corporate leader in 1989 when I was just 24 years old. (It's hard to believe, even for me, as I look back.) How did it happen? To make a long story short, a forward-thinking head-office director recognized my ability to learn and took a risk, placing me in a mid-manager position. He was committed to building talent and felt I was well-suited to the new management style he wanted to develop.

A couple of years later, another director promoted me into a senior-manager position running a large retail operation on the Canadian west coast. He told me at the time, "You have a lot to learn. I am taking a huge risk. But I believe you can do it. Don't let me down." At the time, I didn't question my ability to do the job. I didn't know what I didn't know, so there was no reason to be intimidated.

When I assumed the role, six managers (four men and two women), ranging in age from 35 to 55, reported to me. I was responsible for more than 100 stores spread over a large geographic area; together they generated millions in annual revenue. The culturally diverse and unionized workforce comprised thousands of employees governed by seven collective agreements. At the time, leadership felt natural to me, and I was undeterred by the scope of the challenge before me. In this case, ignorance was bliss!

I rolled up my sleeves and decided I would be the best area manager the company had ever seen. I was out to prove myself, and I wanted to do it my way. I would operate in a style that was authentic to me and that I felt would get the best results.

- I didn't attempt to memorize the seven collective agreements or learn the mind games so often employed at the bargaining table. I would lead by following my own operating principles and trust my managers to guide me regarding the various collective agreements.
- I refused to micromanage. My managers were seasoned professionals; some of them had strong track records and others were considered weak, but they all knew more than me when it came to running the day-to-day business.
- I pushed back on the corporate culture and challenged the status quo. I questioned everything that did not seem to generate productive activity or behaviours. I believed norms had to serve a clear, positive purpose and that there was no sense in being a yes-man, as the business could not grow without fresh thinking.

I chose instead to do the following:

- I developed solid relationships with all the shop stewards and demonstrated my respect for their mandates and mission. My colleagues thought I was naïve and foolish. The union said I was sitting on the wrong side of the table. Regardless, cooperation gradually emerged and tensions eased.
- I created a container for my managers' success. I saw myself as their facilitator, helping them think through issues and challenges, creating a team culture in which we would celebrate and appreciate our individual and collective achievements. In addition—and perhaps most important—I saw it as my role to be a buffer, so my managers could focus their energy on their own duties and responsibilities rather than worry about office politics.
- I looked at everything with fresh eyes and asked "why" questions. The corporation had a very long tradition and well-entrenched practices that people conducted while on auto-pilot. The policies, procedures, systems created a bureaucracy I found mind-boggling. I fought to release us from this mantle of red tape, thus freeing my managers to serve their customers and their communities.

There are probably many other things I could mention, but many years have passed and these are the strategies that stand out to me in hindsight. From this foundation, I developed an earnest interest in leadership and in creating a way of leading that would allow others to be the best they could be in service of themselves and the company. Each time I led a team, they grew from lurking at the bottom of the pile to being top performers or from being inundated by challenges and problems to forging new paths for the company. In all instances, the leadership strategies and approaches I adopted served me well.

As I worked with my teams, underperformers rose to the challenge, broken systems within our control were fundamentally repaired, and new ways of working were created to fill obvious gaps. Work was challenging and great fun! My goal was to create a container that would allow all individuals to use their talents to thrive, and I share many of these ideas in this book.

This book was also informed by my experience with toxic, destructive and selfish leaders. I reported more than once to people who did not deserve to have another's career or person under their influence. These individuals taught me what *not* to do and about the damage one can do to workers, teams and the company. They allowed the company to lose millions to protect their own interests, they created scapegoats to protect their own yes-men, and they treated their employees as assets, much like equipment, to be discarded on a whim. From these men and women, I learned the damage that self-interest, cronyism and abuse of authority can inflict. It was not a pretty sight.

Through such exposure, I learned to take great care with words and actions and recognize that leadership positions are a privilege, not a right. As a leader, it is difficult to overestimate the impact on those around you of your words, gestures and actions. By virtue of your role and position, you hold power. Do not be careless with it. Appreciate that what you do and say (or what you don't do or don't say) will take on more significance than you may anticipate or expect. Understand that your position on the organizational chart is neutral. Your position does not come with a predetermined set of values. You do. People do. Decide what kind of a leader you want to be and make your work an expression of your values and an opportunity to make the world a better place.

Working with your team in generative and positive ways will enrich your life. The many hours invested become hours passed in meaningful ways, seeing real progress. Work becomes a deeply satisfying experience for you and your team. My consulting practice strives to achieve the same. All of us can be exceptional leaders, either officially or by example. The world can never have too many leaders. We simply need to understand that the leader's journey is a learning journey. This quest sometimes requires us to follow and serve to deepen our self-awareness and mature our practices. Leadership and followership are yin and yang—interconnected and interdependent.

My passion is leadership: leadership that supports people's deepest and truest aspirations, that adds value where and when people least expect it, that rallies people to do what's right and not what's expedient. Great leadership makes the world a better place.

Using this book

Every leader I know wants his or her team to be "fired up"—in positive ways, of course! We want our teams engaged with a desire to achieve. I often hear leaders say of a colleague, employee or team, "What happened to the fire in their belly?" In other words, what happened to the passion and the drive? Many people begin their career or job with great enthusiasm and a belief in its worthiness. Over time, this energy and conviction erode or are blocked. Why? People don't one day decide that caring less and coasting are better than investing emotionally in something that matters. People don't decide "Life is better if a job is just a job" and "I'm better off working in a job that leaves me feeling unfulfilled."

The sense of possibility and the joy of contributing to something that matters, which is present for so many people at the beginning of their journey, can fade with life's challenges. But it doesn't have to. It is within a leader's sphere of influence to keep a team focused on possibility, to work in ways that nurture collaborative endeavour and to appreciate and value effort and progress.

Remember: When people move from engagement to complacency, resistance or burnout, they have reasons for doing so. Something happens that leads to a shift in mindset, which in turn leads to a change in behaviour. It's like a domino effect. Most people don't know how to manage through and beyond this kind of process in constructive and healthy ways. As a leader, it's your job to help, guide and support your followers on their journey—when they are cruising and all is well, when there are bumps in the road, and especially when they need a boost over daunting hurdles that stretch across their path.

To truly move individuals and your team collectively from low engagement to igniting the passion that lies within—or, if you are fortunate enough to have a dynamic team, to sustain the fire in their bellies over the long haul—you as a leader need to fully embrace your role and dive deeply into the guts of engagement. Be forewarned: It can get messy, it can be unclear, and it can be uncomfortable. It can also be playful, joyful and deeply satisfying.

Leadership happens one conversation at a time. I recognized early in my leadership journey that every interaction with another person or with the team as a whole was an opportunity to develop the relationship and support a shared goal. Leaders evolve by becoming adept at working with what happens around them, at all times, and channelling the energy (positive and negative) into constructive and productive aims.

For the record, here's what "firing up your team" is *not*:

- being a motivational speaker like Tony Robbins
- spinning truth to get "buy in"
- manipulating your team so they do what you want

Firing up your team may happen in quiet, subtle ways. Sometimes it will happen through a boisterous, tension-releasing celebration. As a leader, learning to recognize what a person or team needs to create or sustain their engagement is fundamental.

The "50 Ways" format

Leaders are rarely taught the art of leadership. True leadership requires a mindset that's authentic, an ability to breathe life into work, honest conversation and vision to see future possibilities but also to see how far we've come. I have used these four elements to divide this book into four sections.

Part 1: Mindset and Mind Games
Always remember: Your mindset leads your actions. If you don't want to become a manager who plays mind games, your starting point must be to lead yourself from within. Getting your own mindset (attitudes, values, operating principles, beliefs) in order will anchor you in ways that are hard to describe. It will allow you to trust yourself and others. With trust, you will have crucial conversations, collaborate with amazing

results and pilot your team through anything the business or marketplace throws at you. Mind games, which are destructive, will be minimized.

For a leader, looking within is a must. At the end of the day, it is who you are as a person that makes people want to follow. It's not about what you *know* but who you *are*. As you will read, many of the 50 ways will invite you to face yourself and see what there is to be seen so that you can make informed choices about how to lead authentically. This section will help you to ground yourself in the reality of today, ask you to reconsider old paradigms and conventions and open up possibilities for moving forward.

Part 2: Inspiration and Action

This section explores the importance and impact of inspiration. Inspiring an individual or your team requires connecting to aspiration. Sometimes it's helping people become clear on their own true desires; sometimes it's communicating why you believe a goal is meaningful and worthwhile. Your role is to encourage action in service of the aspiration, regardless of the current set of circumstances or situation. Your belief in employees' ability to find the path forward will inspire them to persist in discovering the right avenue, either through existing knowledge or creative thinking.

Leaders with self-motivated teams have won half the battle. Their energy isn't absorbed by constant prodding, incessant following up or uncomfortable performance-review meetings. Investing time and energy in figuring out true desires, building a picture of what they look like and establishing connections between personal aspirations and these desired end goals generates self-sustaining energy and enthusiasm. The trick is not to stifle this energy but to allow it to continue to release and to cultivate it. To do so, you must work with ambiguity, leverage diversity, play with possibility, encourage interconnectivity and, above all else, learn how to be truly present as a conduit for your team's success.

Part 3: Feedback and Feedforward

Most leadership programs and books address performance management and coaching with a focus on feedback. There are many, many programs and books on the market to help leaders with difficult conversations— again, usually involving some type of negative or constructive feedback. Few, however, emphasize the need and challenge of "feedforward," which is delivering core information and positive, useful commentary daily to counteract performance issues and, most importantly, to ground people in how this knowledge will inform and support future action.

Building complete feedback loops and working with them all the time usually eliminates the need for difficult conversations, because poor performance is less likely in environments that create true conditions for success. Leaders who work systematically with feedback loops—normalizing the act of receiving and giving feedback to facilitate others' success and oversee the impact of actions—create a dynamic learning environment that breeds high performance. This section gives you ideas for using both feedback and feedforward to improve leadership practices and overall productivity.

Part 4: Progress and Fearlessness

Seeing one's work as meaningful and believing in the vision and values of one's organization fuels team engagement. Meaning is a cornerstone of passion at work. However, meaning alone is not enough. People need to feel a sense of forward movement or progress. If your team invests a great deal of time and effort in a project, team members will want to see that it has made a difference. They will want to know they have contributed to the organization in a way that moves it into a better position or helps it achieve a milestone.

Often, in organizations, we do not nurture a culture that acknowledges and celebrates progress. We might miss the smaller but significant wins and move on too quickly from enjoying the fruits of our bigger wins. Sometimes we are afraid of making the bold moves that will generate real progress. Tracking progress is essential to maintaining engagement. Often, in order to get progress, leaders must help their teams tackle difficult issues or obstacles, and they must encourage their teams to take risks. Seeing progress or enabling progress in difficult circumstances requires fearless leadership. This section is dedicated to sharing ways leaders can help their teams overcome obstacles fearlessly, foster a sense of forward movement and create ways to mark progress visibly so people don't miss the signs of progress that surround them, even seeing progress in mistakes and disappointments.

A learning strategy

This book acknowledges that leaders today often have little time but want to make time to strengthen their leadership capabilities because they value its power to transform. The book is structured in 50 ways to help resolve this dilemma. I have chunked the content into small digestible bites without compromising the depth of the conversation I want to have with you. In addition, at the beginning of each chapter, you will see an upward arrow ⬀ indicating that I have summarized the main message of the chapter and how the technique described will help you fire up your team. Feel free to read the book from start to finish or flip to a page and start to read anywhere. Each "way" relates to many others, but reading the book in a particular sequence is less important than entering the book at a point of interest and exploring its ideas, tips and techniques.

I have also written for leaders who enjoy exploring different concepts and who want help with practice as well. So each "way" has tips and stories to assist leaders in applying the ideas to their own context. In addition, at the end of each chapter (and sometimes within a chapter), there is an  activity. Each activity is highlighted with a text box with an upward arrow. I suggest you do the activities, even though you may be tempted to skip them when reading. When you think about how the ideas apply to your situation, the learning will kick in. Reflection is the key to gaining benefit from the time you invest in reading.

Since there are 50 ways to read and absorb, you may want to take this book slow to fully profit from it. You may choose to undertake one way per week for a year, for example. At the beginning of the week, take a few minutes to read and do the reflection for one way. Then select one idea to integrate into your practice that week, one thing you can act upon. At the end of the week, make quick notes in the margins of the book to create a learning diary. I guarantee, by the end of the year, you will have grown your leadership practice in a deep and meaningful way.

A final note: The many stories in this book are based on my own leadership or consulting experiences. However, I have changed names and merged similar situations into one story out of respect for client confidentiality.

Enjoy and have fun deepening your leadership skills and knowledge. It's a journey—sometimes intense and serious, but more often exciting and fun!

PART 1:

MINDSET AND MIND GAMES

↗ OVERVIEW

Mindset includes perspective, attitude, beliefs and focus. As such, it sets the foundation for all our choices. Seeing mindset as a choice will give you and your team exceptional capacity. Once you recognize this, you can limit and perhaps even eliminate mind games. Your mindset will be one of your greatest assets or liabilities as a leader. Recognizing this upfront may save you from creating problems for yourself and clear the way for stellar leadership practices.

I define *mind games* as manipulations, in that you are trying to influence how another person reacts, acts or generally behaves. Mind games take many forms, such as withholding positive comments to make a different point or persisting in passive-aggressive behaviour rather than confronting issues directly, or trying to make yourself look good at someone else's expense through one-upmanship. Often this is not completely conscious. Our ulterior motives exist only on the periphery of our understanding unless we step back and take a look at why we are choosing certain behaviours.

Mind games inhibit business, block opportunities and stultify productive aims. Mind games play out through passive aggressive or controlling behaviours, jumping to conclusions and acting upon them, taking sides, playing favourites, deflecting accountability and blaming others or circumstances. Once we have stopped such mind games, we are free to move forward in creative, constructive and collaborative ways, improving exponentially our value and productivity.

With a positive, healthy mindset, we can engage in easy conversation, even on sensitive topics; we can stay open to new, challenging ideas; we can ensure our team and colleagues will trust us, making business flow and resolving any conflicts easily; we can resolve rather than intensify "drama"; and we can sidestep office politics and steer a path that maintains our integrity and upholds our values.

1 | REALLY WANT TO

Valuing your role and seeing how you can add value to each person's work experience will increase *your* engagement. Leadership will become something you want to do instead of something you have to do. It will orientate you to offer your gifts to each team member as well as the team as a whole. Your team will appreciate your commitment and respond in kind. (And yes, they will get fired up!)

I have rarely met a manager who is as engaged in developing her leadership potential as she is in growing or supporting the business. More often than not, leadership responsibilities are seen as a nuisance, as "have to dos" that come with promotion rather than "want to dos" that will further one's career. The vast majority of leaders I know began as technical experts—accountants, actuaries, policy analysts, engineers, journalists—or grew with their companies out of entry-level positions as letter carriers, retail clerks, day-care workers, hairstylists, social workers and the like. As a result, leaders often identify with their professions rather than with the discipline of leadership.

> **LEADERSHIP IS PERSONAL, AND IT BEGINS WITH HOLDING IT AS A PERSONAL VALUE.**

A leader contributes in significant ways to the quality of life of each team member. The team culture the leader establishes will fundamentally define how the team works together and how team members interact with clients and with other teams. Whether you consciously choose to cultivate such influence for yourself or not, it happens by virtue of your role within the organization, you hold this power. Who you are and how you are does matter.

Each and every one of us has tremendous, though frequently unrealized, leadership potential. Unfortunately, many CEOs, seasoned managers and even so-called "natural-born leaders" fail to tap into the full power of their inner leader. The potential of many others remains completely undiscovered.

In most organizations, to progress, we must take on a leadership role, whether we like it or not. Rewards and recognition usually come with increasing management responsibilities, which may or may not be the forte of the rising star. You've likely seen examples in your own organization: the brilliant salesperson who fails miserably as a manager, the recently recruited and exceptionally good "numbers guy" who blows up an intact team in a matter of a few weeks or the brilliant technician who has no idea how to align people to a shared vision. Traditional practices of many organizations set people up for failure and inhibit the business's overall capacity and success, both on the team and organizational levels.

Leadership skills and interests, when recruiting and promoting, are often considered "nice to haves," when they should be essential facets of the hiring and succession-planning process. Dazzled by someone's technical track record, we might overlook a lack of leadership and team-management skills and rue the consequences when the individual fails as a leader. It's time we recognized the value of professional leadership in its own right, separate from an individual's technical knowledge and expertise. Leaders with this recognized value are engaged and successful.

See your role and value as a leader

When I work with leadership teams in workshops and one-on-one coaching environments, I make a point of emphasizing the vital role engaged leadership plays in business success. I know from experience that the first step in helping people tap into their inner leader is to help them be aware that their role as a leader has value to the organization. It may seem obvious that people who manage should understand that leadership is an essential part of their role. But they don't!

Here's a reconstructed conversation I had with a senior executive I'll call Andrew, whom I met at a business networking session in Europe:

> *Me:* Pleased to meet you, Andrew. What do you do?
> *Andrew:* I run an insurance company.
> *Me:* Oh? What are your primary responsibilities? (*A follow-up question to prod him to talk about leadership.*)
> *Andrew:* I ensure our parent-company initiatives are properly executed.

Me:	How do you ensure this? *(I'm still hopeful we'll move into a leadership discussion.)*
Andrew:	Well, I have a great team of people, and they really are the ones that run with it.
Me:	What makes them so great? *(Now we're getting somewhere!)*
Andrew:	They're just really intelligent and ambitious people. I don't have to get too involved.
Me:	So how do you invest your time then? *(Since parent-company initiatives don't seem to be it.)*
Andrew:	Well, mostly I work on high-profile projects that help the company expand.
Me:	Like acquisitions?
Andrew:	Basically, yes.

Based on this short conversation, I guessed that Andrew did not identify with his leadership role. Now that we had become better acquainted, I knew that he felt leadership was something that came with the job and something he had to do, not something he wanted to do. It was an afterthought for him, and one that rarely surfaced as he considered how to best serve the company for which he worked.

Andrew was a seasoned professional in the late stages of his career. As he indicated in our initial conversation, he had a team of intelligent, driven, caring and capable people working for him. But he did not yet understand that he had the choice to enter an exciting phase of his career, one that would enable him to share his unique perspective with his team and shed new light on their challenges and opportunities. He had not yet learned to value his inner leader. He didn't yet know how to bring forth his knowledge, perspective and experience—his offering—to support the members of his senior team on their own leadership journeys.

His team members frequently complained that Andrew didn't give them feedback, even when they pressed him for ways to improve. He simply asserted that they were doing great work. He didn't realize he was actually doing his team members a disservice by withholding his observations and insights. Instead of encouraging them, he disappointed them and unknowingly signalled that he couldn't help them become even more successful. Nothing could be further from the truth. Each of us can help another learn, grow and move toward the next stage of development. The time has come for leaders like Andrew to rise to the occasion—to accept the mantle of leadership and give their teams the gift of their knowledge, expertise and wisdom.

ACTIVITY

Take a moment to reflect on your own mindset about being a leader.

- Are you in the "have to" camp or the "want to" camp?
- On a scale of 1 to 10, moving from "having to" to "wanting to," where would you place yourself?
- How could you make leading more meaningful or purposeful?
- Or, how could you help others fully value their leadership role?

....

....

....

....

2 | BE PLAYFUL

To fire up your team, learn how to play at work. People follow leaders who will play with new ideas and possibilities, explore the merits of other approaches and help them strengthen their rough ideas into solid solutions. Ultimately, leaders who detach themselves from their own preferences in order to serve the greater objectives of the team create an openness that enables them to play with their team and seek better paths forward.

I define *playing* as wanting to learn, as detaching from a particular outcome to discover alternate paths, and as having the courage to explore unfamiliar territory when it's the right thing to do. *Playing* involves you in the ongoing evolution of work and life; *knowing* has you pretending you have already arrived and the journey is complete. Playing takes courage; knowing is the easier route. Leaders limit their effectiveness by standing solidly in the "knower" camp. To lead means to enter uncharted territory, to be an explorer and to spend a lot of time *not* knowing.

Being a knower places a great burden on people. The knower expends vast amounts of energy asserting herself, defending himself, positioning herself, masking himself and engaging in a host of other non-functional (and decidedly non-fun!) energy-draining behaviours. I frequently begin my workshops with a discussion about knowing and learning, because I often work with extremely bright, highly educated people who are paid well for what they know. When I invite them to play rather than to know, they become quite uncomfortable. But this discomfort is a reminder of our attachment to what we know to be true and, if tolerated, helps us consider as-yet-unexplored possibilities. When we relinquish our attachment to what we know, we create the space for new insights—which, in my experience, inevitably support us in the pursuit of our goals and objectives.

> **WHEN WE BECOME TOO FOCUSED ON ENSURING WE KNOW, WE FORGET TO PLAY.**

A friend of mine, Mark, left Canada to teach in Singapore. Initially, he found Singaporean students refreshing compared to those he had taught in Canada. They were punctual, polite, diligent and always did their homework. For a Canadian high-school teacher, it was a dream come true. He couldn't say enough about these wonderful young people. However, as the year progressed, he began to notice a pattern. He would begin to teach a lesson on Shakespeare, perhaps tell an interesting story. Either before or immediately following the story, someone in the class would inevitably say, "Will this be on the exam?" If he said no, he noticed almost immediate disengagement. If he said yes, he noticed many pencils to paper. Over time, he began to draw a relationship between the standard testing practices and the learning habits of his students. Basically, if it wasn't on the test, they weren't interested. What about the sheer joy of learning? What about finding something interesting for its own sake? What about exploring a topic based on your emerging interests?

When leaders become too focused on ensuring that we know, we forget to play. We may become single-minded and lose sight of the broader purpose—in this case, learning. Yes, exams (the evaluation) may be a part of the learning process. However, evaluation is not the point of learning. When we grossly amplify the importance of evaluation, we may do so at the expense of its real purpose.

Sophie learns to play

I often work with teams in crisis and was recently involved in coaching a manager—let's call her Sophie—who led one such team in Asia. Sophie was highly committed to her job, her employer and her personal achievements. She was concerned about her performance and how it impacted the company's bottom line.

The first time we met, Sophie told me, "I care about my success, and I don't want to be set up for failure." She shared this with me in the context of having been mandated to "fix" her team, which had become infamous for complaints, negativity and resistance to change. By then, Sophie had managed the team for five years but had gradually minimized her contact with them.

Based on her own description, the image I had of Sophie was of a highly conscientious employee—someone who got to work early, sat down at her desk and stayed focused on her work, rarely looking up to notice or engage with those around her. She felt it best to let her team "get on with their jobs," in the belief (and possibly the hope) that they were doing what they were supposed to do. Most of the team did not feel connected to Sophie, and as a result, over time, some members had become critical of her when speaking among themselves as well as to others. They often resisted her direction and were known to take actions to undermine her credibility. In essence, there was a complete breakdown of trust.

In addition, Sophie's team had developed a manner of interacting with others in the company that often created conflict. This was most obvious between her team and those teams they worked with daily. This fundamentally unhealthy pattern of behaviour had become accepted as the status quo, and Sophie's team was thought to be filled with "difficult employees." Her avoidance of related issues and the needs of her team was palpable.

Company leadership didn't get involved with Sophie or her team until I challenged the premise of "difficult employees," which implied there was nothing that could be done. Fortunately, the new COO, to whom Sophie reported, wanted a department based on true teamwork and insisted that something could be done.

Let's take a closer look at what was going on. How did Sophie think about herself and her team? What was implied by her comments and observable behaviour?

Sophie was clearly more focused on herself than her team. In her mind, their success was secondary to hers. Had that not been the case, she would have talked more about them and their success when she and I met initially. In truth, she had given up on her team and simply hoped they would perform well enough when doing their daily work.

Her comments also spoke to her fears. Her assertion that "I don't want to be set up for failure" implied that she did not believe she had the knowledge or skills to turn the team around. Had she been more honest with herself, Sophie might have discovered that she felt helpless in the face of the challenge. Instead, she saw herself (not consciously of course) as a victim of circumstance—in this case, of having "difficult employees" on her team.

This helplessness was also reflected in her choice to distance herself from her team by minimizing contact with them and focusing on her own work. She had even created seating arrangements that put her as far away from her team as possible. Yet, when confronted with the task of "fixing" the team, Sophie truly made an effort to see a way forward.

As I challenged many of her beliefs and practices, she tried to take them on and reflect on her choices. She was sometimes resistant and defensive, to be sure, but she also recognized that the status quo was no longer an option. She had to make changes, both on a personal and an organizational level.

One day, after we had worked together for a number of weeks, Sophie said to me, "I get it. I get that I can't be successful without my team. I get that it's my job to work *through* my team, not apart from my team."

From that moment on, Sophie began to create ways to engage her team. It was a journey that began with baby steps, but her acceptance of her true leadership role and her own accountability for the dysfunction were the foundation for change and action. She gave up what she "knew" about her team, which also meant she had to give up the need to be right. When she adopted this learning mindset and began to play with other possibilities, she was able to discover another path to success. In the long term, her leadership work would benefit not only herself but also every member of her team. By investing in her own growth and learning to use play to become a better leader, Sophie was doing right to the benefit of all.

I have a great deal of respect for Sophie. She made a fundamental and smart leadership choice: she chose to play rather than to know. When someone places a very high value on knowing, she has come to over-rely on her expertise and believes her credibility depends on her having the answers. Her self-esteem requires her to be right even at the expense of properly considering another's views.

Sophie courageously chose to engage in a learning process and step into the challenge. Had Sophie adopted the attitude of a knower, she would have asserted that her management choices had been, and continued to be, appropriate. She would have been indignant that others were asking her to change her approach. She would have insisted she knew her team best, knew their capabilities and practices and knew she was managing them to their full potential. But Sophie did very little of that. She chose to play.

Understand that you do not need to always know. People don't follow you because you are always right. In fact, when you present yourself as always knowing the right way forward or having the answers to all problems, your team performance will ultimately suffer, as no one wants to hang out with a know-it-all. As a leader, this is a sure-fire way to isolate yourself from your team, as Sophie did. A team labeled as "resistant to change" and "difficult," in my experience, is a frustrated team, made up of people who feel their voice has not been heard and so have given up trying to engage the leader in a different way forward. The team has retracted and feels deflated.

Knowing and playing in life

Looking beyond this specific case study, let's consider how we have been groomed to approach the world. In general, are we encouraged to see the world through play-filled eyes or through the eyes of one who knows? Most of my workshop attendees, upon reflection, say they have learned to value the idea of knowing over playing. Just think about most education systems. What is emphasized and recognized? Knowing the right answers, of course!

Think back to your earliest school days. The teacher stands at the front of the room, tests the class for knowledge, sees who will raise (or not raise) a hand in response, praises those who get it right for their knowledge and encourages those who got it wrong to study harder.

We reward the right answers. We put a glowing spotlight on those who know and admonish those who don't.

Play is especially important for building our knowledge. Play allows us to engage with existing ideas and think beyond them. Play allows us to begin from the place of "not knowing" so our views are not clouded by current paradigms and biases.

One of the greatest lessons I learned in art school (art is one of my other passions) is to embrace my playful side. When I did, unexpected and often wonderful things emerged. "What if I added this to the sculpture?" "What if I took these two images and combined them?" What-if experimentation allows the person who plays to engage fully in rich, juicy and fruitful exploration in which new possibilities inevitably emerge.

When we stay solidly in the knower camp, we often miss seeing the full spectrum of possibilities and opportunities that surround our work and us. A player is a lifelong learner who is confident that she will be able to learn what she needs to know or do to move forward in her work and her life. When we learn, we often become fearless, because as we learn, we experience our own capacity to respond, grow and adapt to emerging challenges or changing environments. Not knowing or fully understanding everything is no longer a problem. It becomes a non-issue because of our ability to engage in meaningful ways, generate new insights and create new things becomes the foundation of our success.

ACTIVITY

Reflect on the notion of play:

- In what ways have your experiences supported playing or entrenched you in needing to know?
- To what extent are you comfortable with not knowing?
- How might play and creating build more resilient leaders and businesses?

....

....

....

ACTIVITY

Try out the what-if approach to help develop the habit of play. This question helps us explore possibility in an experimental, playful way.

- What if we tried . . .?
- What if we combined . . .?
- What if we eliminated . . .?
- What if we reversed . . .?

....

....

....

3 | RETHINK REWARDS

To fire up your team, avoid relying on rewards. Such incentives instantly create a competitive environment. They set up a barrier to thinking creatively, prevent collaboration and ultimately produce ordinary results. Rewards become obstacles to high meaning (working for its own sake, not just because you might get a bonus) and to true progress (working with others to create the best possible result rather than working independently to get all the credit).

Traditional rewards appeal to people who identify with knowing, because rewards reinforce the idea that you have arrived and the learning journey is complete. Knowers are drawn to participate in a "know-compete-reward" triangle. This is an unfortunate by-product of the traditional education system: *I am rewarded if I know. I am special if I get an A. My self-esteem is boosted if I make the honour roll. I get a scholarship if I get the highest average.*

> **RELEASE YOURSELF FROM THE BURDEN OF COMPETITION.**

We consistently link gaining knowledge with getting a reward. We are also taught that rewards are in short supply, and we structure things to prove this hypothesis by only having one prize or limiting the scope or range of possibilities. A bell curve, for example, creates a structure that separates the elite from the average from the stragglers. If I want success, I have to show how much I know. More important, I have to show I know more than you. Competition naturally ensues.

Alfie Kohn, the author of many books including *Punished by Rewards: The Trouble with Gold Stars, Incentive Plans, A's, Praise, and Other Bribes* (1999) and *No Contest: The Case Against Competition* (2006), lobbies against offering rewards for acquiring knowledge, on the basis that it distracts us from engaging in excellence and focuses us instead on competing for rewards by beating our classmates and teammates. In other words, rewards and competition can create environments that prevent collaboration, promote compliance and produce inferior results.

Competition also nurtures fear. If I don't get it right, I might lose my job. If I don't know how to solve this problem, I risk being demoted and/or not getting the bonus that helps pay for my kids' education. If I admit to making a mistake, I will look bad and hurt my reputation and chances of promotion. So I must, at all costs, show what I know, defend my choices and play it safe. After all, it's a game of survival of the fittest in which we must compete for limited resources and rewards.

When your team is motivated instead by a desire to explore new ideas without having to fear loss—when they're playing—the dynamic shifts from one of scarcity to one of abundance. Whereas competition is structured to award only one prize (say, student of the year), we might equally choose to create a different game in which everyone can achieve (all students in the class receive recognition for their contribution and strengths). In this version of the game, prizes are abundant, not scarce. Ultimately, the motivator is not the external reward. Instead, we learn to focus on our intrinsic motivator: the satisfaction that comes from learning, growing and developing.

Or perhaps the goal is not to see who can score the most points with the boss but how the team can create something that surpasses what each individual can produce on his or her own. The prize is overall forward movement for all participants. No one wins and no one loses; these terms are no longer relevant. Everyone advances and benefits. Progress is its own reward.

Activity

Reflect on the role rewards play in your life.

- Are external rewards (motivators) important to you? Why?
- How do you view these rewards? What does it say about you if you succeed in attaining a reward? What does it say about you if you fail to get one?
- To what extent have your decisions been influenced by the pursuit of external rewards versus true wants/aspirations?
- How attached are you to the belief that competition holds intrinsic value?
- What would change if you equally valued cooperation and intrinsic rewards?

....

....

....

4 | LET MORE BE MORE

Fire up your team. Disrupt the idea that competition is good and encourage your team to see ways forward in which no one loses and everyone gains. The world exists in a richer dimension than either/or. Our lives are not binary code of have/have not, win/lose, right/wrong. We live within a spectrum of possibility, a world of abundance. When your team adopts this orientation, they will share their talent, energy and support, knowing their gifts will be reciprocated.

If we accept that rewards and competition create barriers to collaboration, promote compliance and produce inferior results (as discussed in "Rethink Rewards"), it makes sense to challenge their continued use. What if, instead of focusing on scarcity, we took the idea of abundance more seriously? Merriam-Webster.com defines *scarcity* as "want of provisions for the support of life" and *abundance* as "an ample quantity: profusion." Think about those definitions for a minute. Take another few minutes to consider how attitudes around scarcity and abundance impact the way we work.

> **WE REALIZE ABUNDANCE WHEN WE UNDERSTAND OUR CAPACITY TO CREATE.**

There is a distinction between objective reality (facts) and our orientation or mindset. It may be true, for example, that IT professionals are a scarce resource in your marketplace. It is a fact, easily quantifiable. Or maybe water is abundant in your region. Again, an easily substantiated fact. However, this discussion on scarcity and abundance is in the context of how we choose to see the world and run our lives. Let's look at an example showing the two perspectives of a consultant.

- **Scarcity:** There are many consultants in my marketplace, and I get nervous about this and feel threatened by so much competition. I might see the work as scarce and difficult to attain and therefore be very protective of my clients, trying to keep as much work for myself as possible. I may be careful about sharing information even with clients, as they might not need me as much, or I might have a tendency to put down other consultants as I try to differentiate myself in the market.

- **Abundance:** There are several hundred consultants in my marketplace, and we each have our unique strengths and competencies. There is a great deal of potential to collaborate on large-scale projects that require a multitude of skills. If I share what I know with my clients, my role might evolve so that I could do even more interesting work. I might even promote other consultants who could complement my work. There is abundance for everyone. We need not fear and see the world as a competition.

Let's compare and contrast the two mindsets.

Scarcity	Abundance
If I want to get ahead, I need to fight for my share.	There is plenty out there for everybody.
There's only so much available. The pie is only so big.	There are many ingredients available to use, and we can make many types of desserts.
If I win, someone else has to lose, and vice versa.	We can both win or advance or progress.
It's either/or. You have to choose between this and that.	It can be both (and more!). There are many possible alternatives and solutions.
I need to hold and defend my position.	It's okay to explore divergent points of view to see what might emerge.
I am always comparing myself to others to see how I measure up. I need to be better than others in my chosen field.	I appreciate others' strengths. If someone else is better than me at something, I do not feel less valued or less valuable.

We need to focus on outdoing the competition within the bounds of what is acceptable.	We have a never-ending ability to create and generate new ideas, markets and products.
I need to take credit, hold power and make sure I look good.	I am happy to share credit, power and/or profit.
If someone else succeeds, it makes me wonder if there might be less for me.	I am genuinely happy for another's success.

When we compete, we implicitly decide someone must lose and someone must win. As there is only one prize, we must oppose each other in pursuit of it. I win; you lose. You win; I lose. The foundation of this type of thinking is scarcity: there is one prize, there are many competitors, and we fight it out to see who will be successful. The definition of scarcity suggests that when resources are lacking, our very survival (physical, psychological and/or emotional) is threatened. When we feel our survival is at stake, we go into "fight, flight or freeze" mode—a reactionary rather than a creative orientation.

When you google "abundance mentality," Stephen Covey's *The 7 Habits of Highly Effective People* (1989) usually tops the list. Covey has revitalized the concept of abundance over the last several decades. However, the notion itself is ancient: from Epicurus's focus on what we have to Buddha's abundance and happiness philosophy to Christ's multiplication of the loaves and fish, the idea of living life with an attitude of abundance has been with us for eons. Yet here in the 21st century, we remain entrenched in a detrimental, competition-centric paradigm.

I have seen scarcity mentality at play in dozens of companies. Sometimes it leads to a battle (as in union versus management negotiations), sometimes to withdrawal ("I give up on what I truly want because I don't believe I can achieve it if I'm competing with others I view as more talented"). Both are examples of "fight or flight" and are part of the lose/win dynamic. Many examples can be found:

- Executives vie for power and influence: "If I don't show that I'm more business savvy than my colleagues, I might not get the recognition I deserve."

- Managers fight among themselves for resources: "I need to fight for what we need or else we won't be able to meet my objectives."
- Teams work in silos to ensure they meet their targets, regardless of other teams' needs: "We need to look after our own goals first. If we have time or additional resources, we can help others later."
- Employees give up on progressing their careers: "I can't compete here; it's not a level playing field."

In every case, the company loses. People expend time and energy on internal battles rather than on building the business, departments prioritize poorly and miss opportunities to do what's best for clients, and unexploited talent and underdeveloped potential languish in organizational backwaters.

None of these scenarios is extraordinary; we've all experienced at least one of them at some time or another. Others among us have experienced all of them at once. Every day, most organizations waste time and energy competing when an attitude of abundance productively applied to tasks, goals, issues and opportunities could focus efforts and align teams to support what matters most to the organization.

In essence, an abundance mentality sees the world as expansive and able to accommodate creative endeavour. Through seeing how we can complement and augment what has already been created, we cease to see others as competitors who might eat all the pie before we get to the table. We can always create a space for ourselves when we work with what already exists to make further meaningful contributions.

Try these practical things you can do to help your team see abundantly:

- Encourage team members to focus on strengths rather than what they lack compared to others.
- Help them focus on how they can support and build upon the work of other teams to achieve their own goals and objectives.
- Guide them to see where there is synergy to minimize competition for resources.
- Urge them to publicly acknowledge and celebrate others' success.
- Walk the talk by excelling at conflict management. Let your team see you exploring other points of view rather than adamantly defending your own to demonstrate how new and more satisfying solutions emerge when you detach and properly consider and build on others' ideas.

ACTIVITY

Think about your workplace.

- What evidence do you see of a scarcity mentality?
- What evidence do you see of an abundance mentality?
- As a leader, how could you promote a focus on abundance?
- How could you nurture more cooperation?

....

....

....

5 | COLLABORATE YOUR WAY TO ABUNDANCE

Fire up your team by embracing the wisdom of Aristotle, spoken centuries ago: "The whole is greater than the sum of its parts." Recognize the value each team member can offer, and create a collaborative environment in support of the team and its goals.

The strength of competition as a paradigm can make discussions around authentic collaboration challenging. On some level, the notion of the inherent naturalness (if not goodness) of competition is sacred to many in business and in life.

The acceptance of competition as the natural order of things translates into an acceptance of competitive practices at all levels of a company. Mostly, people present a defense of competition and often cite Darwin and "the survival of the fittest" argument as proof that you must compete to survive. Few realize that survival, according to Darwin, is based on the ability to adapt versus ability to overpower. People want to believe competition is natural rather than entertain the possibility that competition is manufactured as a cultural construct that can be challenged and changed.

Currently, most of my clients value collaboration; however, many apply it in rather limited ways. For example, while they may see that it would be good to collaborate across business units for employee-engagement initiatives and specific problems, rarely would they see the benefit of collaborating with other companies in a similar line of business around client needs. Even internally, departments often compete rather than collaborate with each other, fighting for and focusing on their own resource requirements. I also frequently see competitive behaviours between the head office and the field. The language itself is oppositional, with "we" and "they" references peppering every conversation—and

> **COMPETITION IS SO INSTITUTIONALIZED, WE CAN SCARCELY IMAGINE IT ANOTHER WAY.**

each person or group seeing their own position as the "right" one, the "knowing" one.

Although it's not about collaboration, *Blue Ocean Strategy*, a book written by W. Chan Kim and Renée Mauborgne (2005), does assert that we are mesmerized by all things competitive: competitive analysis, competitive advantage, competitive intelligence, competitive pricing. We also promote internal competition: sales competitions, bonus schemes and often budgeting policies and processes. This mindset is so much a part of how we think that we can hardly imagine functioning without this concept as a central tenet of our business models.

The authors of *Blue Ocean Strategy* encourage us to create a new space for ourselves, an uncontested space, through strategic thinking that does not use competition as a benchmark—thereby limiting our creativity and innovation—but instead works independently to create new markets. They propose blue-ocean space as an alternative to a highly competitive space where competitors focus on attacking each other, bloodying the waters surrounding all.

Merriam-Webster defines *collaboration* as "working together to achieve something an individual could not achieve on his/her own, something that has never been done identically before." Collaboration is a collective, creative activity best engaged in by those who play versus those who want to always know.

In the last year, I have been collaborating with other seasoned professionals in the learning and development field, and it has been an amazing experience. I have often seen senior practitioners compete with each other to secure their rank or validate their experience or keep the status quo and stay within their comfort zone. We agreed to instead work collaboratively, accepting all ideas and working with all ideas to see where they would lead. In the end, all ideas became everyone's ideas as we talked them through and explored how they might work. We didn't keep all ideas, as some didn't hold our interest while others became more and more rich.

Accepting another's idea often means moving forward without carrying one of your ideas forward, and that can be hard to do. But once you learn that in playing with someone else's idea you create a new idea, letting go is really about creating space for something new. When we're working collaboratively, this something else is a co-creation that holds the best you all have to give and is inevitably better than the best any one of you has to give.

Recently, a client of mine decided to conduct business planning in a collaborative manner rather than in silos. In order to achieve this, it was important to create an overall goal and focus to keep each business unit from looking solely at its own products. The broader focus forced the business heads to look at how various products interacted in the marketplace from the consumer's point of view. They also looked at profitability by customer rather than by product.

This collaborative process led the VPs to think at a corporate level rather than a business level, which in turn stimulated many new ways of tackling issues as well as opportunities. It also helped them to share resources, change their servicing model and give up some of their own margin to gain business elsewhere in the company. At the end of the day, the business-planning process was far more enjoyable for all involved, as they deepened their knowledge of the other departments' business, solidified cross-company relationships and most importantly created a cohesive business plan for the forthcoming year.

To free ourselves from the limitations of this competitive paradigm, we can look for an alternative path, enabling us to think more constructively and creatively together, play collectively as a team and learn as a team. If we bring collaboration into the heart of our business, from how we work together to how we work with external bodies to how we play in the marketplace, we will see new possibilities.

ACTIVITY

Think about your current interactions.

- Do you see signs of competition among departments?
- Are you overly focused on your competitors rather than your customers?
- As a leader, how could you reframe discussions to foster collaboration?

....

....

....

....

6 | NURTURE GREAT RELATIONSHIPS

You can fire up your team by developing a meaningful relationship with each of its members. Let each person know you so he or she can trust you. Once trust is established, your ability to deliver results will dramatically increase. Your team will interact with you and each other in ways that accelerate how work gets done. Collaboration is much easier with a foundation of trust. Anxiety, hesitation and watchfulness will evaporate as confidence, assurance and faith fuel productive action. Mind games will be replaced by a healthy mindset.

A number of years ago, during a high-level meeting, a senior manager turned to me and asked, "What is the essence of leadership?"

In all my years of consulting, no one had ever asked me this question, so I didn't have a ready-made response. I paused, considered and let my answer surface. What came forth was a single word: "Relationships."

Leadership requires follower-ship. You can't have a leader without at least one follower. You can't escape the fact that this is a relationship.

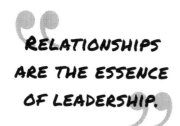

RELATIONSHIPS ARE THE ESSENCE OF LEADERSHIP.

However, we rarely spend time at work talking about the quality of our primary relationships. We focus instead on business plans or urgent "to do" matters. We do not invest much time, effort or financial resources in meaningful, substantial relationship-building. It's true that traditional team-building workshops aspire to improve relationships. Yet because they often do not deal with real, critical workplace issues and team-based challenges, more often than not they fall short of that objective.

As all of us know, significant relationships require attention and nurturing to remain healthy. We are accustomed to making this kind of investment in our personal lives (and if we don't, we suffer the consequences!), but we shy away from discussing the importance of relationships in the workplace. We have created, in most business segments, a left-brain business culture—one that focuses on facts, data and logic rather than people, emotions and relationships. We hesitate to get too touchy-feely. The very idea of having an intimate, relationship-based conversation at work makes most managers exceedingly uncomfortable. Nevertheless, to create the kind of teams and workplaces that produce innovative products and exceptional service, we need strong internal and external relationships. Without them, we lack the rich, fertile ground from which to cross-fertilize, grow and, ultimately, succeed.

Leaders need to nurture existing relationships, attend to those that are more difficult and build new ones, so that the organizational leader/follower collaboration can be brought to full fruition. Doing all of these things requires a certain level of EQ—emotional intelligence, the ability to navigate the emotional terrain of your organization. Mindset is a key component of emotional intelligence. For example, how you choose to see people will determine how you respond to them and therefore will dictate the quality of your relationship. If I believe people are inherently greedy and are out to get what they can, I will tend to treat them suspiciously and behave very cautiously around them, withholding information or help. Such behaviour will not easily build a relationship. On the other hand, if I believe people want to make meaningful contributions during their lifetime, I will respond quite differently. I will trust them and look for ways to support or collaborate.

In his book *Emotional Intelligence* (1995), Daniel Goleman shares research that clearly demonstrates the need to "do" relationships well. Technical knowledge and skills undoubtedly support success, but their relevance diminishes the higher up the corporate ladder one climbs. The more senior or more pivotal your role, the more your non-technical knowledge, skills and perspective become important.

In a research project with a manufacturing company, Goleman was able to correlate a business's productivity with leadership EQ, he wrote in a January 1988 article for the *Harvard Business Review* entitled "What Makes a Great Leader?" He found that, on average, emotionally intelligent managers—those who are self-aware, can self-regulate, are self-motivated, are empathic and have strong social skills—realized 40 percent greater productivity than their counterparts who relied more on their technical expertise. This is a phenomenal result, one we must not ignore if we care about our people and our business success.

ACTIVITY

Talk about it! Relationships are built on how you engage. Take time to figure out how it's working. Is the relationship being supported or damaged?

- With each employee, discuss how the work gets done between you. What works well? Could anything improve to make working together easier?
- What about communications? Does how you currently share information, discuss ideas and gather input work for your employee?
- What about decision-making? Is the current process working for the employee? Does it preserve trust and respect from their point of view?

....

....

....

7 | THINK EQ

At the heart of firing up your team is your willingness and ability to direct emotions productively. Emotion, when channelled appropriately, creates an unstoppable team. Roll up your sleeves and dive in. Stay connected with your team's emotional landscape and work with them where they are emotionally—it will lead to great relationships and meaningful progress for individual members and the business.

Emotional intelligence is the measure of one's ability to navigate the emotional terrain of one's life. In the case of a business leader, it's the ability to navigate the emotional terrain of his organization and/ or workplace. It is not being touchy-feely. It is being able to read a room, knowing when to hug a coworker and when not to, understanding when to address something publicly in the moment or privately at a later time and much more.

"EMOTIONS UNDERPIN SUCCESS."

I often tell my workshop participants, "We like to think we spend most of our time living in our rational, logical, left-brain mind. However, the reality is we are always experiencing emotions along with thought. The two are continually at play as we go about our day: thoughts and emotions, ebbing and flowing, as we take on the day's challenges and tasks."

As much as we might like to, we cannot shut off our emotions when we get to work. They are a part of who we are, how we function and what we need to draw upon to successfully achieve our deepest aspirations.

- The *passion* we have for our products instils confidence in our customers.
- The *caring* we show our employees generates loyalty.
- The *hopefulness* we share with colleagues uplifts them, especially in challenging times. When people are hopeful, they are more receptive to seeing solutions; but without hope, they won't even look for them.

Handling these emotions and channelling them helps your team and boosts their productivity.

Activity

What other examples of emotions in the workplace can you think of?

....

....

....

Emotions underpin success. Just because we don't stop to see it and appreciate it surely doesn't mean it isn't so. We need emotions in the workplace to create experiences of which we can be proud and create the great relationships important to success. We also need to know how to handle negative emotions so they're not destructive.

To be effective, today's leaders must be comfortable navigating the emotional aspects of their organizations to develop relationships necessary for accepting change, supporting key decisions and fostering healthy exchanges—all of which make work fulfilling and successful, both for leaders and their teams. Reticence to wander from the rational, logical and well-travelled road to the less familiar but extremely powerful intuitive, sensing path inhibits success and depresses organizational growth, particularly when it occurs at the most senior levels.

Take senior manager David, for example: he is completely unaware that he needs to address the hopes and fears of his team as the broader organization transitions through a significant corporate downsizing. He continues to run his programs and manage his department as if it is business as usual. In the meantime, his team is crumbling around him. Some members are physically unwell, others are experiencing panic attacks, and a handful are planning an escape route. Ignoring the emotional landscape will be David's downfall if he doesn't take action soon. His team's effectiveness is already compromised, and their poor performance will eventually call his leadership into question.

In such a situation, doing nothing is the worst option. Basic actions can be powerful—for example, sitting down with the team to talk about the situation and how people are feeling about it. In addition, David could share what he knows and be upfront about what he doesn't know. He can get team members to talk about ways to better cope with the uncertainty and help them build resilience. David could reach out for help from experts in change management, either from within his HR department or through external resources. In my experience, just sitting down and talking human-to-human goes a long way all by itself.

Or consider Gordon, a CEO so focused on pleasing the board of directors that he neglects the needs of his own team. Gordon has fallen into a trap: he accepts any and all board challenges to demonstrate his capability. He continually presses his VPs to do more with less and does nothing to demonstrate the extent to which he values each of them. Instead, he frequently cuts off discussions to assert his own conclusions, shows impatience when others try to understand the issue or point of view presented and shoots from the hip when pressured to act, making hasty decisions and using reactionary tactics rather than slowing down to listen to his team and accept their advice.

After months of this, his team is stressed, demotivated and quite frankly fed up. Some VPs are beginning to withhold to preserve their energy and sense of well-being, while others are burning out. Either way, the energy needed to sustain healthy growth is in jeopardy. Gordon needs to tune into his VP team's frustrations and make adjustments. He can do this by checking in with individuals and the team collectively, asking for feedback.

If Gordon proves that he can accept feedback and work with the information constructively, people will be forthcoming. Gordon can also stop worrying about demonstrating his own talents and refocus on bringing his team together to help him, ensuring that he properly considers their suggestions, shares the spotlight and rewards accordingly. In the end, Gordon will feel more supported through stronger relationships, and the company will benefit from diverse thinking and input—a better-quality result that is supported and therefore sustainable.

Many researchers have collected substantive data and demonstrated the value of high emotional intelligence. Leaders who are unable to handle this dimension of leadership must take a deep breath and muster the courage to develop the skills required to shift easily between logical, analytical thinking and emotional awareness and connection. Aspiring leaders take note: the more senior or more pivotal your role, the more your non-technical knowledge, skills and perspective become important to attaining strong performance.

ACTIVITY

What challenging current situation would improve if you were able to navigate the emotional landscape intelligently?

....

....

....

8 | DEEP DIVE INTO AUTHENTIC CONVERSATIONS

To fire up your team, talk to them! Really talk. Communication is the foundation of relationship and builds trust. When you demonstrate what you value, like the importance of communication, you are revealing your mindset, translating it into practice and bringing an awareness to it.

You likely know what matters most to your team collectively as well as to individual members. Don't leave this unspoken. Make it a normal part of your conversation. Talk purpose. Talk aspiration. Talk appreciation. And when times are tough, don't fear the elephant in the room. Everyone knows it's there. As the leader, be courageous, acknowledge it and lead a thoughtful discussion about it. Your team will feel unburdened knowing there are no taboo subjects, only topics that may require gentle handling. When you make it real, people will feel inspired.

> **A LEADER'S ROLE IS TO STIMULATE MEANINGFUL, PRODUCTIVE CONVERSATION.**

How often have you seen people speaking around what they really *ought* to be talking about? Over and over again, I have witnessed people fail to raise topics that might get emotional, bring up concerns requiring sustained time and effort to resolve or advocate for ideas that might be at odds with beloved systems or beliefs. When I challenge the superficiality of my clients' communications, the most common response is, "Why can't we just focus on the work and get on with it?"

Seriously? This is the biggest cop-out I've ever heard. People hide behind the veneer of tasks at hand, action plans and business-as-usual instead of tackling the big issues underlying them. What they are *really* saying is, "I don't have the skills and know-how to sort this out, so I'm going to pretend I don't have to. Anyway, our performance is good enough. We're successful."

On one level, this may be true. There are a lot of mediocre companies and leaders out there. A good number survive, and many are successful in specific ways. But they could be thriving beyond their wildest dreams.

During my years managing teams, I was always amazed by the way authentic conversation always took us to another level. I remember at one strategic retreat, we were nearing the end and were finalizing our agreed-upon actions when I noticed two team members becoming restless and even looking disgruntled. We only had an hour left in the retreat, and we were really just adding the finishing touches. I was very keen to wrap it up and get going on implementing our great ideas. However, I knew by looking at the body language and facial expressions of these two team members that there was concern and even irritation brewing beneath the surface.

I knew that if I pushed forward, it would mean proceeding without the true and full support of two team members, so I stopped the facilitator and said, "Sue and Tom, I can see you are struggling with our plan. Can you tell me more?"

They proceeded to say that although the plan we had created was good, they felt we had passed on some of the best ideas and had not spent enough time trying to figure out how to make them work. They felt we had chickened out and were going to miss some great opportunities to increase our impact.

So with less than an hour left in the session, we opened up the conversation again and revisited the ideas they felt we had too quickly abandoned. I encouraged everyone not to see this as backtracking but as looking more closely to possibly mine a golden nugget.

Everyone took a deep breath, refocused and began to discuss in earnest the two abandoned ideas. Collaboration is a wonderful thing! Within the hour, we had reshaped our plan and incorporated two new and workable ideas that we felt would take our business to the next level. If I had chosen, as the leader, to ignore the signals these two team members were sending me, we would have missed out on an opportunity to dig deeper for workable solutions, communicate more clearly and build something special together.

Avoidance of all kinds is, more often than not, the result of a fearful mindset: fear one might not be able to handle what ensues, fear it might make things worse rather than better, fear it will take too much time and effort, fear it will put other goals at risk, fear that _____ (you fill in the blank). When we say, "It's good enough," essentially we're saying we don't want to take on the challenge. We don't want to put the status quo at risk. But why not? Perhaps because the status quo is known whereas the results of addressing inefficacy are still unknown.

Making conversation safe versus playing it safe

We have been conditioned to know rather than explore, calculate rather than intuit and manage risk rather than effect change. We want to play it safe rather than make conversation safe and communicate in ways that will free us to do greater things. For many of us, the latter feels like an incredible risk, and rather than embrace it, we shy away from it. As Marianne Williamson, author and founder of the Peace Alliance, writes in her book *A Return to Love* (1996): "Our deepest fear is not that we are inadequate. Our deepest fear is that we are powerful beyond measure. It is our light, not our darkness, that most frightens us."

To be fair, most of us haven't developed the skills to navigate complex, emotional and/or abstract conversations. That's why many of the tools in this book strive to support the requisite skills in a leadership context. At its core, being a leader is about being an explorer and spending a lot of time *not* knowing. That may sound counterintuitive, but it's a fact. We will always know less than what is available to know.

What does this have to do with having conversations? In my experience, leaders often fear exploring—"playing"—through real, meaningful conversations. Talk to a leader about business models, strategy, negotiations or tasks, and he is comfortable. Talk to him about his need to give more feedback or address team dysfunction or challenge long-held beliefs, and it's quite another story. The business world does not produce leaders who "deep dive." (Deep diving is a term borrowed from the sport of scuba diving, where deep divers equip themselves—through training, the proper equipment and breathing techniques—to explore the water at great depths, sometimes up to hundreds of feet.)

A number of years ago, a colleague came to me to share that an employee felt I had violated confidentiality. I was surprised but also very concerned, so I spoke to the employee as soon as possible. I simply began by sharing what I had been told and began the conversation by focusing us both on the outcome:

Me: June, I care a great deal about our relationship and your ability to trust me. I don't know what confidence I might have violated, so I would really appreciate hearing about it so we can figure out what happened and what should be done about it.

June: Well, at the meeting we had last week with the other teams, you mentioned to the group that you'd been coaching me. I was uncomfortable with this.

Me: Oh, yes, you're right. I do recall saying that we had worked together to help you address some team issues. Why did that make you uncomfortable?

June: Well, I don't know those other people very well, and I was afraid they would think I was a weak manager and couldn't figure it out on my own.

Me: Ah. Yes, I can see that. Since they don't know your capabilities, they might interpret my helping you as you needing help because you are a weak manager—judging you for accepting support.

June: Yes. And in this company, your reputation is everything. I don't want people forming first impressions of me without all the relevant information.

Me: So why didn't you share that information with the group, since I hadn't made it clear? Why didn't you say something?

June: Hmm . . . I don't know. I guess I was feeling insecure, since they don't know me.

Me: What could you have said?

June: Well, I could have explained the complexity of the situation and why it was so challenging, and I could even have said specifically how you helped.

Me: If you had, how do you think you would have felt compared to how you feel now?

June: I guess I would have been able to alleviate the worry about how they had interpreted your comment. And I guess I wouldn't have been as annoyed with you.

Me: I think you're right. I know you are a strong manager, and I admire you for tackling the tough issues that many other managers fear addressing. I wasn't sensitive to the group dynamics when I made the comment, otherwise I would have taken more care to explain the context. I guess

	if there is a next time, we both could handle the situation differently.
June:	True. I came into this conversation upset with you, but I have actually learned something about myself. Thanks.
Me:	Me too. And, thanks back.

Learning how to listen, ask questions and help another think it through, while owning your own accountability, will enable you to make any conversation safe without playing it safe. In this conversation with June, I could have ignored her concerns. Instead, I told her I was interested in why she felt this way, and when she told me, I did not criticize her for having the feelings or for blaming me.

June didn't see that she'd had an opportunity to turn the incident around. Instead of allowing our conversation to become bogged down in a competitive or negative mindset, I encouraged June to see where she might have done things differently so that going forward, she had more than just an apology. I also took responsibility for my part and shared how I, too, might have acted differently. She now had the tools to create a different outcome, and I had a new awareness. None of this could have occurred without an honest, authentic conversation.

Tips for making a conversation safe
- Don't judge anything the other person says. And if it's about you, don't defend. Simply listen and understand.
- As people speak, they are often sorting things out for themselves as they think it through with you. Help the person you are talking with gain clarity.
- Don't formulate an opinion about what the other person says.
- Step back and be a guide, asking questions that will help the other person share what he or she is thinking and feeling without fear of reprisal or judgment.
- Very importantly, help the other person see his or her personal power.
- If you need to accept accountability for anything, do so unhesitatingly to enable the conversation to progress.

Activity

How can you, as a leader, deep dive into conversations that matter, plumbing depths below the surface?

....

....

....

Build on this list by using the tools and techniques in the next chapter. Once you get the hang of it, it is fun and fulfilling—nothing to dread.

9 | BE PRESENT. LISTEN DEEPLY. ASK QUESTIONS. RELAX.

Fire up your team by remaining mindful and using the four tools of authentic conversation. These gifts demonstrate the extent to which you value the relationship and your team members' perspective and contribution. With this foundation, your team will give back in kind, and together you will find ways forward that build on what's working and remove obstacles that slow you down.

Because leadership is about working through and with people, leaders often find themselves in the midst of misunderstandings, miscommunications and misperceptions. While knowing how to chart a course across an ocean is a useful leadership skill, perhaps more important, leaders must be comfortable navigating the depths and undercurrents of human relationships to successfully reach their destination with the ship's crew and the ship itself intact. (It's also a good idea to avoid mutinies during the voyage.)

Navigating below the surface requires a lot of deep diving so you can have the authentic conversations important to moving past obstacles. The golden rule of conversational deep diving is fourfold: be present, listen deeply, ask questions and relax.

Over the years, I have been practicing and teaching how to host conversations, and I have observed that our formal and informal education often interferes with creating a space where people can be real with each other and tell the truth. We have been taught how to use rhetoric and debate. We have been taught how to assert our point of view or negotiate to get what we want. We listen only well enough

> **EACH MOMENT HAS THE POTENTIAL TO BE A WHOLE MOMENT. EVERY CONVERSATION HAS THE POTENTIAL TO BE FILLED WITH RICH, WHOLE MOMENTS.**

to formulate a response, or we jump in with our point at the other's first intake of breath.

Rarely have we been taught to sit still, absorb what the other is saying, pursue a deeper understanding and suspend our worry or even anxiety about the outcome of the conversation, instead trusting that the right outcome will emerge. In our haste to speak and answer and rebut, we do a disservice to the business. We do not make sure we properly understand and fully explore the dimensions of a topic, thereby leaving the company short-changed.

I recently witnessed two teams blaming each other for a situation. One was primarily defending its processes, and the other was pointing out how they were broken. By trying to allocate blame—"It's your processes!" "No, it's your resistance!"—rather than seeing the interaction as a whole, the teams could not see their way to a new solution. When we are stuck in defending and blaming, we are not putting our energy into exploring better ways for the company and its clients.

Once you begin to practice the four tools of this chapter, you will see instant results. Your conversations will move effortlessly, difficult conversations will evaporate, and issues will surface and resolve in an ebb-and-flow fashion. In the above example, the teams could meet and create a space in which they truly listened to each other's challenges with empathy and understanding. New ideas could be exchanged that would accommodate both needs without compromising results.

Although this sounds very warm and fuzzy, as some of my participants like to say, it is actually highly productive and serves the business very well. You focus on deeply understanding the issues and problems to come up with a better solution for all involved. Let's now dip our toes briefly into the pools of being present, listening, questioning and relaxing.

Be present

This is not a new idea. It's been around for centuries, though it's made a modern-day comeback through a wide variety of channels, including yoga, mindfulness and best-selling books like *The Power of Now: A Guide to Spiritual Enlightenment* by Eckhart Tolle (1999).

Being present is a must if one wishes to engage successfully in truly meaningful conversation. It focuses your brain on the here and now, not on speculating about the situation at hand or imagining how the conversation will go. When truly present in a conversation, you focus exclusively on what the other person says and thus hear it purposefully and purely.

You are listening one word at a time. You are not worrying about your response or what else is on your plate for the day, or what's happening in the office next door. A brain whirring at 100 miles an hour trying to think of a response, or creating a mental to-do list for the day, or wandering into surrounding conversations cannot pay full attention to what's being said. Your listeners know when you are present or when you are distracted. They know when you are putting all your energy into that conversation or when you lack interest and alertness.

When you are fully present, it's a completely different experience for both parties. Your presence affirms the value you place on the conversation, the situation and the person. It underscores that the other person is important to you and that the relationship matters. You are paying that person respect.

As a leader, when you consider the benefits of being fully present when you meet with your team or individual members, doing anything else seems foolhardy. When fully present, you build relationships and work efficiently, as your brain is wholly focused on the issue or opportunity at hand. You generate new possibilities because your brain has the capacity to work more creatively when it's not trying to multitask. We fool ourselves if we think otherwise.

Many years ago, I was attending a conference and the vice president of a telecommunications company was addressing the audience. She was a mother and managed a very large business unit. She often noticed that at work she was worrying about home, and when she was with her children, she was constantly checking her BlackBerry. One day she made a decision: *When I am at work, I will be focused and present for my clients and colleagues; when I am home, I will be mindful and fully engaged with my family. My head will be where my feet are.* When you are interacting with your team or a team member, let your head be where your feet are, and be truly present for them.

Listen deeply

When fully present in a conversation, you listen deeply to what the other person says. You take in the words, the tone and the body language as multiple channels delivering information to you. You tune in to all the channels simultaneously. You bring your energy and brainpower to bear on this single conversation at this point in time. Nothing else is in your mind but listening to what the other person says.

Listening goes beyond being present. Listening is also understanding. When you really take in each word, phrase or sentence, as well as how it's said, meaning emerges more fully and easily. It is a completely different experience than conversational multitasking—listening superficially while mentally preparing a response to what is being said or thinking about your own opinions on the topic. It's a fact that our brains cannot multitask, despite popular belief to the contrary. Our brains are designed to focus. We might be able to rapidly move between different things, but this also involves our cognitive abilities. There are many resources for understanding this further. For a quick explanation, check out a YouTube clip featuring Nicholas Carr discussing his book *The Shallows: What the Internet Is Doing to Our Brains* (2010).

For our purposes, know that our working memory has very limited capacity (two to four pieces of information). If we want to get the most out of our interactions, we need to focus on the information before us to make sense of it and gain the greatest benefit. Allowing our brains to absorb the conversation at hand and make meaning will allow the conversation to progress in an efficient and resonant manner. Instead of revisiting the same old issues or needing to restart conversations or feeling like you aren't getting traction, one conversation through which you truly and deeply listen will produce a much better result. You will be able to get to the heart of the matter, to stay open to possibilities and alternatives and to find sustainable solutions efficiently and thoughtfully. Give it a try.

Ask questions

When you get a good sense of another's meaning through deep listening, you are better equipped to ask questions, which will help you fill in the blanks and lead you to a clearer understanding. Asking relevant questions demonstrates you are receiving, absorbing and processing the information for meaning, and this is leading you to wonder about other, potentially related aspects of the issue at hand. As information comes forward, it creates fertile soil for generating new questions.

When someone asks questions intended to help him understand our meaning and purpose, we automatically become more open and less defensive. We feel supported. We feel as if the other person is on our side and has our best interests at heart, simply because he is taking the time and making an effort to understand. This investment tells the speaker she is worth it and that the listener cares. This, whether the speaker and the listener agree or disagree about the content of the conversation in which they are engaged, is the foundation of trust.

Without trust, authentic conversations are not possible. People withhold information, pretend to know what they don't know and say what they think you want to hear, as well as sundry other things—none of which help you or the team or the company properly deal with matters at hand.

When you remove the barriers to real conversation, you open the door for honest questions and honest answers to gain full comprehension. You will see all the parts in relationship to the whole. You will understand a variety of components, from basic facts to underlying motivations to unspoken assumptions, all of which you will need to hold a clear picture to support your decisions. Without the benefit of all the available information, it is almost impossible to make good decisions or resolve situations.

Take time to ask questions. A few questions can go a long way to furthering your understanding. Think of times when, if you had asked a few more questions, you would have saved yourself a great deal of trouble. Begin today with simple open-ended questions. Before you accept a statement at face value, explore a little and see what might surface. Here's an example of a recent conversation illustrating this process:

Simon (manager): What's on our agenda for today?

Chinh (team member): I'd like to speak with you about a problem with our reporting system. We can't get people to input data quickly enough to meet our deadlines.

Simon: Is anyone inputting the data on a timely basis? (This is an excellent question, as it tests whether the deadlines are realistic and achievable.)

Chinh: Yes, some departments are, like ops and compliance. But sales and marketing aren't. And I'm tired of always following up and not getting a response, and it's starting to cause tension.

Simon: Do you know why they aren't able to meet your deadlines? *(This question enables the manager to assess whether Chinh understands his stakeholder well enough to find solutions.)*

Chinh: Ah . . . no. But if the others are, I don't see why they can't!

Simon: Maybe this is information that would help you manage the process? *(This suggestion helps Chinh to refocus.)*

Chinh: Probably.

Simon: How much flexibility do you have? Could you consider changing how the reports are generated and the order in which you get the numbers? Meaning, perhaps there is a different way to manage this information flow that will align both your needs and the department's constraints, presuming there are some. *(These questions are intended to stimulate new thinking.)*

Chinh: You mean do something different for them? Why does everyone have to kowtow to sales and marketing? Why do we always have to make exceptions for them?

Simon: Let's think about what impact there'd be on you if you adapted the process to accommodate their needs. *(Simon refuses to buy into this line of thinking and keeps Chinh focused on reality.)*

Chinh: You mean extra work and stuff like that?

Simon: Yes, all the pluses and minuses. *(Here Simon provides a simple structure to guide the discussion.)*

Chinh: Well, there'd be the time to meet with them and then figure out what needs adjusting and what is or isn't possible. And it might change how I sequence things and maybe the time it takes to pull it all together. I'm not sure, but probably most of the impact is in the upfront investment of time to figure out why it's not working smoothly now.

Simon: Okay, so that's the big minus. What are the pluses?

Chinh: I get my reporting done on time without stress . . .

Simon: How do you feel about the situation now? *(As the manager senses a shift, he asks for confirmation to bring awareness to the employee.)*

Chinh: Actually, pretty good. I'll meet and see why the current process isn't working for that department and depending what I learn, we can consider making adjustments to accommodate all our needs. Hmm . . . Seems manageable and will reduce my frustrations if this approach works. Thanks.

Importantly, we need to take the time required to explore what is being said, implied or ignored. By doing this, we create a fuller picture and can lead our teams and team members through rough or even turbulent waters in a manner that doesn't have to cause anyone seasickness.

Relax

Relax into the conversation. Your mindset may cause you to experience tension. For example, if you feel the stakes are high and you want to secure a positive outcome, you might feel a great deal of pressure to make sure the conversation goes well. This tension is counterproductive. You can't think clearly when your brain is worried about an outcome. However, if you detach from the worry and relax, the conversation will flow more easily.

When you are very anxious, you may trigger your "fight or flight" response, and your body will respond accordingly. Your heart will pump blood to your large muscle groups, your breath will quicken, your pulse will race, your fists might even clench. You will have a variety of physiological responses, sometimes mild but sometimes intense. All of this fogs your thinking brain and does not create ideal conditions for a fruitful conversation.

If a situation is causing you to feel uptight, the first thing to do is to consciously take deep breaths. Demand that your brain stop worrying about the future and refocus on your current intention, which is to have a meaningful conversation to move a situation forward. When you force yourself to relax, you will find it much easier to know what questions to ask and, when necessary, how to respond.

We are wise beings with a great deal of experience, knowledge and compassion. When we trust ourselves, we let go of the need to prepare for and script conversations as if they were plays and we were actors. When we create such scripts, we are trying to make the conversation go a certain way to guarantee an outcome we desire, when all we really need to do is show up and bring our hearts and minds to the discussion. The solution will emerge collaboratively.

Imagine yourself on a cruise ship taking a leisurely stroll on deck to discover all the interesting areas—both those that are obvious and those that may lay hidden—for the purpose of orientating yourself to the overall layout and flow of the ship. You're in no rush. You'll know when you have enough information because you will feel like you understand the dynamics of the situation. You will feel a sense of knowing or understanding. You are relaxed and languidly deepening your understanding. And, from that understanding, a next step will emerge.

Refrain from jumping too quickly into problem-solving. Without a clear sense of the situation, you may create a quick fix instead of a sustainable result. You can patch the deck boards, but if there's a hole in the hull, the problem won't go away.

Our need to provide answers and problem-solve often stems from a stress response. We are in the habit of putting out fires and reacting to the situations presented to us as if they were all a crisis needing urgent and immediate attention, or we may be in the habit of rushing to the next thing to get through our daily to-do list, so it's easier and quicker to tell someone what to do than to help him or her see it differently and take more strategic actions. Don't try to get anywhere—just keep taking your leisurely stroll until you feel you really have a grasp of the layout and the landscape. How to respond will then be very obvious, and your original worries about getting to a certain outcome will seem frivolous.

Next time you are sitting down with one of your team members, begin by taking a slow deep breath to relax into the conversation. Tell your brain to focus on the matter at hand (big or small), pay attention to all the information coming to you, ask purposeful questions and enjoy the energy and ideas that emerge.

ACTIVITY

Practice having a conversation during which you shut down your own thoughts (mind chatter) and focus solely on what the other is saying. Begin by saying, "Tell me about . . ." Find something you know the other person is interested in or cares about, and then just listen and ask questions to learn more. Use the four tools for deep diving to keep focused, and do not let your mind wander. If it does, gently bring yourself back. Make notes about this experience after the conversation is over.

....

....

....

....

10 | BUILD AND RESTORE TRUST

To fire up your team, make sure they know what you stand for as a leader. Once they know what you are about and that you walk your talk, they can trust you and commit to achieving your shared goals. On the other hand, if your actions contradict your stated values, or if you mismanage a situation and don't make amends, your team will see you as inconsistent and unreliable. The result will be a distracted team that focuses more on how to "manage up" or how to "navigate the landmines." More importantly, the team will feel upset rather than uplifted. Your momentum and achievements will be delayed, if not completely compromised. Living one's values is a challenge, but it is also deeply rewarding and worth the investment.

As a child, I never heard my parents speak poorly of anyone. They always saw the best in neighbours, family members, colleagues and friends. Their door was always open. I remember many people coming to our home seeking help, and to my recollection, my parents always did what they could to offer support. Likewise, they contributed to the community in meaningful and valuable ways, particularly to their church.

Others saw my parents as reliable, capable people with strongly held values and beliefs. They knew my mom and dad were trustworthy and that they were concerned about others' interests. My parents valued the confidence and high esteem in which the community held them.

TRUST MAKES EVERYTHING EASIER.

The simple yet powerful lessons I learned from my parents remain with me to this day. Here are a few examples:

- My mother cleaned homes for a living. She sometimes worked for minimum wage, often less. Yet if she worked an additional 15 minutes and one of her clients tried to pay her for this, she would refuse. She would say, "I don't count my time by the minutes. I am satisfied with three hours of pay. It's enough." Clients knew she would not take advantage of them, and they didn't need to watch their back.

- If anyone dropped by to say hello, even if the timing was inconvenient, warm hospitality (and usually a meal) was offered. A less fortunate neighbour, a cousin, the parish priest, everyone was treated the same—generosity and warmth were shared equally. People learned you could count on being well received at my parents' home. The door was truly always open.
- My father did not tolerate gossip or disparaging remarks. He was a man of few words, and he always chose his words carefully. I recall him raising his voice to me only once, and then because I had hurt my mother's feelings. I learned the value of respecting others and preserving another's dignity. I also learned the value of kindness, understanding and generosity of spirit.
- My parents took trust seriously. It was the cornerstone of all the relationships they valued.

I brought these and other home-grown values with me into the workplace, but at the top of the list was trust. As a young manager of a large team of direct reports (my first true management position), I didn't have experience to guide me. Instead, I had my values, and I used these as my operating principles. I created a mantra for situations in which I wasn't certain of the best course of action: *Trust your team. Trust the person to do the right thing.*

Perhaps my youth was my greatest advantage: I couldn't know every facet of the work, I was new to the profession, and I wasn't in the least bit cynical (I hadn't yet had enough exposure to the corporate "underworld" to become so). All I had to fall back on was my own somewhat limited personal experience, and so, in a way, my parents became my leadership guides. They had no business experience whatsoever, but they had people experience in spades, and, as it turns out, the lessons I had learned from them proved to be exactly what I needed to know.

Navigating team management was no simple feat. Understanding my P & L was easy by comparison! Through their actions, my parents taught me to be trustworthy, and they also taught me to trust. Perhaps the two go hand in hand; maybe you can't have one without the other.

I was never disappointed when I followed my mantra. Upon reflection, I think when people know you trust them because you believe they are trustworthy, they work hard to preserve the confidence you have placed in them, thus creating virtuous cycles through which relationships build and flourish.

The fragility of trust

In his book *The 7 Habits of Highly Effective People* (1989), Stephen R. Covey presents the following analogy:

> An Emotional Bank Account is a metaphor that describes the amount of trust that's been built up in a relationship. It's the feeling of safeness you have with another human being.
>
> If I make deposits into an Emotional Bank Account with you through courtesy, kindness, honesty, and keeping my commitments to you, I build up a reserve. Your trust toward me becomes higher, and I can call upon that trust many times if I need to. . . .
>
> But if I have a habit of showing discourtesy, disrespect, cutting you off, overreacting, ignoring you, becoming arbitrary, betraying your trust, threatening you, or playing little tin god in your life, eventually my Emotional Bank Account is overdrawn. The trust level gets very low. . . .
>
> I'm walking on mine fields.

Over the years, I have seen this played out over and over again in my life and the lives of those around me. However, I have also observed it to be not as straightforward as counting up credits and debits. Credits rarely count as much as debits. It's not a one-to-one relationship. In fact, a healthy bank account built over decades can be bankrupt in one fell swoop with a single severe betrayal, such as a marital affair (on a personal level) or leaking confidential company information (on a corporate level).

Blind trust

Interestingly, the event or situation need not be dramatic or traumatic for the debit/credit imbalance to be observable. During workshops, I sometimes conduct a "Blind Trust Walk" experiential activity. Half the group volunteers to be leaders, and the other half are followers. Leaders and followers are paired. The leaders then leave the room and are told their partners will be blindfolded; their job on their return is to guide their followers around the environment safely, but in a way that allows them to interact with their surroundings.

There are two twists. First, when the leaders go back to the room, they must go to someone other than the follower with whom they had chosen to work, and secondly, they are not allowed to speak. Before rejoining the followers, the leaders shout "Safety First!" three times and then re-enter the room, take a follower's arm and begin to walk them around the room, corridors, gardens or whatever else is in the vicinity. The activity only lasts three minutes, but it is rich in potential learning. Over the years, I have made lots of noteworthy observations, including these:

- Although a few followers are nervous from the onset, the vast majority begin by moving forward comfortably with their new partner.
- Although the leaders remain silent, usually half of the followers suss out quickly they are not with their original partner.
- There is a spectrum of risk-management strategies, from none to full stop, from followers who seem to be leading their leaders (they push forward while their leaders try to slow them down) to followers who barely inch forward with hands stretched out in front to detect as early as possible any obstacles in their path while their leaders literally drag them into taking a full step.

I surmise from these observations that some people are risk adverse while others are impetuous. This also relates to trust. For some, trust comes easily and is freely given; for others, it must be gradually earned.

The other important observation I've made is that it only takes a small stumble to make a huge deficit, regardless of whether trust is freely given or gradually earned. The follower who practically gallops around will slow dramatically if his or her shoulder hits a doorframe. The follower who has just begun to move fluidly will come to a dead stop if he or she walks into an object, even a soft one. For the remainder of the exercise, the momentum never returns to its original high point. The takeaway is that trust is fragile, even when freely given. Many positive steps can be rapidly undone by one misstep.

The fragility of trust should not deter anyone from making deposits in the bank account. My goal in sharing these observations is to emphasize that trust is no small matter. It behoves leaders to think before they act. Ask yourself if your action will build trust or potentially destroy it. Once trust is destroyed, it takes a great deal more effort to refill the bank account the next time around. Whether it's fair or not, some broken trust will never completely heal.

ACTIVITY

In the workplace, what actions build trust and what actions destroy it? Below is a quick checklist, based on my team workshops. While lists like this one are useful, I encourage you to think about your current practices and habits and ask yourself some important questions, such as:

- Do your habits serve you well?
- Do your followers trust you and your leadership?
- What's your evidence?

Reflection Questions	Yes	No
I keep my word. I do what I say I am going to do. I follow through.		
I "walk the talk" and ensure my actions line up with my stated beliefs and values.		
I tell people where they stand with me rather than telling/complaining to others.		
I share information freely. I tell the team what's going on, especially when they might be impacted by a decision or change. Or I tell them when I can't share and why.		
I explain my decisions. I share my underlying motivations as well as reasoning so that my team will understand the "whys" behind the choice.		
I take accountability for my team's actions. I never make team members scapegoats and let them take the blame, distancing myself from the problem, even if ever so slightly. In other words, I never throw them under the bus.		
I forgive errors. I don't hold grudges. I never mention past incidents, especially once they have been addressed. I don't carry baggage and allow it to taint my current behaviour.		
I learn from my mistakes. When I have caused a "debit," I am accountable and share what I've learned about my mistake.		

I apologize and express regret. Or I ask for forgiveness for mistakes through which I caused personal hurt to team members.		
I explicitly value each team member. I know each person's strengths and celebrate them. I encourage team members to learn from each other, demonstrating that their value is worth sharing.		
I treat everyone equally. I share my time evenly and look for opportunities for each of my team members. I don't have favourites.		

Restoring trust

We need to restore trust, at a deep level, in the workplace. We have given people too many reasons to be cynical, and many of us have been transformed into dyed-in-the-wool cynics ourselves. Remember: When you are in power, you may be able to force someone to be compliant, but you can never force that person to trust you. Trust is a gift people may either give or withhold.

It is impossible to cite the myriad situations in which trust may be damaged or destroyed, including the simplest, smallest and seemingly benign things. Add assumptions and personal insecurities to the mix, and a small matter can become very serious indeed. Building, maintaining and restoring broken trust are among the greatest challenges of forging productive and happy human relations.

All of us have relationships that are damaged. We wouldn't be human if we didn't. The question is: How can we mend them? When the damage is the result of broken trust, there's usually no quick fix. Adding a few cents to the emotional bank account is not enough to repair the damage. But that doesn't mean the situation is irreparable. A substantial deposit to the account, in the form of meaningful actions, is required to create a noticeable shift in a depleted trust account balance.

Henry, a regional CEO, was uncomfortable with conflict. As a result, instead of addressing issues face-to-face with his direct reports, he developed a habit of expressing his frustrations or disappointments to others. These were rarely matters of major significance. However, over time, Henry's direct reports became aware of this tendency, usually by hearing through the grapevine what he thought of their performance. It didn't take long before some members of the team began to avoid him, withhold information and generally attempt to stay under his radar. Some presented a supportive, positive face to Henry but criticized him behind the scenes and undermined his authority in response to their own uncertainty about where they stood with him.

The situation came to a head when one of Henry's key team members, Avery, unintentionally gave Henry a taste of his own medicine. While speaking to a group of vice presidents, Avery mentioned the team was struggling to come together around an important business initiative. The group vice president flagged this with the executive team to see how they might help. When Henry learned about the exchange and the result, he felt betrayed. Instead of raising the issue directly with Avery, however, Henry excluded him from strategic meetings and high-profile assignments, thus further degrading the situation.

To avoid such difficulties, here are some steps to supporting rather than destroying trust.

Step 1: Accept accountability for your actions

This is important even if their impact was unintentional. Rather than excusing yourself ("It wasn't my intention to upset you"), accept that your action had an unintended effect for which you are sorry ("I did not want to upset you. Upon reflection, I see how my comments were ambiguous and could have been interpreted as a personal criticism.")

When Avery realized action had been taken at the group level, he did a sensible thing: He spoke to Henry. He acknowledged that rather than making a passing comment to a group VP, he should have expressed his concerns about the team directly to Henry. He explained he had not intended to create group pressure on Henry but was looking for help.

Step 2: Learn more about the context

If you find yourself in a similar situation of broken trust, seek to understand what other forces contributed to the interpretation in question. Uncover the underlying issues. If the other person's reaction seems over the top, chances are it was simply the straw that broke the camel's back. In other words, an issue exists (and perhaps has existed for a long time), but it is buried. An innocent remark trips the emotional wire to the issue and *kaboom!* You blow up the vault containing all your precious trust deposits.

Conversations that truly restore trust are deep dives that answer questions like, "What conditions existed to give rise to the interpretation that broke the trust?" When brewing concerns lie behind a broken trust, "I'm sorry I wasn't clear" will not restore it. The underlying issues must be exposed and addressed to move forward.

For example, Avery—who had a habit of speaking too openly and off-the-cuff, leaving his listeners to draw potentially erroneous conclusions, which in turn made it difficult for his teammates to manage—was surprised by Henry's reaction. He had not been overtly critical of Henry. He had simply expressed concerns about team alignment. Why had Henry reacted so strongly? Why had he given him the complete cold shoulder? After making his apology, he told Henry, "I truly am sorry I upset you. I care a great deal about our work and how we work together, so I was a little surprised by how upset you were and why you didn't come and speak with me. What was it about my comment that created this problem?"

Step 3: Share a different future

An understanding of the past is not sufficient to restore trust. Once you have accepted your own accountability and addressed underlying concerns or misunderstandings, you must describe a different future. How will you ensure the same thing doesn't happen again? If the underlying condition stemmed from a misunderstanding of roles and responsibilities, what steps can you take in the future to maintain clarity? If the underlying condition was a team member feeling undervalued, how can you provide appropriate feedback to ensure people feel confident that they are on track and appreciated?

Once you have attended to your own accountabilities, ask the other person what he or she could do differently in the future. Relationships comprise two people, both of whom must contribute. One person cannot do all the work, even if that person is the leader. The leader can certainly take the first step and show the way forward, but the employee must also help restore soured relations, or vice versa in the case of Henry and Avery.

Sometimes, after having gone through the steps above, an employee will see what they could do differently to avert similar situations down the road. If they don't, you might guide them with a suggestion like, "In the future, if you are not clear about your role and responsibilities, please ask me. And if I say something that seems to be a personal criticism, please ask me to clarify or share with me what you think you heard."

As leaders, we need to demonstrate that we are comfortable with feedback. Also, it's constructive to point out we are not *always* going to be clear, precise or perfect (far from it!), and to invite team members to tell us when our comments are not being well received.

After talking with Henry, Avery understood he needed to consider his choices, meaning how he chose to respond to this and similar situations. As a result of this reflection, Avery began to practice expressing his concerns directly to those involved. Interestingly, this open, genuine and honest conversation also prompted Henry to reflect. Henry recognized his aversion to conflict was in fact creating conflict among the members of his team. The conversation with Avery had been painless, and Henry realized avoiding such discussions was needless.

ACTIVITY

Think about a relationship you value that has suffered from broken trust or had more emotional debits than credits lately. How could these three steps help you repair the damage?

....

....

....

11 | LIVE YOUR PERSONAL VALUES

Leaders face dilemmas and challenges, sometimes daily. Your choices and reactions during these times teach others about your values, which are evident in what you *do*, not what you *say*. A leader may say she values honesty, but when employees hear her spin messages and avoid issues instead of practicing straight talk, they will eventually notice the disconnect. People are not stupid, nor are they easily fooled for long. That's why it's critical to "walk your talk."

In his novel *The Best Laid Plans* (2010), Terry Fallis addresses the issue of living your values in a humorous way. It's a political novel set "today" in Ottawa, Ontario. A sixty-something engineering professor named Angus runs for parliament in order to escape having to teach an introductory English class at his university. He fully expects to lose, as he is by far the underdog; in fact, he *wants* to lose, but extraordinary events catapult him into the winner's seat. He now must attend to his business on Parliament Hill.

Although a reluctant parliamentarian, he approaches this work as he does life—with absolute integrity. In other words, he refuses to play the political game, which becomes the source of comedy for the novelist. Angus has a transparent agenda, no longer cares what others think and sees this as his time to begin a new chapter in his life.

The novel, while hilarious, also suggests some interesting questions: Why is this character such obvious fiction? Why does someone taking the high road cause such mayhem? Why does living one's values wreak havoc?

Although it creates an amusing story line, when one ponders the reason it's funny, it's a little depressing.

> **WALKING YOUR TALK TEACHES OTHERS YOUR VALUES. YOUR TEAM DISCOVERS YOUR VALUES THROUGH WHAT YOU DO.**

In many ways, the novel is a call to action: It invites each of us to step up in our own way and do the right thing. But how do we know what the right thing is? As leaders, we need to know what we stand for and make it clear why we are trustworthy.

We all hold many values, and many of us say we value the same things. For example, I have never met anyone who claims to not value honesty. However, all our values will not be equally important to us— some matter more than others. Sometimes when we closely examine our choices, it becomes clear the values we think are at the top of the list are actually further down than we thought. The opposite may also be true. You might say truth is your highest value, but those who are close to you or who observe you in the workplace see fairness is actually what matters most to you.

Your stated values will never distinguish you—your actions will. Remember the old adage, "Actions speak louder than words"? It applies doubly to leadership. Whether you realize it or not, your team discovers your values through your actions, not your words. I learned this lesson firsthand years ago.

I managed a team of professionals for a large retail chain. The team, which had members in the field working with large regions, led learning and development initiatives across the organization. I intentionally structured the team so they reported directly to their regional general manager (GM), with a dotted line to me. I wanted to ensure the field offices owned the learning and development programs we created, especially as they were responsible for the implementation and follow-up.

This structure worked exceedingly well for a number of years, until the regions were asked to scale back on personnel in a cost-cutting measure. In one region, my learning and development professional, Wade, was targeted. Wade was a loyal senior employee who had worked hard for the company for decades. He was doing a good job but was seen as slightly old-fashioned and a bit of a whiner. Wade was admittedly a little fussy, but he cared a great deal about his work and the organization. Plus, he executed our programs well and always received positive performance appraisals.

I intervened, and it wasn't pretty! We discussed and debated, and it became a hot topic. It was obvious Wade was not one of the GM's favourites. He was viewed as a bit of a nuisance, and combined with the fact that learning and development were seen as a "nice to have" rather than a "must have," his position was the logical one to cut—according to the GM, anyway.

Although I was a manager at the head office and relatively senior, I was two levels below a GM. So I took a deep breath and held my ground on two counts: 1) Wade was being unfairly targeted because of his personality quirks, and 2) the function was being undervalued at a time when we needed to ensure our personnel exceeded customer expectations, and training and development was a critical component in achieving that goal. In the end, I had to put my own job on the line to save the position.

Once the crisis passed, one of my junior but more experienced and mature employees, Gwen, came up to me and said, "That was a tough situation. You've always said you would fight for us and our work. People were watching you to see if you'd give in, but you didn't." Then she walked away. I was 30 years old at the time, a novice leader. Some 20 years later, I still remember the lesson I learned that day.

The power of walking the talk can never be underestimated. It feeds a leader's credibility unlike anything else. Your behaviours must align to your stated beliefs and commitments. Without this direct connection between words and actions, leadership has no right to ask people to enter follower-ship.

ACTIVITY

What are your top values? List them below. Are your current decisions and actions congruent with them? If not, what adjustments must you make to align them?

....

....

....

12 | CREATE A CULTURE OF ACCOUNTABILITY

Fire up your team by holding them and yourself accountable. This isn't about creating a blame game—this is about empowerment. When you foster a culture of accountability, people understand they have the power to create things that matter most to them. You instil in them a way of seeing the world that provides them with choice so they can always see a way forward. When a team embraces accountability, they know they can take action in service of their goals and aspirations. Such a team rarely feels helpless or victimized. Instead, they see they have the power to drive forward toward goals that matter.

It's all well and good to create workspaces that connect people to aspirations, encourage collaboration and reward those who are engaged, but we can't forget that with all those things must come a willingness to take responsibility. For leaders to share power, and for employees to gain more freedom, leaders need to implement the fundamentals of accountability. Managers who insist on accountability can relinquish a great deal of control because their employees recognize—and, perhaps more important, *own*—their choices.

> **Face into your freedom. Accountability is all about seeing your choice.**

What you permit, you promote

A thoughtful actuarial client, Larry, shared a quotation during one of my leadership development workshops. He told the story of a fellow manager who complained about his team's performance and behaviour to a group of peers, one of whom responded with a provocative statement: "What you permit, you promote." Larry, who was part of the circle, said the complainer stopped mid-conversation, and the whole group paused to reflect on the wisdom of these words.

When frustrated with results, leaders often blame employees for performance issues. I suggest they ask themselves some tough questions instead: Who holds the formal power and authority? Who's responsible for managing performance issues? Where does the buck stop? Unless the team is a self-directed work group, responsible for giving each other feedback and doing peer evaluations, leaders who point the finger at their teams have it all wrong. They would be better served looking in the mirror and reflecting on how they have failed as leaders.

This is not to say employees need not be held accountable for their work. They absolutely should be! However, managers are wholly accountable for the team's results. If a team member or the entire team misses targets or behaves unprofessionally, the manager needs to apply his leadership knowledge and skills to turn the situation around. If the manager does not have the knowledge or skills, then she needs to either acquire them or seek the advice and support of others who do.

Managers create a culture of accountability when they are accountable for their leadership responsibilities, and they make employees accountable for the execution of their own work. Ultimately, this allows everyone more freedom, thereby stimulating engagement through empowerment. *Everyone* owns workplace accountability: Successes and failures are co-created, and accountability is shared.

What does this mean in practical terms? When I ask people what first comes to mind when they hear the words "you are accountable," the most common response is, "It means my head's on the chopping block if things don't work out." The implication is, "You will be held responsible if it doesn't work out," and worse, "there might be consequences" for failure.

However, accountability is much more positive and broader than that. Take a look at the chart below. This is an assessment you can use for yourself as a leader to help you stay grounded in what it means to be accountable. You can also use this as a tool to bring awareness to your team. The statements can also be a source of coaching material for you. When you hear people making excuses, you can shift them into looking at what was within their sphere of control. When people feel powerless, you can help them see alternative paths forward, and when people can't see the choices before them, you can help point them out.

ACTIVITY

The following is a self-assessment for reflection purposes. We will look more closely at the term *accountability*. Before we do, I invite you to complete the following questionnaire.

Self-Assessment

	Not at all	Rarely	Some-times	Usually	Always
1. When things go wrong, I look to myself first.	1	2	3	4	5
2. I often find myself arguing to prove I am right.	5	4	3	2	1
3. I am good at seeing alternative paths to a goal.	1	2	3	4	5
4. I have a tendency to blame others.	5	4	3	2	1
5. I complain about my boss or colleagues.	5	4	3	2	1
6. I pursue professional development opportunities whenever possible.	1	2	3	4	5
7. I take initiative regularly. I don't wait to be asked.	1	2	3	4	5
8. I am resourceful. I find ways of doing things.	1	2	3	4	5
9. If I accept a goal or objective, I never make excuses for why it wasn't achieved.	1	2	3	4	5
10. I can always see how I contributed to an outcome or a situation.	1	2	3	4	5
11. I easily make decisions and stand by them.	1	2	3	4	5
12. I spend my time wisely.	1	2	3	4	5
13. I know when I have acted against my principles.	1	2	3	4	5

14. I can clearly articulate my sense of purpose.	1	2	3	4	5
15. I like to have clearly laid-out guidelines and rules to follow.	5	4	3	2	1
16. If I disagree with the group's decision, I speak up.	1	2	3	4	5
17. I like to challenge the status quo.	1	2	3	4	5
18. I consider myself an independent thinker.	1	2	3	4	5
19. I create my own goals and objectives and am motivated to accomplish them.	1	2	3	4	5
20. I know I always have a choice.	1	2	3	4	5
Subtotal (Add each column)					
Grand Total (Add the subtotals)					

Scoring

81–100: You have embraced accountability. You understand you have choices and you know you have power over your own life. You know this isn't always easy, but it is preferable to having others control your life.

61–80: You have partially accepted working with accountability. With an increased understanding of accountability, you will likely choose to fully work with your freedom.

60 and under: You likely see yourself as limited by the organization's systems and practices. You are probably not happy at work; you frequently feel frustrated or negative. You don't see the actions you take as choices.

The self-assessment is a reflective exercise to introduce you to what accountability might look like in your workplace—perhaps even in your life. In my experience, accountability cannot be easily defined in a sentence or two, perhaps not even by an itemized list of 20. I see it as a cluster of actions, such as:

- embracing your own power to create
- seeing and owning your choices
- using *I* rather than *you*
- refusing to blame or play the victim
- not making excuses
- recognizing your own independence

Avoidance strategies

As a leader, once you have gained an understanding of what it means to be accountable, you can begin to mentor your team. The first step is seeing the avoidance strategies in action and knowing how to get people focused on their own choices and what they can control. By insisting that your team members look at their work through the lens of accountability, you will create an empowered team. They will see how they can act on their own behalf. This will lead them to see how they can create the type of workplace they most desire, as well as produce results of which they are tremendously proud.

It is not unusual for human beings to distance themselves, at least at times, from fully owning the situation before them. Sometimes these situations are opportunities (for example, I can choose to be proactive or I can choose not to engage) and sometimes they are addressing what has gone wrong (for example, I can speak to the role I played in missing a deadline or not). When confronted by such situations, we may choose either to accept ownership or to avoid it. In my experience, when we accept ownership of a situation, positive results ensue.

Here are some typical things we do to avoid accountability and some everyday examples of what they might sound like. No doubt, you've heard many of them before.

Be passive instead of proactive. (Note: Passive choices are choices nonetheless.) We choose to let others take action, choose not to take action ourselves or choose not adjust a course of action when it's failing. We say things like:

- "I'm waiting for the numbers to come in."
- "I don't get any feedback from my project lead."
- "The market is not responding, so we missed our goal."

Make excuses. We claim change is beyond our control and that obstacles are too difficult to resolve, pointing to others' inaction, tough situations or conditions. We say things like:

- "I was on the road, so I didn't know about the meeting."
- "The CEO did not ask for the report in reasonable time."
- "We couldn't finish, as we're not getting clear direction."

Deflect. We change the subject by saying things like "yes, but." We create distractions (such as red herrings) and say things like:

- "It's just how it is in the business world."
- "The company's goals are not communicated effectively."
- "He's never going to change, so why bother?"

Blame (especially people or circumstances). We focus on others' mistakes and failures—the boss, our team, the organization, the client—and judge what others should or shouldn't do. We say things like:

- "I have a difficult boss."
- "Sometimes I can't be productive because of my depression."
- "My coworkers are apathetic and negative."
- "She's so disorganized I didn't get the info on time."
- "The nepotism around here is out of control!"

Play the victim. We highlight our powerlessness, demonize others and allow our circumstances to confine us. We say things like:

- "My last manager was verbally abusive, so I can't trust."
- "My manager has it in for me."
- "The market is soft; we won't get new business."

The vast majority of people do not realize when they forsake their personal power. Their mind is so focused on the circumstances and external factors of the matters at hand and the possibility of discomfort—confrontation, consequences, punishment—that avoidance strategies are easily adopted. We need to diligently listen to our words and pay attention to our behaviours so that we can observe when we shy away from accountability and choose to lean into it instead. Why? Because once you recognize your choices and consciously choose, especially in favour of your values, you will feel a sense of freedom, the strength of empowerment and the understanding that you can be the driving, positive force in your own life.

ACTIVITY

Spend a day noticing how often you might subtly or explicitly choose to be passive, make an excuse, change the subject to avoid discomfort, blame others or think "poor me." Each time you notice yourself avoiding accountability, shift gears, own it and make a different choice. At the end of the day, make notes reflecting on your experience.

....

....

....

....

....

....

13 | AVOID BEING HIJACKED

You can keep your team fired up by helping them self-regulate so they don't become reactive to certain situations and people. Self-regulation keeps energy directed on what is most important and supports strong decision-making and interpersonal relationships, moving the business forward efficiently. For leaders, it's key to self-regulate so your team sees you as calm, cool and collected in challenging situations. It's even more important that you don't allow your own assumptions and biases to trigger you with your team members. Preserving relationships is key to your success as a leader.

Human beings have a survival instinct. Part of our brain is programmed to protect us from threats and dangers. It's called our limbic system—also known as our emotional brain—and it houses the "fight, flight or freeze" mechanism designed to support us in emergencies. When we perceive a threat, our rational, thinking brain (neocortex) is made subservient to our limbic system. In other words, the thinking brain is hijacked in favour of the emotional brain, and our "fight, flight or freeze" system kicks into gear. We are ready for action: adrenaline and hormones are released, blood flow is directed to our large muscles groups, our peripheral vision diminishes, our fists tense and our jaw clenches. We are built for survival, wired to respond to threats.

In today's business world, we typically don't fight for our physical survival. No mammoths barrel down the corridors at us, no poisonous snakes lurk in corporate doorways, and no predators prepare to pounce on us as we approach their hiding places. But do our brains know this? Researchers tell us that the limbic system, an ancient part of the brain, functions today much as it did centuries ago. Many of us experience the physical symptoms and the unthinking behaviour that accompanies an emotional hijacking triggered by a perceived threat.

> **HIT THE STOP BUTTON AND THEN RELAX, REFLECT AND RESTORE YOUR CLEAR THINKING.**

In surveying my workshop participants, I get a wide range of responses to "How often do you experience an emotional hijacking?" Some participants say they're hijacked multiple times a day; others say once a year; most fall somewhere in-between. One thing is certain: the limbic system is alive and well, and with it comes a whole host of fear-based responses. Our modern-age challenge is to recognize this fact and to self-manage our emotional reactions, a key message of Daniel Goleman's groundbreaking book *Emotional Intelligence* (1995).

If we accept that fear is a natural response that will show itself in the workplace, despite physical survival not being an issue for most employees, we can learn to manage it. When leaders do not understand that fear—and, as a result, emotional hijacking—is present in the workplace, just as it was in the savannahs of our prehistoric ancestors, they cannot effectively manage their teams. First of all, they deny their own fears and remain blind to their own response to perceived (or real) threats. Secondly, they most definitely cannot support their employees in developing self-awareness around emotional hijackings, which is essential to the creation of healthy relationships.

Self-awareness is the ability to understand why you react the way you do; self-regulation is the ability to channel fear constructively. We all experience emotional hijackings. They elicit instinctive behaviours intended to protect us and prepare us for action, specifically reaction. When we're hijacked, our heightened state inhibits our cognitive capacities, making it difficult to consider, reflect or discern. When we behave in ways that appear illogical or over the top, the odds are that an emotional hijacking lurks unseen beneath the calm, or not-so-calm, surface.

Here are some examples of situations that can trigger emotional hijackings in the workplace:

1. A boss "nitpicking"
2. A colleague showing up perpetually late for meetings
3. An employee rolling her eyes when you speak
4. Your team excluding you from an event, such as a social gathering
5. Unrealistic targets
6. Ever-changing rules
7. Being overlooked for a project
8. Decisions being made that impact your department, by fellow employees, without your input

Why can these situations trigger our limbic system and shut down our "thinking brain"? What are the perceived threats? What creates the fear response? Let's look at each of the examples listed above and surface the possible underlying thought that triggers the hijacking:

1. If my boss doesn't like me, my success will be compromised.
2. Punctuality is a sign of respect; my colleague doesn't respect me. My credibility is at stake.
3. Passive-aggressive employees are undermining my ideas and jeopardizing our goals.
4. This team does not see me as an equal partner. I do not really belong.
5. I am being set up to fail.
6. I cannot make proper decisions because I don't know the boundaries. I will inevitably make mistakes.
7. I am not seen as a valuable player and contributor on this project. I am not valued. My future is not secure.
8. My team's goals and objectives do not matter to this organization. I do not matter to this organization.

As leaders, we must understand our own triggers and fears. It is one thing to realize that our team members are subjected to hijacking, but we all must learn to self-regulate so that our limbic systems do not run amok. How often have we reacted to a person or event and later regretted it? How often have we hit "send" and immediately wished we could retrieve the message? It happens more often than we might care to admit, and the result is havoc in the workplace.

Let's look at a real-life example. One of my coaching clients, Joanne, leads a departmental team. About a year ago, a new department was formed to assist all departments, including Joanne's, to improve the company's workflow processes. Joanne's team was interviewed to gather their views and ideas on workflow; they were asked what worked, what didn't and how the process could be improved.

When the new workflow process was implemented, however, Joanne's team did not see how their feedback had been incorporated. To add insult to injury, Joanne's team members felt the new process, rather than being *better* than the old one, was actually *worse*; they saw it as a significant step backward rather than forward. It was more laborious and increased the odds of data-processing errors; as far as they were concerned, it was almost completely unworkable.

Not surprisingly, the team reacted strongly and objected vociferously to the change. Joanne tried to pacify them by explaining why the process had been created in the way it had been, but to no avail. Her team members continued to complain, and their anxiety—not to mention their attitudes—seemed to grow worse by the day.

As the new process was fundamental to the team's day-to-day deliverables, Joanne's department descended into chaos, with the team perpetually on the brink of emotional hijacking. Other teams that worked interdependently with them began to dread interactions with Joanne's team. Tension between her team and other teams escalated by the day. It was a disaster!

What was the threat that led to this heightened, reactive state? Not feeling heard caused Joanne's team members to feel devalued; increasing inefficiencies made it harder for them to meet their performance standards; and the ongoing need to correct errors hindered their sense of progress. All in all, it added up to one disgruntled team, to put it mildly!

Joanne tried to calm the troubled waters by telling her team members that "we all have to do things we don't like," which is of course true, but not the way to resolve the situation. In fact, Joanne's comments only made it worse. Not only did the team feel unheard and devalued by their colleagues in other departments, they now also felt unsupported by their own manager, even though she was doing what she felt was best to help them cope.

Relationships within the team and with other teams were at risk of devolving into serious conflict from which it would be extremely difficult to recover. Achieving day-to-day targets was next to impossible under the circumstances. At the end of each day, Joanne's team left feeling exhausted and depleted rather than uplifted by the day's work.

If any of this sounds familiar, you are not alone, believe me. Leaders face these kinds of situations with alarming regularity. I've heard scores of similar stories during my consulting career, and, like me, you may also have experienced them firsthand.

Although it would be nice to think we can always avert such situations, sometimes things spin out of control quickly. At the very least, as a leader, you can address the situation as soon as you become aware of the tension or misunderstanding. Many leaders do not intervene at this initial stage of awareness, however. They hope it will pass or that the team will work it out or that the events will be of little consequence. In reality, there is always a cost, and over time, if not addressed, emotional hijacking can become debilitating for a team.

The golden rule? As soon as you become aware of tension and conflict, begin one-on-one or team coaching. It is important that you hit the *stop* button and help people relax and reflect to restore their rational thinking and provide them with the tools to work through the situation constructively.

As a leader, what would you have done to resolve the situation Joanne faced? There are three key steps you can take:

1. **Acknowledge** your team's disappointment and frustration. Demonstrate your empathy clearly and authentically. Joanne might say, "I know you spent many hours sharing your ideas on how to improve the old process. I know that when you make such an investment, it's very disappointing not to see your ideas reflected in the solution and then to have the solution create new problems. And, since you work with this process daily, it's now making it tough for you to keep up with your workload."

2. **Fact-find** to uncover what is working and what needs to be fixed. If emotions are running high, do not delegate this task. As the senior person and as the objective participant, support your team by investigating what benefits have been derived from the system and what new challenges have emerged. Liaise with the sponsor of the new process and work together to evaluate the current state of affairs. Keep your team updated on your findings or even involve them so they work alongside you and learn how to handle such situations for their own development.

3. **Advocate** for change. It is your responsibility to ensure your team's working conditions enable success. If the new process generates unnecessary work or creates stress and confusion, you owe it to your team to ensure the situation is addressed. You cannot accept a process that reduces performance. You must believe there is a solution or an alternative, and you must advocate for finding it. Otherwise, you compromise your team's ability to succeed and their sense of well-being.

Leaders who understand the mechanics of how human beings react to others, as well as to circumstances they perceive as threatening, have far greater insight into the potential causes of problematic events and situations. Greater understanding and insight in turn enable leaders to address emerging situations and reduce the chance of conflict occurring, prevent it from escalating when it occurs (because there will be times when it does), resolve it when it escalates (because there will be times when it does that too) and shift people back into a positive, forward-looking mode whatever does or doesn't happen. Equally important, when leaders better understand how fear operates, they can more easily self-regulate and reduce the likelihood that they themselves will end up in an emotionally hijacked state.

This is not to say that life becomes a bowl of cherries when we have a better handle on emotional hijackings. We are only human, after all. However, leaders who are armed with a deeper understanding of fear and of how the brain and emotional hijackings work are infinitely more competent, courageous and confident in dealing with whatever they may encounter. I know, because I've seen it work wonders with my clients. But don't believe me—try it for yourself and see.

ACTIVITY

Reflect on the following:

- Think back to a time in life when you experienced an emotional hijacking.
- What did it feel like emotionally? What did it feel like physically?
- Recall an occasion at work that evolved into a difficult and tense situation. To what extent did emotional hijacking(s) make the situation worse?
- Knowing what you know now, what could you have done differently?

....

....

....

Activity

Identify an area of building conflict to "nip in the bud." Use the acknowledge, fact-find and advocate steps outlined above to plan your strategy.

Acknowledge: What facts or feelings do you want to acknowledge?

....

....

Fact-find: What fact-finding do you need to do or assist your team to do?

....

....

Advocate: For what change do you want to advocate (either external to your team or within your team)?

....

....

14 | DON'T JUMP TO CONCLUSIONS

To fire up your team, be vigilant about team or team-member assumptions and ways of seeing the world that interfere with reality and positive inquiry. People, often unwittingly, interpret events through a biased or distorted lens. When the interpretation holds negative meaning, a strong reaction may ensue, causing conflict and possibly derailing the team. Identifying potentially problematic assumptions and/or interpretations quickly helps your team rethink their reactions and choose positive ways forward to avoid wasting time and energy on imagined problems.

The Stairway to Conclusions is a tool I created with my business partner, Lorie, to help people distance themselves from emotional situations to better analyze and constructively address them. It's similar to, but simpler than, the Ladder of Inference, a tool developed by Chris Argyris and presented in Peter Senge's bestselling book *The Fifth Discipline* (1990). Our tool embraces the popular adage, "Don't jump to conclusions!" It works with this conventional wisdom in a modern context.

The Stairway to Conclusions is a way for us to identify how we are reaching conclusions so we can manage ourselves and situations with more finesse and effectiveness. It helps us break down our thinking in such a way that we can see and understand our own unique mental models and what makes us reach incorrect conclusions.

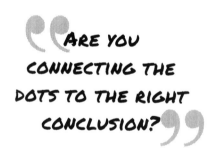

ARE YOU CONNECTING THE DOTS TO THE RIGHT CONCLUSION?

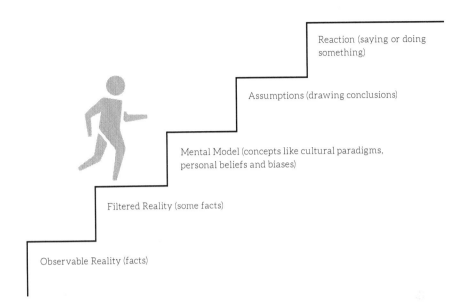

Reaction (saying or doing something)

Assumptions (drawing conclusions)

Mental Model (concepts like cultural paradigms, personal beliefs and biases)

Filtered Reality (some facts)

Observable Reality (facts)

Jumping to conclusions is an instantaneous and unconscious action, and it is extremely difficult to control. In fact, when it happens as a result of an emotional hijacking, it cannot be controlled. Once the amygdala releases large quantities of peptides and hormones (including adrenaline), they flood through our system and create a heightened emotional state during which we are primed to act or react. The best many of us can do is force ourselves not to react when we are pretty certain there is no real threat.

This chemical reaction needs time to subside. My mother always used to tell me, "Count to ten." Or, if I was really steaming, "Go take a walk around the block." These pieces of everyday wisdom are very good advice.

Even though the match has been lit, it does not have to be used. Instead, we can allow our self-regulation to kick in. Until the adrenaline stops pumping, we're best to keep still, because what we do or say during an intense emotional hijacking will likely be irrational and negative, or even destructive. As we keep still, we can call upon our rational, thinking brain to help us back down the stairway and re-examine all the facts.

The stairway has five steps:

1. **Observable Reality:** These are the facts. Reality is about what actually happened. It's about the entirety of what happened. It is the whole cloth, not fragments, but it's always about what we know and can prove because it's observable. It can also be about

seeing what we don't know so we can go on a fact-finding mission to better inform ourselves.

2. **Filtered Reality:** In filtered reality, there are only *some* facts. Instead of developing the discipline of observation so that we can gather all the relevant facts, we take shortcuts. We might only observe as much as we think we need to understand the situation of interest. Although we might think the facts we have gathered are sufficient, when we select only a narrow slice of reality, it often leads us to the wrong conclusion because we are missing too much relevant information. So learning to be diligent about our fact-gathering will serve us well in our people-leadership practices. It will keep us on track rather than take us down an unproductive garden path.

3. **Mental Model:** This is the paradigm we apply as we evaluate what we see. This is the most critical step of the Stairway to Conclusions, and so I have dedicated a section to it below. In brief, a mental model is a learned view or perspective that we overlay on reality to help us make sense of reality and know what to do or how to behave. The challenge is that these mental models sometimes are congruent with reality, but sometimes they distort reality.

4. **Assumptions:** These are the conclusion we draw. Once we have applied a mental model, we interpret what the facts mean within the specific situation. In other words, we make assumptions. If the mental model is congruent with reality, our interpretation will lead to an accurate understanding and therefore lead us to an accurate conclusion. But if the mental model has distorted reality, and therefore our understanding, we will conclude incorrectly.

5. **Reaction:** Regardless of whether our conclusion is valid or not, we will now decide on a response. This response is a reaction to our conclusion. Sometimes our response will align with the facts and sometimes it will seem illogical to others who have not applied the same mental model and made the same assumptions. Learning about your own mental models will help you choose wisely rather than react to false information.

Mental models

We all have unique and shared mental models that shape how we see the world. A mental model is like a camera lens: it frames how we interpret what happens around us. Each of us experiences the world differently for a variety of reasons, including how we focus our lens and which filters we adopt. Our lenses and filters determine our view of reality: what we notice, what grabs our attention and what we ignore. We may notice many details, or we may notice few. We are all unique. Our interpretations of the world depend on our mental models—like camera lenses and filters, they determine what is absorbed or rejected and what finally registers onto our internal digital screen.

Our mental models are shaped by a number of factors.

- **personal experience/history:** what we observe, encounter and undergo over the course of time
- **values (personal or cultural):** concepts of worth
- **ethics:** a set of moral principles
- **beliefs (personal and cultural):** opinions or convictions held personally or collectively
- **biases:** prejudices in favour of or against things, people or groups compared with others, usually in a way considered to be unfair or inaccurate.
- **assumptions:** things we accept as true or as certain to happen, without evidence or proof
- **judgments:** opinions or conclusions

When we use mental models, we create, in our mind's eye, a representation of the real world—or, as is often the case, a representation of imaginary situations. Kenneth Craik first described the notion of mental models in 1943. He talked about how the brain constructs small-scale models of reality that it then uses to anticipate events.

Mental models exist below our level of awareness. They are powerful and have a tremendous impact on how we respond or react to the events around us. They allow us to make sense of the world. For example, a mental model might be: "People are trustworthy." It's a belief we might hold because of our values or because of our personal experience or because we were taught it at an early age. This mental model then puts us out in the world with this point of view. As our camera lens takes in information, it passes through this filter of "people are trustworthy," influencing how we engage. Chances are, if one of our mental models is "people are trustworthy," we will be open and expect only the best from people when we first meet them. It's unlikely that we would be guarded and cautious.

On the other hand, if our mental model is, "People will always take advantage of a situation for their own gain," we are likely to behave in a completely different way, because it colours how we view another's actions. For example, a colleague may offer us help, and we would wonder about hidden agendas or how he planned to get something out of this situation.

Our mental models also help us recognize patterns. Being "street smart," for example, is a form of pattern recognition. You know not to go down a dark alley in a bad neighbourhood at night. Or, if you know a person well, you might understand that certain expressions or behaviours mean something is going on for that person, based on patterns you've learned from being in her company. For example, when a particular friend is quiet, you might recognize that this behaviour indicates something is bothering her; furrowed eyebrows and a tense forehead might mean that she is not at ease about something and feels insecure.

So how does this concept apply in a leadership context? As a leader, it is key for you to be able to help yourself and your team deconstruct mental models so you are all grounded in the same observable reality. To do that, it's important to understand how our mental models can interfere with our ability to engage effectively with others in an organizational environment.

To illustrate the power of mental models, I want to share a personal example of how a mental model got in the way of me being able to solve a puzzle. First, try linking these nine dots using no more than four straight lines, without lifting your pencil off the paper.

I played with this for a while, trying all sorts of options to no avail. Finally, the facilitator invited solutions. There was a pause, and then one lone participant said, "I think I've got it." Standing up at a flip chart, she took her pen and connected all dots by zigzagging outside of the imaginary box formed by the nine dots. (See YouTube for the "Nine Dots Four Lines Solution.")

Ah. The power of our educational system and conventional approaches! It never occurred to me to go *outside the box*! We're supposed to stay *inside* the box, aren't we? In fact, the "stay in the box" rule in my head was so firmly entrenched that it didn't even *occur* to me to question it. I made this assumption completely subconsciously. Mental models are powerful.

When I first encountered this puzzle, I was surprised by my inability to solve it without assistance. My mental models were so strong that my brain wouldn't let me consider the "out of the box" solutions to either of them. Mental models define our experience of the world more than we realize.

Using the Stairway to Conclusions

The examples below use the stairway to show how a conclusion can be reached.

Example One: Special K Plays

A number of years ago, Special K launched a commercial that played with our mental models. The scene opens with a large, boisterous Italian family sharing a meal. The energy diminishes as the family finishes eating and settles in for post-meal relaxation. Everyone pushes back their chairs . . . and then all the men stand and begin clearing the table and doing the dishes. Meanwhile, the women remain seated, stretch and bring out their cigars. The first time I saw the commercial, I laughed out loud. The punch line had inverted my assumptions and expectations to make a point.

Our cultural mental model cues us to view the commercial through the lens of traditional male/female roles. As we follow the story line of the commercial, we begin to anticipate how it will go. The commercial overturns our assumptions by having the men wait on the women. Playing with mental models in this way helps make them more visible and allows us to see them more objectively.

Reaction (saying or doing something): We laugh at the surprise twist.

Assumptions (drawing conclusions): When everyone pushes back their chairs, we assume the women will stand.

Mental Model (concepts such as cultural paradigms, personal beliefs and biases): Women clear tables and do dishes while men sit, smoke and talk.

Filtered Reality (some facts): We focus on everyone pushing back their chairs.

Observable Reality (facts): We notice the meal is winding down and will soon finish.

Example Two: The Punctuation Exercise

Punctuate the following: A woman without her man is nothing.

Upon first seeing this puzzle, while attending a professional development workshop, I punctuated the sentence like this: "A woman, without her man, is nothing."

The feminist within me thought, *What a stupid exercise!* and *How dare they use this in a training session. I'm going to have to speak to the program's sponsor.* My brain prattled on to myself, *In this day and age, I can't believe a facilitator would use this material. This company is supposed to be reputable. I'm really surprised they are allowing this in the program.*

Our brains think fast, and mine would have continued along the same line of thought if the trainer hadn't called time and asked for our solutions. Another participant immediately offered the same solution I had constructed. When no other ideas were forthcoming, the facilitator turned to the flip chart and punctuated the sentence as follows: "A woman: without her, man is nothing."

I could feel my face redden as the solution sank in. My internal rant and rave had been all for naught. I wondered why I hadn't been able to see the second possibility, especially as it fit more closely with my feminism. In time, I understood. Our cultural mental model is a very strong bias, and the phrasing of the first solution is arguably the more commonly accepted expression or sentiment. This mental model was so strongly ingrained in the minds of all the participants (including me!) that we were blinded to the possibility of other solutions. Even my feminist values were not sufficient to counteract the more prevalent cultural filter that informed my punctuation.

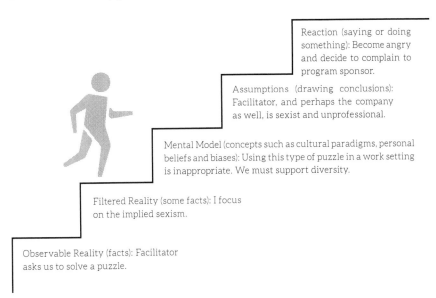

Reaction (saying or doing something): Become angry and decide to complain to program sponsor.

Assumptions (drawing conclusions): Facilitator, and perhaps the company as well, is sexist and unprofessional.

Mental Model (concepts such as cultural paradigms, personal beliefs and biases): Using this type of puzzle in a work setting is inappropriate. We must support diversity.

Filtered Reality (some facts): I focus on the implied sexism.

Observable Reality (facts): Facilitator asks us to solve a puzzle.

Fortunately, before I had a chance to react, the facilitator debriefed the exercise. Otherwise, it would have been a very embarrassing moment!

When we run up the stairs, our brain does not question its beliefs and assumptions. Rather, our brain is convinced that it's right, and we move forward with determination and confidence to address the situation. Tentativeness vanishes, and we move to assert ourselves.

It's pretty much guaranteed that if you observe someone overreacting to a person or a situation, he or she is in the midst of an emotional hijacking and has run up the stairs, leaving known facts on the steps below and filling in unknowns with beliefs, biases and drawn conclusions based on assumptions.

Our brains like to know. We don't like gaps. We want to figure it all out and make sense of our world. It's a form of order. Ambiguity doesn't sit well with most brains. As a result, we often move away from the facts and create our own complete picture, which almost always distorts the objective reality of what is happening.

This is also the nature of gossip. We speculate about what a fact means and create stories that can be quite harmful. "We saw her come out of his house" might be all we know. But we want to know more—we want to fill in the gaps. A speculative question follows: "So what do you think they were doing?" and so it all begins.

We greatly benefit when we learn to control how our brain operates. We are much more than runaway neurochemicals! We have the power to stay at the bottom of the stairs until we know all the facts, but it requires awareness, knowledge and discipline to do so. These skills lie at the center of emotional intelligence.

Example Three: A Leadership Example

In my work with teams, I've noticed how often the source of a conflict is rooted in team members attaching incorrect meanings to a word or gesture—and how often this is reciprocated, making the tension more intense. Let's consider the example below.

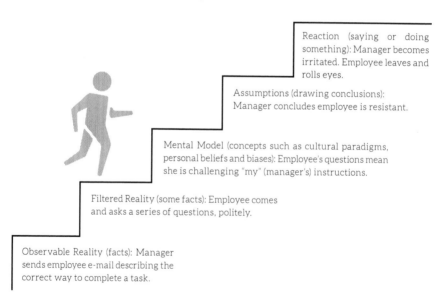

Reaction (saying or doing something): Manager becomes irritated. Employee leaves and rolls eyes.

Assumptions (drawing conclusions): Manager concludes employee is resistant.

Mental Model (concepts such as cultural paradigms, personal beliefs and biases): Employee's questions mean she is challenging "my" (manager's) instructions.

Filtered Reality (some facts): Employee comes and asks a series of questions, politely.

Observable Reality (facts): Manager sends employee e-mail describing the correct way to complete a task.

In this example, past experiences and personal biases create the leap to the top of the stairs. Over the years, this employee has challenged a number of changes executed by management. As a result, his manager has drawn the conclusion that the employee is disrespectful and insubordinate.

Once this type of conclusion is established, it becomes a strong filter, and from that moment forward, the manager interprets the employee's actions through it.

Such interpretations become a vicious cycle. The stronger the filter, the more our brain sees evidence that supports our conclusion. And the more evidence we accumulate, the more proof we have that our conclusion is correct, which then reinforces the filter.

This example is a case in point. Even once I pointed out these "brain facts" to the manager, he refused to give up his judgment of the employee. In order to improve the relationship between the manager and the employee, the past had to be left in the past. New experiences had to be taken at face value by both the manager and the employee so that the habitual responses—irritation, rolling eyes—would stop and be replaced by healthier, more constructive behaviours. As you might imagine, this is much easier said than done! Nevertheless, once we are determined to be true to the facts, it is doable.

Keeping our feet on the first stair

The question now becomes, what do you do about it? How do you stop yourself from running up the stairs, especially if your limbic system has been triggered? We all jump to conclusions at one time or another—it's part of being human. Your brain operates at lightning speed: it filters facts, applies mental models, jumps to conclusions and reacts in the bat of an eye. Before you know what's happening, your brain is racing up the stairs, so quickly that it can take some time to figure out why you reacted the way you did.

When you allow your brain to run up the Stairway to Conclusions, you risk arriving at a good many erroneous conclusions by the time you reach the top. Sometimes you are right about your conclusions; however, often you are wrong. Best practice, especially in the leadership arena, is to stop before you step up the stairs.

To stay on firm ground at the bottom of the stairway, stay focused on facts. A good way to do that is to ask two simple, basic and important questions:

- What do I know?
- What don't I know?

Train your brain to examine both. Otherwise, it will just run with what it knows and likely make up the other stuff through associations and speculation. I use this part of the stairway tool deliberately and systematically in challenging situations. If it is a particularly important matter and I want to stay clear and calm, I take a sheet of paper and, at the top, write what I want to be clear on. Then I make two columns by drawing a line down the center of the paper. I label the column on the left, "What I know—the facts," and the one on the right, "What I don't know—unknowns." Then I make two lists. Using the previous example, my lists might look like this:

Why Did He Come and Ask Many Questions?

What I know—the facts	What I don't know—unknowns
• I sent an e-mail with fairly detailed instructions. • When the employee came to my desk, he was polite. • He asked many questions, about 10. • Some of his questions were "why" questions. For example, "Why do you put that information in that folder?" • When he left my desk, he rolled his eyes.	• I don't know his motivation for asking so many questions. • I don't know his reasons for so many "why" questions. • I don't know why he rolled his eyes. • I don't know if the eye rolling was directed at me.

Going through this exercise may open up possibilities about the situation that you had not considered, ones that were hidden from you previously because of your own belief system. For example, it may occur to you that perhaps the employee simply did not understand your instructions, or more likely because of the nature of the "why" questions, wanted to understand the rationale behind the steps in the process to deepen his understanding. He might simply have been trying to inform himself. You may want to add these to the "unknowns" column.

The next step is to clarify the facts around what you don't know. Since the employee is back at his desk, clarification will require a conversation.

If new possibilities occurred to you during the process of analyzing reality, you can "test" them when you speak to the employee. It's key to check back with people and gather the facts that will help you manage your thoughts and emotions appropriately so that your decisions and actions are worthy of your leadership position. The conversation in this example might go something like this:

Manager: Jim, would you mind if we spoke for a moment?

Jim: No problem.

Manager: I was just wondering why the instructions I sent by e-mail led you to ask so many questions. I am wondering if I wasn't clear enough, or perhaps, you simply wanted to know more?

Jim: Your instructions were fine. It's just that the process didn't quite make sense to me, and I wanted to understand why we were putting certain pieces of data in one folder and why other data went in a different place. It didn't quite make sense to me.

Manager: Did my answers help?

Jim: Yes, but I felt like I was bothering you. You seemed irritated.

Manager: I'm sorry about that, Jim. I'm glad you're clear now though.

Sound unrealistic? Well, it isn't. This is a real-life example. The conversation actually happened, and the manager in question recognized that he was reacting to past events instead of staying true to the current moment. His baggage from the past had impacted his ability to see the present clearly, without bias. By going back to the employee for clarification on the facts, he was able to make sense of the interaction.

Also, notice the tentativeness of the questions (i.e., "I was wondering…" "perhaps…"). It's important when you are trying to fill in the blanks that you ask questions in ways that are comfortable for the recipient. You don't want to put people on the defensive by coming across as if you are interrogating them. That would just make matters worse, not better!

Using the Stairway to Conclusions tool is a great way to avoid potential conflict. It will help you to stay calm, be clear, ask the right questions, get the facts straight and diffuse tension *before* it becomes problematic. Our brain is an amazing thing; we just need to make sure it doesn't cause us to race up the Stairway to Conclusions without even thinking.

Remember: Stop before you step up the stairs, and use your leadership communication skills to get the outcome you desire.

ACTIVITY

Consider a situation that is a source of conflict or tension or even simple disagreement as objectively as you can.

1. Sketch your steps on the stairway.
2. Make visible your beliefs, biases and assumptions.
3. Bring yourself back to facts.
4. Make a chart of what you do and don't know.
5. Open yourself up to new possibilities.
6. Confirm and/or fill in the blanks.

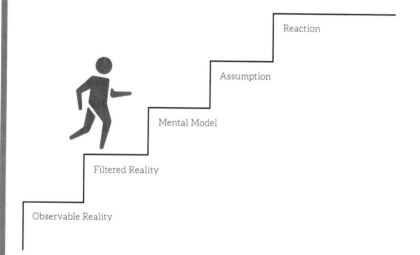

Reaction

Assumption

Mental Model

Filtered Reality

Observable Reality

Ask yourself what you know and don't know. Once you have done this, hold a conversation to fill in the gaps to build your understanding.

What I know—the facts	What I don't know—unknowns

15 | QUIT BEING A VICTIM, VILLAIN OR HERO

Keep the fire in your team's belly by refusing to allow them to take on dysfunctional roles that create the foundation for mind games. As a leader, be vigilant. Listen for expressions of the victim-hero-villain triangle and address them each and every time. You want your team to know how to thrive *despite* the circumstances in which they find themselves.

People often perceive themselves as victims as a strategy to avoid facing their own choices and/or the challenges before them. Whenever there is a victim, there must be a villain. You can't claim to be a victim unless you create a villain. And then, of course, you have a nice set-up to create or invite a hero in to rescue you. A victim sees himself or herself as powerless, at the mercy of a villain and needing to wait for the hero.

Playing the victim is probably the most harmful of the accountability-avoidance strategies and deserves a deeper dive than the others. Playing the victim is somewhat complex, as it often involves creating a villain and usually a hero for the story you are telling yourself. This victim-villain-hero triangle impacts others in significant ways, depending on the situation.

> **KNOW THAT YOU AND YOUR TEAM CAN ACT ON YOUR OWN BEHALF.**

Archetypes

To fully understand the triangle, it's useful to be familiar with the concept of archetypes. Merriam-Webster.com defines archetype as "the original pattern or model of which all things of the same type are representations or copies" and "an inherited idea or mode of thought in the psychology of C. G. Jung that is derived from the experience of the race and is present in the unconscious of the individual."

Jungian psychology interested me throughout my undergraduate and graduate studies. I came to see archetypes as mental models that play a significant role in defining how we see ourselves and the world. In *Man and His Symbols* (1964), Jung defined an archetype as "a universal and recurring image, pattern or motif representing a typical human experience." It is not my intention to debate the merits or difficulties with the work of Jung's or others'—such as Joseph Conrad, Northrop Frye and Caroline Myss—but simply to share with you a new way of seeing workplace dynamics.

Archetypes show up in the workplace and can play havoc if we are not aware of the typical patterns they represent. We often become so engrossed in the details of a workplace drama that we miss the overall patterns playing out before us. Here's one from my own experience:

Person 1: I can't believe my manager is giving me a hard time over my numbers! He knows I have a lot on my plate right now. He's so unreasonable and is always breathing down my neck! And just yesterday, he insinuated I might be sloughing off when I'm on the road. I can't wait for him to retire.

Person 2: Look, I know you work hard and care a lot about your clients. Your manager can be a little too demanding, and everyone knows he's a bit quirky. I might have an opening in my department. Would you be interested in a sales support role? It might be a nice change for you.

It's not hard to pick out the victim, villain and hero in this scenario. The sales manager is of course the villain. He causes suffering and victimizes his employee, who is being rescued by another manager. A nice little triangle. Whenever people present themselves as victims, there is either an identified or unidentified villain. You can't be a victim without a villain. And, the victims usually make their terrible situation well-known in the hope that some hero will provide them an escape route.

Denial of accountability

It's crucial to remember that the foundation of this triangle is a denial of accountability. The victim, in this case, claims he is an innocent and is being hard done by. He cries "poor me" and looks for validation, and possibly a rescue, from another.

Please don't misunderstand me. In life, there are true victims. Bad stuff happens to good people. Real events create real victims. However, in many instances, we have a choice to either see ourselves as a victim or a victor—someone who has the power of choice. A victor knows she can choose differently and thus create different results.

In the exchange above, Person 1 wants his listener to believe he is a victim of a demanding micromanager. If others accept this claim, he doesn't need to accept any accountability for the situation with his manager—he's off the hook. He can simply lay blame at his manager's feet, lick his wounds and remain passive.

The alternative is for this employee to accept that he has co-created the situation and has made choices that have resulted in tension with his manager. He might examine his actions and decisions. Let's break it down:

- "I can't believe my manager is giving me a hard time for my numbers!" *Well, I did commit to those numbers, and I am falling further behind each month without explaining my current challenges. My manager has a right to be concerned.*
- "He knows that I have a lot on my plate right now." *I'm actually not sure I have thoroughly explained my situation. And I probably could do a better job of managing my priorities. Time management isn't really my strength.*
- "He's unreasonable and is always breathing down my neck!" *My manager likes to know what's going on. When he doesn't feel he has enough information, he gets nervous. Because I'm not making my numbers, I have been avoiding him a little.*
- "And, just yesterday, he insinuated that I might be sloughing off when I'm on the road." *I am a little down about the number of rejections I've had lately, and the market is really tough right now. I must admit I am less energetic than normal. And what he actually said was, "I'd like to speak with you about how you're organizing your appointments on the road. I think you could work your schedule more efficiently." I might have read too much between the lines.*
- "I can't wait for him to retire." *It's not his fault I'm not making my numbers. He'd be willing to help, if I asked him.*

When we vent and do a little ranting and raving, we don't really want to engage our rational brain. It's much more satisfying to give in to our inner victim and feel sorry for ourselves in the moment. Being an adult and taking full responsibility is a bit of a drag sometimes!

However, when we understand our own choices, we gain the power to choose differently to get a better result. As long as we stay in the role of victim, we make ourselves helpless and powerless. As uncomfortable as it can be to look at our own choices, the upside is we feel in control of the quality of our lives. We give ourselves the ability to create positive outcomes for ourselves.

Making yourself a victim and someone else a villain is a strategy to deflect your own accountability. Next time you hear yourself complain about someone else, ask yourself how you might choose differently: *What can I do about this situation? What positive actions can I take to create a better outcome for myself and possibly for others?* Next time you want to make someone the bad guy, ask yourself: *What do I gain by making the other person wrong? What responsibility do I have? What accountability am I trying to avoid?*

No one's perfect. You can always find fault with someone else. Villains are available in the millions! The question is, do you want to be a victim? Or do you want to see yourself as a competent, capable person who has the ability to make healthy choices that lead to positive outcomes? Personally, I prefer to think of myself as powerful rather than powerless.

To the rescue

What about the hero in the triangle? Heroes are the good guys. Or are they? Most of us actually don't need rescuing. We need instead to confront our choices and accept our accountability. Heroes deprive us of the opportunity to see our choices and to choose differently.

Whether well-intentioned or not, heroes do not serve us well unless we are truly in crisis and powerless—as in dangling off a cliff, for example! Often, heroes are self-serving. They get their sense of self-worth by helping others. They rescue because there is something in it for them, even if it's just feeling good about being a Good Samaritan.

When we rescue someone, it's usually in the form of a Band-Aid solution. In a true crisis, this may be exactly what's needed. However, heroes can become addicted to being heroes. If a victim doesn't present himself for rescuing, many heroes go looking! This is why we sometimes see people in organizations fabricating a crisis. Saving the day can be a buzz, after all.

Rather than rescuing, it is often much better to support those in difficulty by helping them take action on their own behalf. Acting or removing obstacles for them takes away the learning experience that could help them choose differently moving forward. As the Chinese proverb says, "Give a man a fish and you feed him for a day. Teach a man to fish and you feed him for a lifetime."

Heroes, unwittingly in many cases, impair our ability to increase our independence and personal power. They amplify the sense of powerlessness the victim already feels by underscoring to the victim that he or she doesn't have the strength or power to act on his or her own behalf, but needs someone else—the hero—to do it instead. So heroes get to feel good about their roles, as do victims *in the short term*. In the long term, however, victims continue to see themselves as incapable.

Heroes, ask yourselves: *Is it more important to feel good about helping someone or to support them in becoming stronger and more autonomous?*

Leaders, listen for victim-speak and challenge it. Help victims discover how they can choose differently. Don't be the hero. Be the coach who challenges and refuses to allow them to dis-empower themselves. Don't buy into creating villains. They are just that—creations or illusions, a mental trick we play to avoid our own accountability.

Activity

Spend one day listening for examples of hero-victim-villain. Notice how often you or others place themselves in the powerless victim role and create villains out of others. Also, watch to see if anyone emerges as the hero to rescue the situation. At the end of the day, reflect on what you have observed. Once you see them in action, you can choose to interact differently and move beyond these confining roles.

....

....

....

PART 2:

INSPIRATION AND ACTION

➚ OVERVIEW

A little inspiration can go a long way to helping us take action in support of our aspirations. Far too often, the world (or even our family and friends) tells us why we can't do something or shouldn't do something. Sadly, it is uncommon for others to tell us to "go for it" or to challenge us to be true to our heart's desires or to support our risk-taking, even if we might fail.

This is true for the ordinary person as well as for the famous. For instance, as told in the 2012 movie *Hitchcock*, director Alfred Hitchcock had to finance *Psycho*, his most acclaimed film, by mortgaging his own home because the studios wouldn't take the risk, even though his previous work had been very successful. *Psycho* didn't follow the known "Hitchcock formula." It was a departure, an experiment, and as a result Hitchcock found himself surrounded by naysayers and critics. He nevertheless insisted. He persevered. And with the help of his wife, Alma, he pulled it off and created a film that would be studied evermore by critics, students and filmmakers.

As leaders, our role includes inspiring those around us to reach their highest aspirations, to take risks and to see possibility in all things, including challenges. Help your team see the purpose in their work, the worthiness of their goals and the value of their efforts.

Remember, inspiration kick-starts action and helps people persist in the pursuit of meaningful goals.

16 | ASPIRE TO SOMETHING

When we aspire to something, we have a strong desire, even a longing, to bring into being a goal that is meaningful to us. Meaning is the cornerstone of passion. To light a fire in the hearts and minds of your team, you need to instil in them a sense of purpose. It's impossible to be fired up as individuals or as a team without a deep sense of why it all matters. As a leader, it starts with you. Begin by aspiring to greatness yourself.

What are aspirations? And why should you care about them? Let's deep dive into the associated verb and its roots.

According to Merriam-Webster.com, to aspire means "to seek to attain or accomplish a particular goal; ascend, soar." Looking at the origins of *aspire* and *aspiration* reconnects us to their true nature. The verb *aspire* comes from the Middle French *aspirer* and from the Latin *aspirare* (which means, literally, to "breathe upon") and *spirare*, "to breathe."

When we connect the roots of the word *aspire* to our modern definition of aspiration, the importance of purpose-filled goals to help us lead inspired lives becomes crystal clear. Breathing enables life; breath itself is life-giving. As newborns, the first thing we must do to survive is to breathe. Interestingly, the difference in temperature between the womb and our new environment triggers our first breath, thus kick-starting life on "the outside."

> YOUR WORK IS GOING TO FILL A LARGE PART OF YOUR LIFE, AND THE ONLY WAY TO BE TRULY SATISFIED IS TO DO WHAT YOU BELIEVE IS GREAT WORK. AND THE ONLY WAY TO DO GREAT WORK IS TO LOVE WHAT YOU DO. IF YOU HAVEN'T FOUND IT YET, KEEP LOOKING. DON'T SETTLE. AS WITH ALL MATTERS OF THE HEART, YOU'LL KNOW WHEN YOU FIND IT.
> —STEVE JOBS, STANFORD COMMENCEMENT ADDRESS, 2005

Aspirations give us a sense of purpose and inspire us to take action in service of them. They are the starting point for motivation.

Human beings are designed to create, and through the act of creating, to lead purposeful lives. When we get in touch with our true aspirations and desires and conceive goals based on these, we tap directly into our life force and breathe more energy into it. Through the act of realizing goals that represent our purpose and aspirations, we fully engage in life—we become players rather than spectators in our own existence. When we aspire, we are "breath-fully" alive!

To attain a true sense of fulfillment at work, it is essential to see how our personal aspirations align with what we do—that is to say, your personal aspirations and your role at work must be congruent. If your current work does not support your long-term aspirations, you will lack a sense of purposeful direction and therefore passion for what you are doing.

ACTIVITY

Some of the most important questions we can ask ourselves as leaders are:

- Do I feel a deep sense of alive-ness?
- Am I engaged in my life?
- Am I connected to my truest, deepest aspirations?
- Have I articulated goals that support these aspirations?
- Does my current role support me in achieving my goals?

....

....

....

Here are some practical real-life examples (including my own) to show what living one's purpose looks like:

1. My aspiration has always been to live a more conscious, fulfilling life and to support others in doing the same. Essentially, this means choosing in favour of my values and things that matter most to me. As a young leader, I worked hard to ensure people loved coming to work and had the opportunity to contribute

fully once they got there. I challenged people to stop settling for anything less than a great work experience! Life is just too short to aim for less. Now, through my workshops and coaching, I encourage people to create the life they want and truly desire, both at work and at home. Throughout my career, I have felt connected to the same purpose, regardless of where I worked and for whom I worked.

2. A client of mine, Fatima, is a learning and development professional. Fatima strives to create more diversified workplaces. She seeks opportunities to support this goal through all of her assignments, and over time, she has seen results. She helped a women's network blossom; she facilitates powerful conversations about race and gender issues within leadership workshops; and she lobbies executives advocating for a workforce that reflects local demographics. Every day, Fatima works toward the goal of diversity in the workplace. Sometimes her actions are modest; sometimes they are bold. Small or large, she takes a daily step forward and in the process experiences huge personal fulfillment in her life.

3. Another client, Roland, wants to ensure people in his community feel supported through their work relationships. Employees at Roland's insurance company know the company will "be there" for them. He nurtures a culture that encourages colleagues to treat each other as family. Roland sets the tone. For example, whenever an employee goes through a personally difficult time, he offers comfort and support. I have known him to attend a funeral wake, not for a token 20 minutes, but to sit with the family evening after evening. I have known him to entertain the children of his overseas executives to make sure they felt connected to the community and their parents' workplace. I have known him to bring a staff member lunch because he knows the worker did not take breaks that day. His respect for each and every person with whom he works is consistent and apparent to anyone who spends time with him. He is a member of the community first and a CEO second.

How can you make sure you are living an aspirational life? How do you know if you're "aligned to your purpose?" The first step is to check in with yourself and take stock of where you are vis-à-vis where you want to be.

Your purpose need not be grandiose; it can be modest. Meaning is not about magnitude. Small can be significant; big can be irrelevant. Don't think size. Think: "Does it matter?"

When you, as a leader, feel grounded in a true sense of purpose, you are in turn able to support your team members to achieve that to which they aspire. In fact, helping your team members realize their goals in life is one of the most important aspects of your leadership role. When you are clear about your own aspirations, you will be better able to help your employees connect with their own. It's virtually impossible for someone who is not aligned with his or her own purpose to support others in achieving theirs.

To ground yourself before work each day, remind yourself of your purpose. Consider asking yourself (and answering!) these questions at the start of each day:

- Why am I getting up today?
- What do I hope to achieve today?

When you are grounded, you can help ground your employees as well. "Why bother?" you may ask. The answer lies in the bottom line. When people—you, your employees, your peers, your organization—feel their work is aligned to their life's purpose, they are naturally motivated to give fully of themselves. They won't hold back. They will go the extra mile. They will add value to the company wherever they can, because in so doing they will add value to their own dreams and aspirations. It's a win-win scenario in which everyone comes out on top. And, we should always remember that organizations were created for people to do great things together. Organizations exist for people. We do not live for the organization. It lives for us!

Activity

Ask and answer a few fundamental questions to clarify or assert your purpose. Take note of whatever comes to mind. "I don't know" is a legitimate answer, but don't stop there. Ask yourself, *What* do *I know*? For example, you may not be able to articulate your purpose simply and clearly, but you may know that you care deeply about community. So start with whatever you know and develop your ideas from there.

- What is your purpose?
- What would you like to be known for?
- What difference would you like to make in the world?
- What impact do you want to have on the people around you?
- How would you like to contribute to making your workplace or community a better place?

....

....

....

17 | LET GO. SEE. CREATE.

Fire up your team by letting go of control, seeing possibility where others see constraints and creating a shared aspiration. Giving people greater autonomy is key to engagement and inspiration. It requires managers to learn how to guide without controlling, however. In addition, leaders need to recognize that in any difficult or challenging circumstance, when there is a letting go, there is also an opening, providing possibilities for moving forward. Seeing alternative paths enables leaders to explore what the future might look like, eventually formulating a shared goal or aspiration. Once you have found your aspiration, let your love for your goal displace your fears and your need to hold on and control.

This chapter examines, one by one, each action listed in the title. In brief, letting go is the antidote of unnecessary controlling behaviours. Seeing is the act of looking, without bias, at the many possibilities before us. Creating is choosing one to bring to fruition.

Let go

We try to control when we want the illusion that we can determine outcomes. A controlling person is really a terrified person, fearful the future will not be kind. For example, micromanagers fear objectives won't turn out as planned, and hierarchical command and control systems worry employees will take advantage or won't have the will or ability to drive the business forward. Control therefore is seen as a solution in an unpredictable and volatile world. However, it will be impossible for your team to get truly fired up if it lives under a cloud of apprehension and fear.

FEARLESS LEADERS EMBRACE POSSIBILITY AND PROPEL TEAMS FORWARD.

Teams will struggle under leaders who need to know and be involved in all the details—or, worse yet, need to dictate how things get executed to give themselves assurance that the results will be achieved. Everyone needs some latitude, and some people need a lot of latitude. Ultimately, the leader and the organization benefit, because when you give people space to use their judgment and talent, you build organizational capacity and create the conditions for high-calibre performance.

When you let go of the fear of failure or of not knowing or of loss, you are able to also free your team to reconnect with possibility and aspiration. One of my clients has undergone tremendous change over the last two years, with a new mission and a new organizational structure. A number of managers have responded by creating new policies, adding in new levels of approval and creating a cost-management system that has practically paralyzed some key departments. These leaders have been trained and indoctrinated in industrial-age management practices that fundamentally view employees as untrustworthy and incapable. As you can imagine, the employees have not responded well to the additional controls. Many are stressed, others have checked out and some are planning their escape.

What is the alternative? To invest time and energy in internalizing the new mission and understanding what it means to each team as well as spending time building new relationships so work can flow easily across the new organizational structure. Such efforts open up possibilities rather than constraints.

ACTIVITY

Take some time to reflect on your management practices and your ability to let go. In what ways do you try to control? Do you insert yourself in your team's work unnecessarily? Do you require employees to check in with you constantly? Write your answers below. Then challenge yourself to question whether these actions truly add value, or is their purpose to give you comfort and a false sense of security?

....

....

....

See

Once you let go of the need to control, you must orientate yourself to see opportunity. Fearless leaders embrace possibility and propel teams forward at lightning speed. They inform their teams about organizational purpose and ensure everyone is fluent in the big-picture goals of the organization so that the teams can explore ways to offer support.

By concentrating on fulfilling organizational aspirations and expressing the organization's purpose in meaningful ways, teams will find exciting and unique paths forward. As you explore this new territory, it may feel uncomfortable, as not everything will be clear; however, helping your team navigate this stage will bring rewards. Fearless leaders don't channel energies into managing unwanted circumstances or creating the illusion of security. Instead, they encourage their team members to explore uncharted waters to find their own solutions and opportunities to take their work to the next level.

In the instance of my client mentioned above, I encouraged a senior manager to begin slow and deliberate conversations around the new mission and the team's new mandate to help members work together to explore the exciting opportunities offered by the change rather than leaving them feeling only a sense of loss for what no longer existed. Helping the team see all of the new possibilities is an important transition to creating a shared aspiration, which will ultimately allow the team to move forward.

ACTIVITY

When was the last time you met with your team and discussed the company's purpose, mission and core strategies? When do you last discuss how your work supports these? When did you last challenge whether your team was focused on the right things to generate the best value? When did you last hold a meeting to simply explore new possibilities? If it's been more than six months, plan to host one within the next month. Draft your meeting invite below so you can action this immediately.

....

....

....

Create

Fearless leadership is creative and generative. It focuses on what can be brought into being rather than on safeguarding the status quo, managing risk or incessantly problem-solving.

It is in our DNA to create. We are destined to evolve. Robert Fritz, an author whose books include *Creating* (1993) and *The Managerial Moment of Truth* (2011, with Bruce Bodaken), says this so well: "Every artist knows the world doesn't need another painting. Every composer knows the world doesn't need another score. Artists bring their creations into being simply because they want to."

As leaders, I believe we need to ask ourselves (and honestly answer) tough questions like: "Do I have a creative orientation to achieving goals? Or am I reactive and fearful? Do I take bold actions? Or do I hesitate based on a fear of failure, a fear of inadequacy or a fear of things falling apart? Am I willing to challenge my team to go beyond the ordinary to support our organization's purpose?

How does one become fearless? The most powerful antidote to fear is to direct your brain's attention to your deepest and truest aspirations—to take control of your mind and not allow it to live and work from a place of fear. This takes discipline, determination and a clear focus on the end results. This does not mean we ignore real threats. It means we are grounded in reality and able to discern real danger from perceived threats.

As much as fear is a part of being human, there is another force within us that is just as (if not more) powerful: the desire and need to create. We all want to develop and grow. Although we may be comforted at times by the status quo, we are never fully satisfied by it. It's human nature to progress, to stretch, to reach for the stars, and each of us has a creator within.

Communicating a shared aspiration: your picture or story

I have always been fascinated by the visual and performing arts, and for years I studied fine arts, culminating in an interdisciplinary degree. In the process, I learned how much human beings want to express themselves. We have hands to build, sculpt, draw, paint, play musical instruments and more. We have language to express thoughts, share ideas and collaborate. We can bring others to tears with a painting or create a revolution with a slogan.

As leaders, we have the opportunity to create something out of nothing, working through people to produce beautiful, useful or life-changing works of art: products, services and ideas that express our purpose and aspirations as individuals and organizations. The ability to create is available to everyone. Tapping into it results in fulfilling work experiences—for ourselves and others—and enables us to make a difference in the world.

ACTIVITY

Try visualizing. Imagine yourself a masterful artist with a blank canvas and an unlimited palette of vibrant colours. Your job is to paint your aspirations so that your team can envision them. In creating this painting, you visually and dynamically represent the future and establish expectations around which your team can align. Your vision is a masterful work of art: bold, inspiring, beautiful!

Or try storytelling: Create in your mind's eye a picture of your aspiration as it exists in the future. Describe in detail (verbally or on paper) what it looks and feels like. Create a story around your imagined future and share it with your team. Storytelling is an extremely effective tool used by some of the most charismatic leaders. Telling the story of the future as you see it helps your team members also see it in *their* mind's eye: a future that is desirable, enticing and attainable. Well-crafted stories put us in that future moment. Our imaginations are powerful, and as the story unfolds, we "experience" that future.

18 | BE TRUE NOT SAFE

Inspiration often comes from a compelling purpose. To fire on all cylinders, your team members need a catalyst that captures their imagination and motivates action. Sometimes, to manage disappointment, leaders strive for goals that, while realistic, are too easily reached. These are often uninspiring and leave a team feeling flat and unmotivated. If you hold back from speaking your or the organization's purpose, you do your team a disservice. Team members deserve to know the hopes and aspirations that guide you and your organization. There are no guarantees of success, but trying will be infinitely more fulfilling than playing it safe.

An aspiration communicated through a compelling vision—once created, communicated, shared and internalized—drives strategies and actions and inspires people to work together to create. Most human beings want to engage in work that generates "good stuff" and positively influences the world. Leaders and employees alike often tell me, during workshops as well as coaching sessions, that their most challenging goals have produced their most fulfilling work. Living purposeful lives makes human beings "tick" and inspires them; that's why creating a real purpose is such a vital leadership function.

> **WE OFTEN DENY OURSELVES THE JOY OF TRUE ASPIRATION BY SETTLING FOR WHAT SEEMS REALISTIC.**

As a leader, you have an opportunity to present your team with exciting possibilities that draw upon their talents and allow them to create and contribute in exciting and challenging ways. People want to make a difference. People want to contribute to something meaningful. As a leader, you can be a creator-artist and ask your team to help you paint a canvas that will become a creation of which you can all be proud.

Leadership is not about setting the bar so low that success comes without challenge and is easily achieved. Leadership is about taking people outside their comfort zones and telling them that together you can achieve something special. This unique group of individuals, your team, can bring their talents to bear and work with you to progress toward a desirable and exciting future.

Steve Jobs, the late CEO of Apple, is a perfect example of the leader as creator-artist. He began with a blank canvas and imagined future technologies that would change the way we conceive of our world. Further, he demanded his products be aesthetically pleasing as well as functional and innovative. He was not afraid of failure, nor did he set safe goals. He pushed the boundaries of current thinking, presented his team with clear challenges and set about creating desired outcomes. "Following" Jobs was not for the faint of heart. He offered fellow players seemingly impossible challenges. They had to play in the arena of new possibilities and wild imaginings. And Apple is wildly successful as a result.

I can't envision Jobs being realistic and saying the kinds of things I frequently hear leaders say:

- "Ahhh, it's a great idea, but I don't think we could get the chair's support."
- "We have to be realistic about these things!"
- "I think we need to look at best practices and ensure we're keeping up."
- "This company isn't progressive enough to take on such a goal."
- "We need a contingency plan, and we need to invest in risk management."

Creating is about holding a vision and having faith it can be achieved. Faith is key. If a leader lacks conviction, team members will not bring all of themselves to the project.

The CEO of Starbucks, Howard Schultz, wrote in his book *Pour Your Heart Into It* (1999) that the only reason he succeeded in finding investors during the start-up phase of the company was his passionate belief in his vision and his willingness to put everything on the line to see it realized. As Schultz says, "Passion is, and always will be, a necessary ingredient. Even the world's best business plan won't produce any return if it is not backed with passion and integrity."

Neither Jobs nor Schultz would compromise on his vision. Each held his vision strong, planted his feet firmly in the here and now and figured out what next steps to take to attain his visions as things unfolded. This takes courage and tenacity, to see in your mind's eye your distant future clearly and not know how you're going to get there.

The easier route? Modify your vision—diminish it—so that it seems easier to achieve because you can already see the path you could take to get there. Or decide you don't really want it and find a substitute, an easier-to-achieve but less desirable end result. But as Robert Fritz says, "You can't not want what you want." Compromising your vision will never lead to a sense of well-being.

Knowing what you want but not how you will get there can be challenging. Learning how to be comfortable with this *not knowing* is key to remaining committed to your truest aspirations, both personal and professional. Your team needs to know you believe in your vision, even if you don't know how to achieve it. As you take action, what you can do is pay attention to what's working and what isn't and keep strategizing as you learn. Your team will support you, and this collective wisdom will serve you well.

You may also find that, when you stay focused on your vision, serendipity will befriend you. Be prepared to be surprised! Don't let your worries, anxieties or uncertainties deplete your energy. Focus on the end goal, take positive actions and keep learning! If you reach one dead end, keep exploring other unknowns, and you will discover new options and pathways. Telling ourselves to be realistic is a pre-emptive strike on possible failure. Don't do it! In Steve Jobs 2005 Stanford commencement speech, he says:

Remembering that I'll be dead soon is the most important tool I've ever encountered to help me make the big choices in life. Because almost everything—all external expectations, all pride, all fear of embarrassment or failure—these things just fall away in the face of death, leaving only what is truly important.

Activity

Use reflection to create a vision.

- If failure wasn't a possibility, what would you do?
- What would happen if you stopped worrying about being realistic and just went for your vision?

....

....

....

19 | HELP OTHERS ASPIRE TO SOMETHING

Through meaningful conversation, you can help each team member—and your team as a whole—discover what matters most. Once people face their deepest desires, they will naturally move toward them, especially with your support and guidance. And what will that do? Fire them up, of course!

Exploring your employees' aspirations is an important first step to deeper, more meaningful leadership conversations, as aspirations function as the North Star for many other issues, opportunities and decisions. In one experience in particular, these conversations led to dramatic changes on my team. Over the course of three years, half of my team departed to pursue their true desires; the other half reorganized their work so they could live more in their "passion zone" while still achieving their objectives.

I gained by recruiting new folks who really wanted to support our team's mandate. It was a win-win for everyone, especially for me as the leader. By the end of the five-year period, my work was easy. I had a highly motivated, self-directed team, which in turn gave me the time and space to take the group to the next level and expand our offering. Trying to ensure adequate performance with a team that was not fully engaged had taxed my energy. After the changes, I reaped the rewards of a team in true flow.

> **TAKE EVERYONE'S PASSION PULSE AND LEARN ABOUT HIS OR HER DEEPEST ASPIRATIONS.**

Learning about your team's aspirations is key to fostering purposeful engagement. When people understand how today helps create tomorrow, they are naturally motivated to give fully of themselves. Knowing that you, as their leader, understand the connection and will support them in building further connections is also powerful. Our most meaningful goals take time to execute, so when your leader supports your journey, it uplifts and encourages your heart. It's energizing to know someone is on your side, especially when the person is in a position to see opportunities you might otherwise overlook.

As a leader, you can extend someone's reach into other networks or project areas. This provides value to the company as you help find the right fit, matching people (with their unique talents and motivators) with the work at hand. People get to progress toward their longer-term goals and other parts of the organization gain an employee with the right attitude and skills to do the job well. Again, a win-win.

You may have slightly higher turnover and need to recruit a little more often than your peers, but you can use this to your advantage as well. Every person brings strengths as well as blind spots to a position. When I replaced people, I revisited the position requirements and recruited to take the work to the next level. In this way, my recruiting wasn't discouraging; instead it built my bench strength and improved my overall team performance. Another win.

When you help others aspire, you may uncover hidden talents. Rebecca, an assistant in a communications department I managed, did her job efficiently but without "oomph." As she reported to one of my managers, I did not have a great deal of contact with her. However, I still made it a point to check in. One day, I asked her about her long-term goals and the work she most enjoyed. To my surprise, I discovered she was a finance person! I asked why she wasn't working in her field. She said the market was tough, and she had not been able to find something that paid well enough.

At the time, I managed a large budget and had a hefty amount of onerous (at least to me!) financial reporting to do as part of my management position. Hmm ... the wheels started turning. I met with her supervisor, and we created a new position that took on all the financial analysis and reporting duties for the department while maintaining capacity to back up the communications team when needed. Rebecca was thrilled to be back in a finance role, and I was delighted to have the support I needed. Both of us were much happier as a result.

Another one of my team members, a project manager, Lucy, enjoyed her work but wanted to move into a consulting role in the long term. As a single parent, flexibility was her top priority, and she felt self-employment would be the best solution for her. Although I did not want to lose Lucy from my team, I knew that she would eventually leave to support the lifestyle she required. I decided to help her build the skills she would need to be a successful consultant, and, while she learned the skills, I gave her special projects rather than contracting them out.

The company saved money, and Lucy gained a skill set. After she left, she became one of my key resources and consulted for my team for many years. In the end, we didn't lose anything; we gained a dedicated, high-performing consultant.

Disconnection from aspiration

Once you know what people aspire to, you can help them form links between their personal sense of purpose and their work goals and/or opportunities. A word of caution: When you start to have such conversations, don't be surprised if people are unclear about their long-term goals. Sadly, many of us are completely disconnected from our own aspirations. In my experience, there are three common reasons for the gap: falling into, giving up and overspending.

Falling into
People fall into jobs, get on a particular track and become comfortable with the status quo. Soon, it's easier to stay than to leave. In fact, many people don't explicitly *choose* to either leave or stay; they simply saunter down the easiest path, largely oblivious to the fact that they've left their dreams and aspirations behind in the dust. Then, when they revisit their deepest desires, they believe they can no longer achieve them.

Clients frequently tell me, "I can't change now. I've already invested years in this career; it's too late to start all over." Challenging that kind of assumption can lead to fruitful discussions. Furthermore, strategies to support an individual's underlying aspirations within their existing context may emerge as a result.

Giving up
People give up on their truest aspiration because they decide it's not realistic. They do not see how they can make it happen. Because they do not know what steps to take to get to their end goal, they settle for their current situation.

I once worked with an underwriter named Betsy in a small-island market. Betsy really wanted to be a yoga teacher and open a yoga studio. She decided there was insufficient demand for yoga in her location, so she couldn't make a living teaching it. She stayed in insurance for many years, switching companies a couple of times.

In the end, because of changing personal circumstances, she made the move by fully involving herself in the yoga community in various ways. She now happily works as a yoga instructor. Had her personal circumstances not forced a change, it might have been many more years before she took a leap of faith into her dream.

Overspending

People overspend, acquire debt and then feel stuck. Making a change that requires a temporary or even permanent reduction in income becomes too overwhelming, so people feel they cannot make a move toward their aspirations. Within my first week at one organization, I met a half dozen people who said to me, "Only [X] years until retirement!" Sometimes it was a couple of years, for others it was 10 or more. I vowed then and there not to live my life counting down the years and months to retirement.

I also promised I would not let a big mortgage hold me hostage to my job. I often meet people who are "mortgage poor" and feel stuck in their current job because of it. Clearly, keeping up with the Joneses sometimes comes at a substantial cost—sacrificing your freedom and your dreams. In my opinion, living within one's means and leaving room for choice enables one to live a more fulfilling life.

Helping employees who are disconnected

Many people settle for the status quo or feel powerless and trapped by their current circumstances. I once spoke with a neurologist who really wanted to abandon his private practice and do research at a university. He was keen to be part of finding solutions instead of only helping people cope with their symptoms, which would continue to worsen anyway. His office manager was also his spouse, so all their household income depended on his practice. He had multiple financial commitments and couldn't see how a research position would ever cover his expenses. He felt stuck.

When I asked how he could reduce his living expenses, there were many options: sell the large house and buy a smaller house, sell the building that housed the practice, trade in the car for a used one. In the end, we discovered many ways to make the research position more feasible. It's empowering to know that you can make things happen. You may still choose not to make a change, but at least you see it as a clear choice and can therefore feel less of a victim of circumstance and more of an empowered person making conscious choices.

Once people see options and make choices accordingly, they create the space for further engagement. The baggage of "if only . . ." is lifted, and people can *own* their choices, knowing they can choose differently another time.

What can you do as a leader to empower an employee to make choices rather than feel like a victim of circumstance? How can you help your employees reconnect to their aspirations? Before we look at the *hows*, let's look at why you would want to.

As a manager, it is important you have people on your team who want to be there. Those who don't will weigh you and your team down. They will be incapable of giving of themselves fully because their true desire lays elsewhere. It is better to know this and help these individuals either transition or gain an appreciation of their existing situation.

Your role is key: If you assist them in moving to another internal or external position better suited to achieving their long-term goals, you demonstrate to the team your commitment to team development. If you help them see how their current situation serves them well (in relation to their aspiration) by functioning as a stepping-stone to the future goal, you demonstrate your ability to see the big picture and support both individual and team interests. Either way, the organization benefits, through the employee's renewed engagement or by showing transitions will be handled with dignity and care. In the case of the latter, someone who better fits the role will assume the vacated position, so there is no downside.

Managing scenarios like these begin with asking the right questions at the right time. Here's the sequence I have found works best.

Step 1: Get the picture
Always begin by helping the individual paint a picture of his or her desired future. Sometimes this is pretty straightforward. Ask variations of the following: "If you had no limitations, what would you most like to be doing in 10 years?" (Retirement is not an option.)

When I ask such questions, I'm often surprised by the answers, because they frequently have nothing to do with the individual's present circumstances. An underwriter wants to return to playing in an orchestra.

A school superintendent wants to weave. A learning facilitator wants to sell real estate. People also respond less dramatically with the likes of:

- "I'd like to be managing a department by then."
- "I'd like to have my full qualifications and be running my own book of business."
- "I'd like to be consulting to our industry."

These are good starting points. Asking questions to flesh out these goals is equally important. You want the employee to paint a *full* picture so you can really get a sense of it. The more detail, the better. Ask more questions:

- "What kind of an orchestra?"
- "What area of real estate?"
- "What type of work would you lead?"
- "Do you have a preference for a particular region?"
- "What type of book of business would you like to manage?"
- "What type of clients would you like to attract?"
- "Who would you like to have as clients?"
- "Would you have a specialty?"

If people are able to paint a clear picture, it shows they have given considerable thought to the goal. They know their destination. But be prepared as well for people to say they don't have any further career aspirations and claim they are okay with the status quo.

In the late eighties through to the mid-nineties, my experience working within a government-oriented organization heightened my appreciation of the need to find meaning and purpose in work. Many people I knew came to the organization because it paid fairly well and employment was relatively stable. It was perceived as "a good government job."

However, as a result of this, many people weren't there because of an authentic desire. Over time, they felt they couldn't leave, and they stayed because of underlying fears: fear of leaving and not finding other work that paid as well, fear of losing a secured retirement (and maybe a pension) or fear of being rejected by other employers.

Fear-based reasons put people on shaky ground. Such reasons are barriers to feeling capable of creating the life one wants. Building from a place of "I know what I want and I am able to take big and small steps to move myself closer to my goals" is extraordinarily powerful. It moves you toward something that matters deeply (rather than away from a problem or an undesired set of circumstances). Running away from and running toward something are very different experiences. One feeds fear and the other hope.

Ask further questions to help people think it through. For example:

- "If you weren't worried about your retirement income, what would interest you?"
- "If you weren't living in a remote location, what would be your turn-on work?"
- "If you could do your education all over again, what would you pursue?"

These questions help people step outside of their worries and entertain possibilities. It's important to help people see that most things are possible.

Step 2: Find the motivators

Once people have tapped into an aspiration, the next question needs to be "Why?" so you can get a sense of the underlying motivations and the extent to which this long-term picture speaks to authentic desire. For example, does the person truly want to create this life? Or does she want it because she is running away from a situation she doesn't like? Or does she feel obliged because of others' expectations? Or is it simply a matter of keeping up with the Joneses? Building on the above examples, you might ask questions like:

- "What is it about weaving that captivates you?"
- "Why real estate?"
- "What is it about managing a department that interests you?"
- "How is running a book of business different from being a key player, for you?"
- "What's appealing about consulting?"

Beware! People often *think* they want things they truly do not desire. Their motivation is not self-generated but externally driven. Sometimes they see what they want as an escape route out of an undesirable job or situation, so they pursue it as a fix or a Band-Aid. ("There's so much bureaucracy around here, I want the independence of self-employment!")

Sometimes they see what they want as a symbol of success, so they pursue it to support their self-esteem. ("You need to manage a business in order to be truly respected here.") Sometimes people see what they want as a way of pleasing others, so they pursue it as a way to reduce conflict. ("The company wants me to take a new position to help out with a new initiative, and saying no isn't really an option around here.")

Intrinsic motivators present themselves very differently. They are not reactive to circumstances but are grounded in sincere interests and a sense of purpose. For example:

- "Weaving enables me to create beautiful things that are also functional. I love that!"
- "I really enjoy helping people find spaces that they can call home."
- "I'm interested in bringing people together around tough business problems to find compelling solutions. It's challenging but fun too."
- "I value strategy, and I think shaping a book about business would be very satisfying—linking individual deals with the big picture point of view."
- "My natural abilities seem to lie in project and client management. Consulting might be a good fit for me."

Step 3: Offer support

Once people paint you a picture of their long-term goals and connect to authentic desires, then you as a leader can offer clear support. You can be one of their champions along the road, supporting them in various ways. I always find the best question at this point is, "How can I best help?"

People may have some specific things in mind, or they may simply express their appreciation of your support. At the very least, you can try to match their current objectives and responsibilities with their future desired state and align development opportunities. For example, you could:

- give them a temporary leadership role around a particular task or project
- offer them study time during work hours to help them complete their qualifications
- fund training in consulting skills to help them in their current work but also to build toward their future.

One of my previous employees, although committed to the organization for which we worked, was not happy in the head office. She wanted to relocate to a field office. There were many reasons for her desire, which she shared and I respected. I agreed the move would serve both her and the company better, and I began to look for opportunities for work in the field. I encouraged her to do the same. Eventually an opening emerged, and she was the successful candidate. In addition, her replacement loved the head-office environment. It was a win-win for everyone.

Once an employee knows you are supportive of her long-term goals, she will trust you even more. She will also support you in your goals and objectives. People do not want to let down those who help them. It becomes a mutually supportive work environment through which personal and corporate goals move forward.

Assisting your employees to gain clarity for the long term always helps you in the short term through heightened engagement. It also results in retaining the right people, those who truly want to be on your team for the long haul.

Before I established my own consultancy, I worked on the client side in several different government and private-sector organizations. As a leader, I took particular care to have regular "beneath the surface" conversations with my team members, and I always took the opportunity during annual performance reviews to revisit each person's deepest aspirations. I made it a practice to spend a half-day at year-end one-on-one with each of my direct reports.

We began with a meeting in the office, during which we would look at "the year in review." We assessed both successes and missed objectives so we could improve our planning for the upcoming year. I kept discussions focused on "lessons learned" so they would be non-judgmental and forward-looking. Feedback came in the form of seeing what could have been done differently as well as what practices and actions could lead to further success.

After a couple of hours of discussion, we went out for lunch. I chose restaurants that made it easy to talk and have private conversations. I thought of it as having lunch with a friend I cared about and wanted to support in the journey of life. That made it easy for me to keep the tone conversational and somewhat personal. I might kick off the conversation by asking one of the following questions (whichever seemed most natural or appropriate):

- "So, Craig, you're new to our team, and we haven't had a chance to talk about your career goals. What are some of your long-term aspirations?"
- "Lily, since last year, we haven't taken the time to revisit some of your career development goals. Let's chat about those now."
- "Tom, based on this morning's discussions, it seems to me you have been frustrated this year with your tasks. Your job is quite technical and requires lots of Excel work as well as detailed action plans. How do you feel about this type of work? What would you like it to evolve into?"
- "Mel, how did you come to be in this career? Where would you like to see it take you?"

Once you get people talking and sharing about their longer-term goals, it's important to check the extent to which they have passion for those goals; don't simply accept what they say at face value. It's not hard to take someone's "passion pulse." Usually, as people talk about things that matter to them, they become more energized and animated, even if they are generally quiet. Pay attention to their level of engagement in the conversation—if it intensifies, they likely feel more passionate about the topic. If, on the other hand, the conversation is flat and they themselves seem disinterested in the topic, it may be a good opportunity to deep dive a bit further to uncover what lies beneath.

ACTIVITY

As a leader, you can play a key role in helping people grow and progress. It's your job to help your employees achieve their aspirations. When you do so, everyone benefits: they do, you do, and your organization does as well. Ask them:

- "Where do you want to go?"
- "Why do you want to go there?"
- "How can I help you get there?"
- "What is it you like about your work?"
- "What is it about your career that's meaningful to you?"
- "I'm interested in how your career goals connect to your life goals, if you don't mind sharing."
- "To what extent is your chosen career/work fulfilling for you?"

....

....

....

↗ 20 | SET GOALS

Another way to keep your team fired up is to ensure that everyone is absolutely clear on what you are collectively trying to achieve. We think people know. We think we've communicated. Often this is not the case. Make sure people have goals and know the significance of those goals. People need to know the whys behind the objectives. They need to know which goals truly matter. And they need to know if they achieve them, it will make a difference.

You likely have experience formulating goals for yourself, and likely for your team as well. You probably hold conversations on an annual basis to set goals and objectives for the year as part of the annual performance management process. You may also create personal goals for yourself around health, relationships, adventure or hobbies and other facets of your life.

> **BE EXPLICIT WHEN SETTING MEANINGFUL GOALS.**

Or maybe you don't. Maybe you haven't thought about goals much at all. Sure, you do what's required to comply with workplace requirements, but beyond that, you don't really concern yourself with targets. If that's the case, it's time for a change!

Having clear end results matters because it helps you craft the life you truly desire. It's the foundation you need to achieve your aspirations. Spend time to set goals for yourself, and do the same for your team members. Don't take a superficial approach. Take the time necessary to get to the heart of the matter. Here are a few tips on goal-setting at work.

- **Create a meaningful context with clear and highly desirable end results.** Your goals must be meaningful to you; they don't have to be meaningful to others. Once you locate meaning in a goal, you will be naturally motivated to move it forward. Self-motivation begins with meaning. Planning comes next, followed by action.

If you need to work with goals others have given you, take time to think about how you can find meaning in them. A goal may not be highly meaningful to you as a stand-alone goal. However, if it supports a greater goal, then the meaning is derived from the broader goal. For example, meeting your budget may not be intrinsically meaningful, but meeting your budget may support another, more meaningful goal. When thinking about the less-meaningful goal, always attach it to the more-meaningful goal.

- **Create a baseline with concrete facts about the current situation to help you plan.** Knowing where you are today, in concrete terms, creates a point of reference for your future state. A clear understanding of where you are today enables you to create targeted, relevant action plans that will generate the best result for you.

Seeing your current situation (strengths, weaknesses, helps, hindrances) supports you in taking the most effective action steps to get to your goal. Without this, you are not making progress; you are just taking lots of action, which may leave you feeling unfulfilled and tired.

- **Create easy, small actions that build momentum and a sense of progress.** Plan at least three action steps that are clearly relevant to your goal, based on your current situation. Make sure these action steps do not rely on others but are ones for which you can be 100 percent accountable. Take high-leverage actions that deliver a jolt of progress, and afterward, assess whether the action had impact. Include celebrating in your action plan.

Don't take action for action's sake. You will just end up busy. Your actions need to move you toward meaningful end results. Consistently creating and executing personal, leadership and business goals will give you the insight, knowledge and credibility to coach your team.

ACTIVITY

If you could only accomplish one thing at work this year, what would it be?

- Describe it so others can see, feel and taste it.
- Note all relevant aspects of the current state.
- What strategies could you employ to get you to the end goal?

....

....

....

ACTIVITY

Go through the above exercise with your team as a whole and each of your team members. The litmus test is to answer the following questions: "If nothing else happened this year, would I feel I had made a valuable contribution to my organization?"

....

....

....

21 | EMBRACE AMBIGUITY AND "JUST ENOUGH" ACTION PLANNING

Fire up your team by helping them see the value in ambiguity. Our complex and intricate world defies being "known," leaving our knowledge incomplete and the future unpredictable. Support your team by encouraging them to explore, play and intuit through ambiguity. Help them refrain from overdetailed action planning, as this will create a culture of doing as opposed to a culture of thinking. If you encourage people to create space for pausing and thinking rather than going from one task to the next to the next, you will see creativity and innovation blossom as they respond in the moment to emerging opportunities and situations.

One of the greatest challenges for leaders today is comfort with ambiguity, primarily because their education and experience ill equip them. Many leaders with whom I work hold professional designations. In general, this kind of formal education values left-brain, linear thinking, which involves fact-based logic, standards and precedence. It uses the part of the brain that likes to "know" and to ensure everything is concrete and tangible. This part of the brain works well in repetitive, predictable situations. For example, you may have a goal to create two new products this year. You currently have a proven, successful methodology for doing so. The process feels comfortable and familiar. It's easy for you to create new products.

On the other hand, you may have a goal that is new for both you and your organization, such as how to grow in a tapped-out market. This may put you and your team in unknown territory.

> **IF YOU INSIST ON CLARITY AND CERTAINTY AT EVERY STEP, YOU BECOME AN OBSTACLE TO ACHIEVING THE END RESULT YOU DESIRE.**

Nevertheless, people still want to know exactly what the end result is going to look like and how to achieve it—what strategies to adopt. They want it to be predictable, like their tried-and-true process for creating a new product. Unfortunately, no one can foresee what lies ahead. You may have a goal, but if you are in unknown territory, you will have to modify your plan as you make your way toward it. As you learn, you adjust. In this process, the end result may take on a different form than you anticipated.

We must pay attention and adjust based on what we observe and experience. Expect moments of great clarity and moments of great confusion in equal measure. Learn to trust the process; I have done so, and I guarantee it works. I've learned through personal experience and by observing and coaching countless others that the best way to navigate ambiguity is to tune in to the situation and trust in your ability to learn and respond in the moment.

It may seem counterintuitive, but if you insist on clarity and certainty at every step, you become an obstacle to achieving the end result you desire. Put certainty on the shelf, tap into your right-brain competencies, and at least for a time rely more on intuition than logic. Practice creative thinking rather than analysis-paralysis, and make decisions with key information instead of all the information.

While some leaders find it refreshing to let go of reliable, well-known management tools in favour of 21st-century leadership practices, my observation is that it's a challenge for most. Why? Because it requires leaders to take on a somewhat playful attitude and to take themselves a little less seriously. It means saying to yourself, *Let's see where this will take us*, rather than *I want to know where this is going!*

Closing ideas down too quickly because they don't seem practical precludes stumbling upon potentially excellent ways forward. Why not stay open and allow an idea to build so you can see how far the team can take it? It may lead to some brilliant, new, henceforth hidden strategies. As with improvisational theatre, let the story unfold and only judge it once it has landed and is complete. As a team, you may decide you need a stronger story and begin anew, but you will have learned along the way, and your next story will be richer because of it.

Action plans give only an illusion of control. We are never truly in control. We cannot know what the future holds. We cannot know how people or markets will respond. In fact, the future is unknowable.

What *is* knowable is the past. That's why many management decisions and actions are rooted in previous experience. Most of us accept this as a legitimate approach to managing present circumstances. Unfortunately, this paradigm is flawed. Although past experience can inform us, old solutions may not be appropriate for present-day challenges. Relinquishing the need to "know" and to control opens leaders to new possibilities and new solutions. Ambiguity, spiced with a dash of chaos, actually fosters innovation.

Truly creative leaders learn to ignore the temptation to plan it all out. They understand that having two feet grounded firmly in reality while confidently facing into their imagined future—despite not knowing how that future will unfold—increases the chances of success. They know individual actions shape end results by generating lessons along the way.

Each action is part of a process made up of questions, answers and further actions. Did the action taken generate the expected result? If so, what is the next logical action to be taken? How can we leverage this result? If we can't leverage, what can we learn? What alternative action could we take to achieve a result that brings us closer to our goal?

Throughout the implementation, consistent and frequent analysis enables us to re-evaluate our actions to ensure progress. Adjustments are almost inevitable as we create the most effective and efficient path to the goal.

Ironically, when I do action-planning with groups, we actually spend little time planning detailed actions. In fact, we only create a broad plan to begin the process. We then spend the bulk of our energy during the implementation phase looking closely at what is and isn't working. The planning is more around thinking through the implications of an idea and how it will work in reality. Planning for things that are unknowable is a waste of time and can take you off track.

An example of this is planning a large marketing campaign when you don't know how clients are going to react to the first ad. If you create an elaborate plan around the success of the ad and it fails, it's a lot harder to change course because so many plans have to be undone. On the other hand, analysis that allows us to respond authentically in the moment and select the best actions for the emerging situation keeps people on a course for success.

It's important to know your starting point and your goal, but actual situations change constantly, so our actions must be tested or generated to ensure relevance and appropriateness. Because the future constantly unfolds, so must our action plans.

To be successful, today's leaders must be comfortable with the notion that we need to create every day, coming up with new solutions, new ideas to action, new strategies. We must relinquish attachment to old rules, old practices, old mental models and insanely detailed action plans. We must trust ourselves and our teams to navigate the turbulent and highly complex waters of this new world. But we cannot do it alone. One person's thinking will never be enough for the challenges at hand. We must also look to those around us and invite them to work with us as collaborators in creating a bold new global future.

ACTIVITY

Ask and answer a few fundamental questions:

- What old rules and practices are you reluctant to replace with new ways?
- What action plans (written or held in your brain) are habits that you rarely re-examine or question?
- How can you work with your team to find new paths?

....

....

....

ACTIVITY

Think about an issue or an opportunity currently at play that has no obvious path forward. Perhaps it's complex or exceptionally challenging. Possible opportunities or issues:

....

....

....

Now pick one item from above to work on for this exercise. Instead of creating a detailed action plan that has no guarantees, create an explicit end result (a clear goal). In other words, after all the yet-to-be-taken actions are accomplished, what will you have achieved? What will the future state look like? Write your goal below:

....

....

....

Identify one meaningful action step that will take you toward this end goal:

....

....

....

Execute it. Once the action step is completed, reflect on your results and what you learned from that action—what worked, what didn't.

....

....

....

Based on what you learned, create the next action step. Again, sit back and reflect. Then determine the third action step. And so on.

....

....

....

Build a tolerance for not knowing exactly how you are going to achieve your goal. Learn how to be vigilant about learning through reflection to assist you in navigating uncertainty and the unknown.

22 | DIVERSIFY AND CATALYZE

Fire up your team by stimulating them to think in new ways and exposing them to diverse points of view and strategies. Diversity is a great asset. It pushes a group beyond the obvious and is likely to bring challenges to the surface. When we stimulate and provoke, we are creating a catalyst for change. Insist on deep listening so people fully understand ideas and can thus build on them more easily. Teach acceptance rather than judgment to allow the best thinking to emerge as discussions unfold. Nothing will get people more enthused than feeling their perspective is valued and contributes to the team's success.

Most of us prefer to hang out with people who enjoy what we enjoy, to share dinner conversation with people who have similar views and to confide in people who "get" us because they have had similar experiences. It's reassuring and provides a sense of belonging. But if your goal is to find the best solution or create something new and exciting, homogeneity is usually not the best way to go. To leverage the best available thinking, we need to engage with people who have divergent views, different thinking preferences, experiences unlike our own or a different cultural background.

DIVERSITY FUELS CREATIVITY AND INNOVATION AND DISRUPTS NORMS, THEREBY CREATING THE CONDITIONS TO CATALYZE NEW CONNECTIONS AND INTERACTIONS LEADING TO CHANGE.

Creating conditions in which diversity is an asset rather than a barrier can be challenging. Homogeneous groups, at least on the surface, appear more efficient and productive. They tend to work more quickly, for example, because they share so much common ground, agree more and are less likely to get bogged down in conflict. Heterogeneous groups, on the other hand, often require more time to discuss and arrive at decisions and conclusions. However, results are frequently superior because they emerge from a broader knowledge base.

"Mixed" groups are more likely to identify and challenge assumptions, and participants must stretch the normal boundaries of their thinking to accommodate others' ideas, thus providing a rich environment for creativity and innovation. In the face of complex or difficult challenges, group solutions almost always outshine individual ones because they require group members to collaborate—and collaboration, when well-managed, will lead to superior results. Another benefit is that diversity pushes the group's thinking beyond the obvious.

I was working with a team that was killing themselves to compensate for a broken system. Their personal efforts were keeping the system functioning, but without this commitment the system would collapse. Their efforts were creating a Band-Aid that was camouflaging the issue and burning out the team.

I introduced a new idea that, given the team's culture, would not have entered their thinking. I suggested they let things break. As soon as the words "Why don't you just let it break?" left my mouth, every person bar one on the team said, "I could never do that!" "I'd never let someone else down!" "It's never going to happen!" Once the dust had settled, I shared more of my reasoning behind my suggestion and also gave them examples of how something like this could be managed responsibly. By the end of our discussion, they could see the merit in the action, and it stimulated their thinking around how to handle a particular challenge.

If I, as the outsider or diverse agent, had not been present for that discussion, the team on its own would never have generated that idea, as it was anathema to them based on their current culture. Adding diverse points of view into the mix can open up new avenues and solutions.

When diverse groups take on collaborative behaviours, such as those taught in improvisational theatre, the risk of diversity becoming a barrier quickly diminishes. Instead, it sets the stage for creativity and new beginnings. Without specific techniques and tools to exploit diversity, however, most groups stay in the comfort zone of the tried and true. Today's business challenges cannot be tackled with old thinking. We must create new solutions for new challenges. The beauty of collaboration is that we can take old ingredients, combine them in innovative ways and season with new spices to create gourmet recipes for success.

Consciously developing diverse teams and diverse ways of thinking is a powerful method for serving the needs of our teams and organizations. In so doing, we develop a profound ability to generate new ideas as well as the capacity to critique those same ideas, once fully developed, through the multiple perspectives available within the group. In the process, we avoid groupthink, a more common phenomenon than many leaders realize.

A whole host of studies explore and document the downside of groupthink, which Merriam-Webster.com defines as "a pattern of thought characterized by self-deception, forced manufacture of consent, and conformity to group values and ethics." In working with teams, it's productive to strive for constructive discontent and to separate the creative act from the evaluation thereof. Too often we muddle the two and end up in premature debates in which fledgling ideas flounder in favour of the status quo and/or the path of least resistance.

When we collaborate, we leverage diverse talents and perspectives to generate the best ideas possible. We can also use diversity as a framework for rigorous evaluation. To do so, we must temporarily detach ourselves from our creation and thoroughly evaluate its merits using a wide breadth of perspectives. We must embrace both emergence and convergence—and allow each its own space—to produce the best-possible end results.

External catalysts disrupt autopilot

Our brains sometimes run on autopilot to complete mundane tasks and thus create capacity to engage in new, more challenging activities. We can't rethink things continuously; we need our brain to quickly process routine stuff, like our route to work in the morning or the answers to frequently asked questions. Otherwise, our capacity would be severely limited.

Furthermore, our brains are trained to think and do things in certain ways, and many of us have natural preferences for how we like to think. We might even go out of our way to avoid other thinking styles. Sometimes we just plain get stuck in ruts. But when we want to change our habitual ways of thinking and doing things, it can be hard to get our brains to shift gears, even when we know other approaches have produced better results. To think and do things in new ways, most of us need prompting, sometimes in the form of external catalysts.

What does this have to do with leading your team?

In some ways, teams work like our brains. They also get stuck in ruts. When we rely exclusively on our usual teams and advisors, we might miss opportunities to generate out-of-the-box thinking because of blind spots and overfamiliarity. When that happens, adding fresh perspectives through diversity can overcome inertia by creating catalysts that disrupt the team norms. Bringing outsiders in generates juicier conversations, provides new perspectives on challenges and delivers the stimulus to kick-start new thinking. Because outsiders don't see things the way we do, their input disrupts our routine thinking and may call into question the efficacy of our tried-and-true approaches.

Of course, every outsider interaction will not catapult us into wild and wonderful territory, but it can help. At the very least, outsiders offer provocations—questions or statements that challenge our thinking—that act as catalysts, enabling us to connect ideas in new and interesting ways. Appropriate provocative statements or questions depend on the situation, but they may sound something like: "What would happen if you stopped developing that product line?" "Why don't you abandon all titles and corner offices to promote your core values?" "What if we went 100 percent online?" You get the idea.

Diversity gives us a better picture of reality as we see beyond the frame of our normal lens, as well as a better chance of coming up with new ways forward by changing the dynamics or thinking in ways that open up possibilities. Bringing divergent voices together sometimes creates tension and conflict as people inevitably disagree, but that's the point really. At the same time, when this coming together catalyzes new ideas or speeds up our thinking process, it can be incredibly energizing and stimulating. Diversity also often leads to unusual synergies.

Don't be afraid of disruption and difference—embrace them. Try to mix it up as much as you can when you want to catalyze new ways of seeing problems and approaching goals. No matter the outcome, it surely makes for interesting conversations!

Five Ways to Put Diversity to Work for You

1. Integrate customers informally into your meetings to help you keep your feet grounded in their reality. We often try to imagine the customer's voice "at the table," but what if customers were actually there to partner with us in new and exciting ways?

2. Invite new employees to tell you about the company's culture and brand, even if they are not members of the employee engagement task force. They are seeing things without much company experience, and they may see things you have become accustomed to blocking out.

3. Bring employees of all ages into a meeting to look at the redesign of your website, even if this is not within their area of expertise. Everyone can inform you about his or her needs.

4. Include the union in a strategy meeting to share members' views on the market and economic stressors so as to incorporate front-line insight into planning. This way you build ideas as well as relationships.

5. Bring uninitiated employees in to test your thinking. Have them ask lots of "why" questions and probe for assumptions. Queries may be simple questions, such as: "Why do you think that is true?" "Have you asked your customers yet?" "What impact will your plan have on other departments?" You don't have to be an expert in an area to ask good questions, and good questions can be hugely helpful in clarifying a group's thinking.

ACTIVITY

What other ways can you think of to put diversity to work for you?

....

....

....

23 | LET'S PLAY!

You can fire up your team by giving them the tools to truly collaborate. Like a theatre troupe, your team can work together seamlessly to tell their story. When teams play together positively and productively, exceptional results follow. Energy is directed toward team performance rather than petty conflicts or self-interests.

Those of us who care often care a great deal. As a result, it can be difficult to *not* take ourselves and the task at hand too seriously. We can easily lose perspective and forget that, in the big picture, the discussion we are having is likely not that important. In fact, there are many other things that are much more important. When we take things too seriously, we are intense and often rigid. This makes it more difficult for us to enjoy our work, and it surely makes it unpleasant for those around us, because we take all the fun out of life and work!

A number of years ago, I stumbled upon improvisational theatre. The more I learned about it, the more convinced I became of its potential value as a leadership tool. Using improv techniques, leaders can teach their teams the fundamentals of collaboration—an essential component of exceptional teamwork—as well as shared leadership.

IT PAYS TO PLAY.

A friend and colleague of mine, Evan Carter, is a professional stand-up comedian and teaches for Second City in Toronto. He has been a great source of information as I continue to develop ways to incorporate the wisdom of improv into my work. Below are typical rules most improv theatre troupes follow.

Improv Rules

- Don't deny. Accept the gift.
- Don't ask questions. Build on what has been offered.
- You don't have to be funny. Be authentic.

- Don't compete. You can look good if you make your partner look good.
- Tell a story.
- Focus on the goal.

Following these rules paves the way for intriguing and unusual interactions, which in turn lead to productive sessions. The goal of improv is to tell a story. When someone in your troupe offers an idea to move your story along, you never refuse it, you always build on it. You accept it as valid and build on it so the story can advance.

The ensuing comedy is natural, not forced. By responding to what is offered in a spontaneous manner (no "trying" to be funny), humour emerges. As you are working as a troupe to create a successful story, the rules also stipulate you do not compete for the spotlight or the biggest laughs. Instead, you try to offer your partner an idea upon which she can easily build, ultimately making *her*, not *you*, look good. It's all about focusing on others and the common goal rather than being self-conscious about your own performance.

This approach to collaboration requires people to remain in the present moment, as it is impossible to anticipate what your partners will say or do next. You are forced to listen, to respond as much intuitively as logically and to remain focused on moving the story to its natural and successful end.

Example of Improv in Action

The scenario: Shopping in New York City

Player 1: Once upon a time, a father and his twins went to New York City for a weekend of shopping.

Player 2: Yes, and they visited all the hotspots and found amazing deals!

Player 1: Yes, and they were especially blown away by a two-for-one special: "Buy one baby gorilla and get a second one free!"

Player 2: Yes, and the baby gorillas were also twins, so now they felt compelled to buy.

Player 1: Yes, and when the father returned home, now with *two* sets of twins, the mother screamed . . .

And so the story builds.

Imagine using the principles of improv in your workplace to create more energized exchanges. Picture this: You are at a management team meeting. There are a number of items on the table for discussion. There have been some challenges in the operations area, so business leaders and support-unit managers are meeting to brainstorm possible solutions. The energy around the table is electric and ... playful! People eagerly anticipate the collaborative effort that is about to begin. No one is concerned about defending past decisions, no one is anxious about needing to protect his or her turf, no one is fearful about having lost credibility over a role in the current situation. Rather, people are gathered to attain a common goal: a way forward.

The brainstorming session starts. Someone offers an idea. No one challenges it; no one debates its merits or risks. Instead, someone else embraces the idea and augments it by refining it, adding to it and using it as a springboard to another idea. Someone else takes the second offering and sees how it could open up a whole new avenue for exploration. And so on, and so on, until the solution emerges and the brainstorming comes to a natural end.

Does that sound like fantasy? It's not, believe me. When groups follow certain rules of engagement, magic happens. I have seen new products, high-powered business strategies and better ways of using old stuff created using improv principles. So, why in the world isn't the use of collaborative technique more widespread? Because we are trained to compete. We are taught competition is healthy. We are told the pie is only so big, so we had better grab our fair share or be left with nothing. We are hammered with the idea that being without a competitive advantage threatens an organization's very survival.

Meanwhile, we are rarely exposed to the virtues of cooperation, nor do we learn the skills and techniques to collaborate effectively. Most business leaders believe these approaches are warm-and-fuzzy, touchy-feely techniques designed to make people feel good. I admit they do make people feel good. Is there something inherently wrong with feeling good? Not in my book.

More importantly, these tools represent a legitimate way of growing businesses and offering greater value to customers and clients. The research around cooperation is so compelling that business leaders who do not seriously consider its use are hog-tying themselves and their teams.

If you aren't giving collaboration and cooperation their due, I invite you to reconsider your assumptions about how to thrive in today's global business environment.

The five "Improv Rules" applied

A diverse team has been tasked with creating a strategy to dramatically improve employee engagement. Here are the rules:

1. **Don't deny. Accept the gift.** The gifts are the ideas that come forward. All ideas are accepted and carried forward. Receive them with a, "Yes, and . . ."
2. **Don't ask questions. Build on what has been offered.** Don't ask the person who has offered an idea a question. Instead, add to the idea to make it stronger. Build on it.
3. **You don't have to be funny. Be authentic.** Don't try to be the problem-solver or even try to perform in any particular way. Listen, consider and be present. You will know when you have something to add or contribute.
4. **Don't compete. You can look good if you make your partner look good.** Don't try to be the one with the best idea or the one who needs to lead the discussion. Rather, try to support those around you. When you work with another's idea and demonstrate how to move it forward, you both look good!
5. **Tell a story. Focus on the goal.** The story the team builds is the engagement strategy. That's the goal. Stay focused on the end result, not on how you are performing or how your ideas are moving forward. Let go of being self-conscious and enjoy the creative process.

Here's how the application of the rules might sound:

Player 1: Okay. We're here to figure out how to improve employee engagement. How do we want to start?

Player 2: Let's brainstorm. (First offering)

Player 3: Okay, I'll throw out an idea. I think we need to focus on improving our communications. (Next offering)

Player 4: Yes, I think we need to ensure we keep our employees informed about key priorities. *(Yes, and...)*

Player 1: I know my team would really appreciate knowing how other departments are progressing with their objectives and how we might support. *(Building)*

Player 3: Keeping everyone informed about core objectives might help us compete less for resources and clarify what must happen versus what is less critical. *(Building)*

Player 2: We could work with these dilemmas differently as well. Rather than always choosing between two priorities, we could bring groups of employees together to find better solutions. For example, how two projects could move forward with the same resources. We could really open up the conversations. *(Yes, and...)*

Player 4: We could have regular employee gatherings both to provide information and to ask for input on many different things. *(Building)*

Player 1: We could call these gatherings "The Breakfast Club"! We could put on a fully catered breakfast and employees who are interested in the topic could come to listen and participate. *(Playful)*

Player 3: The CEO could host, and the executive team could serve up the pancakes and eggs! *(Playful)*

Player 4: We could have our communications team document the breakfast meeting so everyone who couldn't attend can still learn about what was discussed and decided. Maybe we could still give others a chance to add to the discussion through an online chat room. *(Building)*

Player 2: I think the younger employees would really appreciate more engagement through social media. What if we took a key corporate priority and created a social-media program around it, targeting our up-and-coming talent? *(Building)*

And so it continues.

The energy of such a session is positive because everyone feels validated and heard. Plus, the flow is forward-moving. There is no going back-and-forth on a topic.

When you focus on "Yes, and . . ." and the act of building, you must attend to what has just been said. You don't pre-plan your ideas or wait for an opening to speak. You keep your mind filled with what is happening in the moment by listening carefully. You respond intuitively (and authentically) as you stay open to what emerges through the discussion. Try it! I think you'll like it.

ACTIVITY

How often do you:

- Begin a sentence with "No, I think . . ."
- Say, "Yes, but . . ."
- Compliment an idea, followed closely by "however . . ."
- Contradict another's idea before you have fully understood it or looked at how it could work?

....

....

....

24 | JUST SHOW UP

Fully show up in all interactions. Showing up means that you arrive intending to participate to the best of your ability and allow your heart and mind to engage with what happens. This is an active state. You are receiving a gift—an idea, a comment, a question—and then you are working with that gift. When you use this guideline, you will present yourself to your team as a co-collaborator. As a leader, it is essential to be open to receiving the offerings and demonstrate their value by responding with an action: You do something with the gift. It's an active state. Even if the idea changes and evolves, you give tribute to it as your active participation demonstrates the value you see in it. You are then co-creating, and your team is sure to get fired up as a result.

Many years ago, when I first started to facilitate, I spent hours and hours with clients planning agendas and processes to achieve our desired ends. I was comforted by this preparation; I felt it guaranteed satisfying outcomes. And, truth be told, we did achieve our objectives. Still, on many occasions—even those in which the goals were met—I felt dissatisfied with both the process and the outcome. Had I served the real needs of the group? Was I just an accomplice in a process to control outcomes, albeit with positive intent?

What would happen, I wondered, if I simply introduced the overall objective and any relevant concepts or tools and then let the group explore, guided by my impromptu questions, comments or provocations? Would it lead to richer learning experiences and better outcomes than sticking to an agenda and completing every planned activity? What if I planned less

> **LEADERS WHO OVERPREPARE AND OVERPLAN TO ENSURE THE CONVERSATION UNFOLDS WITHOUT A HITCH INEVITABLY STIFLE WHAT MOST NEEDS TO BE DISCUSSED OR DONE.**

and gave the group, including myself, space to fully participate in achieving the objective? What if we all just showed up and brought our hearts and minds to creating the outcome we desired?

The answers were clear as I transformed my approach to coaching, facilitating and conducting workshops. How I work today looks nothing like the way I worked initially. I keep planning to a minimum, only what is required to create the right conditions for a fruitful interaction. In essence, I now show up and focus on what is happening around me.

I always have a plan, but I'm not attached to it. In fact, the plan is often a jumping-off point or springboard into a session. I prefer to share the leadership of the session with the group, and I know the process will take us where we need to go. I leave space for what will emerge and have faith that the group will handle it.

I know from experience that even the best needs assessments do not always reveal the underlying concerns or enthusiasms of a group. Sometimes it's not until everyone gathers, interacts and exchanges ideas that the real stuff or best stuff surfaces. As a facilitator or workshop leader, I serve my clients best when I show up prepared to take action based on how the group responds. Showing up means hosting a conversation or activity that encourages everyone present to engage and participate. I know without a doubt this methodology ensures that opportunities to work with what matters most to the group will not be missed or lost to overplanning and a predetermined agenda.

I have never had a group complain I didn't stick to the agenda. Why? Because ultimately their goal in hiring me is to help them deal with what's important. When, as part of the process, they resolve critical issues, no one cares if the agenda went out the window, or even if there was an agenda to begin with.

The only exception is if the group doesn't want the real stuff to surface (which happens on occasion). However, in my experience, the vast majority of people appreciate it when one addresses the "elephant in the room" skilfully and respectfully. It may feel a little scary at first, but once an elephant is tackled, the sense of relief within the group is palpable.

In *Improv Wisdom: Don't Prepare, Just Show Up* (2005), Patricia Ryan Madson writes: "A good improviser is someone who is awake, not entirely self-focused, and moved by a desire to do something useful and give something back, and who acts upon this impulse ... And the password— it is yes!" This quotation truly speaks to the spirit of collaboration and it emphasizes the starting points: Show up, be present, and be ready to contribute!

As a leader, I follow the same principles. Overpreparing and overplanning is a control strategy to ensure the group ends up where you want them to end up rather than where they might need to go to truly address underlying issues or to identify exciting opportunities. Stifling this inquiry and interaction will not serve you well. Instead, communicate a clear outcome, provide any essential resources or information, and let the group engage.

When everyone shows up prepared to accept each other's offerings and take action to move forward, the group will come together to act in unity. Creating plans and agendas that constrain and play it safe will not give you the results you ultimately desire.

ACTIVITY

For your next team meeting, don't overplan or overprepare. Instead, show up and host a conversation. Follow these steps:

1. Invite your team to a conversation about a topic that's important to the group. Tell them the conversation will revolve around this topic. Give them a start and end time as well as a location, but that's it.

2. At the front of the meeting room, on a flip chart, post the topic with a question. For example, "Given the current market conditions, how can we collaborate more across the business to deliver better value to our customers?

3. If possible, place chairs in a circle and don't use tables. Otherwise, try for a u-shaped arrangement so everyone can see each other but there is also a sense of open space.

4. Use the flip chart to record the discussion's main points. Keep it low tech.

5. As the leader, engage with every idea and move it forward. Build on it. Encourage everyone to do so.

6. If sensitive topics surface, know you and the group can handle it and take a deep dive. Respond and guide the conversation forward in constructive and fruitful ways.

7. Bring your complete focus to each gift offered, and be an active participant even when you are not scribing or speaking. Coach team members to build on every idea.

8. When it's time to bring the session to a decision, if consensus has not already been reached, ask the group to select the ideas that resonate the most and try to come to a conclusion about which idea to act on first. If you need to, people can vote, but try to have a conversation first, allowing people to advocate for what they think is best. Often the group can reach consensus on its own. Leave 50 percent of the meeting time for this process.

9. Use the lines below to draft your invite.

....

....

....

25 | GIVE UP PERSONAL AGENDAS

You ignite the fire in your team's collective belly when you connect them to goals that are bigger than their own personal interests. Yes, people want to achieve their own goals. However, they also want to be part of something important or special. When they feel connected to a worthy cause or exciting vision, it's easy to give up personal agendas.

What if we let go of our own agendas and concern with outcomes? Although an agenda can be helpful in keeping a meeting on track, there is also a time to keep agendas very simple and allow ideas to emerge and take shape through a healthy and vigorous exchange of ideas. What if we said, "This meeting is dedicated to finding a solution to our most pressing issue. We are here today to answer the following question: How can we address [issue X] while ensuring we stay within budget?"

This sounds straightforward, but it can be very challenging to set aside our own agendas for the good of the whole. For example, one of the business leaders of a client company had to give up some of his profit margin to make a company-wide project work. He knew that in doing so, he would need to place more pressure on his sales force to increase revenues in other product categories to meet his annual targets. He saw the project as an important opportunity for the company, however, and so he was willing to set aside his own self-interests.

> **WHEN WE FOCUS ON WORKING FOR THE GREATER GOOD (OR SOMETHING BIGGER THAN US) RATHER THAN FULFILLING OUR OWN PERSONAL AGENDAS, WORK BECOMES MUCH MORE FULFILLING.**

Here's the challenge: recognizing that we all have desires and goals that we want to fulfill, yet at the same time separating ourselves from these so we can objectively consider what's good for the whole group. In the novel *The High Road* (2010) by Terry Fallis, the protagonist, a politician, is very clear throughout his campaign that national interests will take priority over local interests when needed. He considers it an honour to represent his constituency and will do what's right on their behalf, except if it jeopardizes the greater good, in which case he will support the federal action and consider local interests secondary. This is a fine balance and not always easy to execute. When we take on this approach, we will face dilemmas. Better to face dilemmas and work through them, though, than be myopic and only focus on self-interests.

Why do we get so attached to our agendas or ideas? I have frequently facilitated meetings during which people were obviously resisting the ideas coming forward in favour of their own preferences or refusing to support a solution because it contradicted current practices or habits. To the observer, the position taken by the objector seems illogical because no facts support the position taken. What motivates this behaviour then? During coaching sessions, I have discovered that most often, the reasons are based on uncertainty about the future or concern that they will lose out. Here are the most common answers:

- **"I believe there is a right way to do this, and I can't agree to something I think is wrong."** In other words, there is an ideal that the person feels a need to uphold, even if it is not a corporate standard. For example, people may believe that "Shortcuts are wrong. They compromise the process."
- **"I need to ensure that I look after my own objectives. If I give in, I will risk my own success."** In other words, fear of failure or fear of not finding other alternatives creates the resistance. "If I agree, I may not be able to come up with a Plan B for my own team."
- **"I don't see how I could make it work with the way they are proposing we go."** In other words, the individual doesn't want to reveal insecurities about execution so fights the proposal for fear of looking bad. "I'm not sure I can figure this out."

Of course, every situation is slightly different, but when there is resistance to change or attachment to an idea without clear fact-based reasons, people are usually motivated by personal concerns or fears. As leaders, it is crucial that we see and acknowledge when this is happening within us or our teams and pull back.

When we call ourselves out on our own behaviour, we can detach ourselves from these concerns and participate freely in collaboration. We might even table our concerns as part of the discussion: "I am willing to support the proposal; however, I will need to revisit my own business plan and explore alternatives for achieving our targets, as this proposal puts our current course of action at risk." You never know—people might offer to help or see a solution on the spot. It happens!

Once you begin to work collaboratively, you will be amazed at how emerging solutions can be accommodated. Say, "Yes and . . ." to an idea, build on others' ideas, and offer new challenges as well: "How can we execute this new proposal while maintaining the integrity of existing business plans?" When we open up rather than protect, ideas come forth with support from all around.

ACTIVITY

As a leader, how can you suspend the need you may sometimes feel to protect your own interests? How could you support or encourage others to do the same?

....

....

....

26 | USE OPEN SPACE TECHNOLOGY

Replace the "tip and drool" zombie pose typically seen in countless meetings people endure during a day with a dynamic, energized coffee-break atmosphere to fire up even the most lethargic team member. Give people control over the agenda, freedom of choice and movement, and you're off to the races.

In the 1990s, the concept of self-directed teams was a hot item. I embraced it and worked with my team (I was employed corporately) to develop the requisite skills and a culture that would eliminate the need for a manager—me or anyone else in the same role. My vision was never realized, however, largely because my team members, although happy to work independently, still wanted a leader to support them and focus on areas they eschewed, such as navigating organizational politics, managing certain external relationships and cutting through the bureaucracy of a vast, traditional organization.

> **OST BRINGS THE ENERGY OF A GREAT COFFEE BREAK INTO YOUR MEETINGS.**

I accepted this outcome—admittedly, reluctantly at first—and continued to search for a leadership approach I could sink my teeth into, one not based on a traditional nineteenth-century manufacturing model. My goal was to leverage the talents of individual team members and create an environment conducive to innovation and meaningful progress. I eventually found part of the solution in Open Space Technology (OST), a meeting methodology that aligns people's passion and their willingness to take responsibility while giving participants choice.

The first time I experienced OST, I immediately saw its potential. Imagine being invited to an important corporate meeting that has no agenda. Your invitation specifies a broad theme and asks you to consider related topics you think are important and/or merit discussion. You don't have to attend if you don't want to. If you do, you and the others who show up on the day of the meeting will create the day's agenda. No single participant has greater privileges than another, and there are no leaders, so the day's proceedings rest in your and your fellow participants' hands. Unorthodox? Perhaps. Innovative? Absolutely. Effective? Yes!

The basic principles and rules of engagement in OST further set the tone and encourage dynamic behaviour. Four principles, one law and a single provocation govern OST sessions. They are simple and memorable:

The Four Principles

1. Whoever comes are the right people.
2. Whatever happens is the only thing that could have.
3. Whenever it starts is the right time.
4. When it's over, it's over.

The One Law

The Law of Mobility or the Law of Two Feet: When you feel you are no longer learning from or contributing to a conversation, move to another discussion.

The Single Provocation

Be prepared to be surprised!

Harrison Owen, the creator of OST, observed that people become highly engaged and more likely to take action around topics about which they feel passionate and for which they are willing to take responsibility. He added the element of free choice and devised a meeting model that invites people to participate and contribute. To learn more, I highly recommend reading *Open Space Technology: A User's Guide* (1997).

OST meetings are not mandatory; potential participants self-select, so only those who really want to attend and work on the issues participate. This one difference changes the energy of the entire gathering. Generally, people arrive excited and energized—although sometimes a little nervous if it's their first OST—and ready to get involved. OST sessions may take place in a single day or a portion thereof, but more often than not, they are held over two or three days to enable participants to thoroughly explore a topic and create priorities to action.

The topic, structured using the phrase "Issues and Opportunities," opens the door for myriad conversations. For example, I recently held an OST session for a client under the theme, "Issues and Opportunities for Making Work Easier for You and Better for the Client." All company employees were invited, and many came. Scheduling requirements were a challenge, but the CEO made the commitment that if someone wished to attend, managers would find a way to make it work, at least for half a day. The supportive approach and tone created an invitational space. Such optional yet important meetings tend to attract those who truly care about the theme, as the methodology asks people to invest themselves to move the issue forward in constructive, productive and innovative ways.

When I first learned of OST, it struck me as a stunning way to move organizations forward. It is natural and organic and creates conditions in which people can fully engage and participate. I was convinced the results of such sessions would be superior to traditional meetings, which have a reputation for being huge time-wasters. In fact, I have repeatedly witnessed OST's powerful impact: It produces surprising (sometimes *exceptional*) and always meaningful results wherever and whenever I have used it.

Furthermore, I learned from both attending and facilitating OST sessions that leadership does not reside with a single individual or even a leadership team. In OST conversations, leadership emerges from unforeseen places:

- People who are normally withdrawn and quiet at meetings become passionately engaged.
- Those with highly specialized skills often help innovate in areas completely outside their knowledge base.
- Participants demonstrate an ability to inspire their peers to take action in particularly intimidating situations.

Managers sometimes host the sessions, but more often, relatively junior employees take the opportunity to lead, express their views, share their ideas or demonstrate their expertise.

From the outset, I recognized the huge potential of OST methodology, far beyond its usefulness as a meeting format. OST is a way of working and serves as a model for shared leadership, even within a hierarchically structured organization. It doesn't need to invert the hierarchy but can complement it to help formal leaders become playful and let go of the pressure to always know.

Within this model, people can choose if and when they want to lead or follow. No one is forced to always do one or the other. Leadership and follower-ship become dynamic, organic and fluid to meet changing needs and circumstances. OST methodology also taught me important lessons about the true nature of collaboration:

- No one owns the outcome, no one owns the process, and no one owns the facilitation. Everyone owns it and shares it willingly and respectfully.
- People show up open to possibility and fully present. People don't have to be uptight about their performance because no one places expectations upon you beyond "show up ready to put your passion to work and take responsibility for the work generated during the day."
- There is always "buzz." People don't have to listen to endless speakers or prepare by reading loads of irrelevant background material.
- People don't have to stay politely in conversations that are of no use to them or to which they cannot contribute. In fact, in OST, if you do not feel you are learning or contributing, the Law of Two Feet *mandates* that you move to another conversation. In a nutshell, participants are invited to bring their full selves to the meeting and contribute to the best of their ability and learn as much as they can from others.

Typically, OST sessions generate a range of outcomes, such as stronger connections and better rapport, a high volume of innovative ideas and focused action plans—all of which add up to a satisfying end result. I have seen people create new products, develop new growth strategies, solve complex problems and heal broken departmental and individual relationships using OST. The productivity of the OST format compared to traditional meetings is, quite simply, astonishing.

Why OST works

On the surface, OST may seem simplistic and not very businesslike. In true fact, OST takes a powerful combination of ingredients and combines them to create a unique meeting experience. Of note are three particularly essential ingredients that work to create the magic of OST: an increase in volunteering and diversity and a decrease in structure. Let's look at them in more detail here.

Everyone is a volunteer

OST asks employees at all levels to be volunteers, as the meetings are not mandatory. This is rare in organizations. When my clients ask if we can make the session mandatory, I always refuse. If you communicate clearly and frequently before an OST meeting to ensure that people are fully aware of its purpose, and you genuinely convey your conviction that the time will be fruitful and everyone's input valued, the right people will come.

It is a tremendous way to "see" your workforce in a new light. Who is truly passionate about the theme, regardless of title? Who is willing to give more of themselves to this topic? Who is fired up by the theme and chomping at the bit to contribute? Where is the energy in the company to move the theme or issue forward?

Make your support system visible.

Minimal structure

The openness of the OST format does not mean there are no parameters. Although OST may look chaotic and potentially unproductive—no agenda, no control over who attends and no predetermined outcomes—there is in fact a solid structure within the methodology. That framework provides boundaries within which creativity emerges and flourishes.

Yes, that's correct. Research proves we can be more creative when we work within specific givens or constraints. See Kevin and Shawn Coyne's book *Brainsteering: A Better Approach to Breakthrough Ideas* (2011) to explore this idea in detail.

Diversity mixes it up

Diverse attendees create a dynamic environment. Together they will light a few sparks and perhaps even ignite a big idea. When passionate and responsible people share information, diverse experience, perspectives and ideas, they find creative ways to move forward. It's a foregone conclusion.

On occasion, besides getting lit, the sparks may also fly! That's always possible within diverse groups. However, in my experience, a shared sense of purpose moves people through disagreements toward resolution. In fact, I have seen many individuals and groups reconcile using OST because it gives them the space to move through conflict.

Shared leadership in OST

Open Space Technology is a meeting methodology. However, its principles can be extrapolated and integrated into how work gets done every day.

In an open-space format, people come together with a clear purpose under conditions designed to facilitate passionate engagement. People *want to* contribute, have an impact and make a difference. People also desire a certain amount of freedom to use their talents to create for their organization for mutual benefit. Employees are appropriately rewarded for their contributions, and the organization grows its business.

OST encourages and, in fact, provides an environment for shared leadership. Without consciously organizing our workplaces in new, non-hierarchical ways, we cannot expect employees to embrace their own potential and take on full accountability. As long as companies are organized strictly around traditional patriarchal structures, we will get more of the same. We need to invite employees to get involved, to create *with* us and to make their own choices—with the knowledge, of course, that all choices produce their own unique consequences.

Let me be clear: OST is not about altruism. It is a collaborative endeavour through which everyone gains. OST is valuable because it can help us think in pragmatic ways to create a more dynamic, meaningful workplace. There are many ways to do this. OST is one of them—a powerful and transformative leadership tool to help you help your team members contribute, apply their talents, take on new challenges and make a difference.

Tips and techniques

Three ways to apply OST principles in your leadership practice:

1. **Create an invitational space.** Think of yourself as a host who is inviting people into your home for an evening of stimulating conversation and fun.
2. **Give people freedom to choose how they will participate in meetings, events or projects.** When people participate because they have chosen to, a different energy and commitment emerge.
3. **Cast your net wide.** You never know where the talents you need might reside. As leaders, we often over-rely on a few team members and deny ourselves the opportunity to tap into all available resources.

ACTIVITY

To what extent, as a leader, do you rely on the following:

- Compliance versus volunteerism?
- Detailed agendas?
- The same people?
- How might relinquishing these attachments benefit your business?

....

....

....

27 | EMPLOY ELEMENTS OF OPEN SPACE TECHNOLOGY

Your team will love it when you apply the principles of Open Space Technology to your everyday meetings. Keeping your gatherings fresh, meaningful and spontaneous will set their energy on fire.

Open Space Technology is based on three key pillars: passion, willingness to take responsibility and free choice. It is natural and organic, and it creates conditions in which people can fully engage and participate. OST themes are developed in advance, and the event agenda is built by participants at the start of the event itself.

An OST meeting opens with everyone seated in a circle (or if numbers are large, in concentric circles). The sponsor and the facilitators set the stage, introduce the theme and review the four principles, the one law and the single provocation. The opening culminates in an invitation to all participants to post their own topics relating to the meeting theme.

> **MINIMAL STRUCTURE CAN PRODUCE AMAZING RESULTS.**

Participants offer a topic by writing it and their name on a large piece of paper, announcing it to the group and then "posting" the topic on a highly visible wall by approaching the wall-grid and selecting an available time slot and location. The day's agenda comprises the totality of the posted topics. Whoever posts a topic agrees to host that conversation.

Once the agenda is created, the marketplace opens and people sign up for the discussions for which they have passion and are willing to take responsibility. The hosts takes notes as the conversations unfold (perhaps on paper, with shared laptops or on an electronic notepad). These "convener notes" are then compiled into a "book of proceedings" that captures the main ideas and actions for follow-up.

The structure for OST events is made up of the following elements:

- **Theme.** The event's theme provides focus and purpose. It asks people to bring their attention to bear on the challenge and to focus their energy on fully exploring it. This is the North Star by which we navigate the conversations toward a destination. The theme functions as a question. "Issues and Opportunities for Growth," for example, invites the brain to resolve a challenge (growth) by identifying barriers and possibilities. The brain, which is designed to be creative, loves this kind of a challenge. It's like saying, "How can we?" Presenting your brain with powerful, relevant, compelling questions stimulates the creative juices and enables you to collaborate easily with others around this central question.

- **Opening.** The opening sets the tone, focuses participants on the work at hand, stresses the importance of their participation and affirms that great things will happen. Setting the right environment is a form of structure. You are establishing certain norms for the meeting. It's a form of pep talk but less rah-rah and more thoughtful, so the meaning and significance of the day is foremost. This, combined with sitting in a circle (no tables), establishes a sense of community and brings forward a different energy, one that is open and collaborative.

- **The book of proceedings.** During the opening, an empty binder is held up (or a blank CD if that's more relevant). This creates a concrete vision for the end result. It represents the actual work that will be done during the day. Although an unconventional meeting, it is intended to be a productive working session, and everyone is invited to roll up his or her sleeves to fill the binder (or CD). The convener normally takes the notes from the conversation using headings like "Name of Topic," "Highlights of Discussion," "Future Action/Next Steps/Recommendations," and "Resources Required."

Making the outcome tangible in this way helps to inspire and mobilize people. During the opening, it is important to say what will be done with the book of proceedings after the meeting is over. People need to know their work will matter beyond the day.

- **The Four Principles.** These principles provide structure in the form of meeting practices or norms, and they emphasize why this format will be different.

1. Whoever comes are the right people.
2. Whatever happens is the only thing that could have.
3. Whenever it starts is the right time.
4. When it's over, it's over.

I often frame the principles by saying something like, "We are not going to worry about who isn't here because the people needed to get the work done are in the room now. We are complete. [principle 1]. We are not going to be bound by the time and place we have chosen to host our meetings. If they need to run longer because people are still engaged and productive, then they continue. If the energy and interest peters out, then they should wrap up. It's all about letting things happen in a natural way rather than holding conversations hostage to normal meeting conventions [principles 3 and 4]. Whatever happens is okay, and we are here together to work through it—the good, the bad and the ugly! [principle 2]."

- **The One Law.** I love the Law of Mobility (also called the Law of Two Feet). It is completely freeing. The law throws out polite conventions around attendance. It says that you have a responsibility to leave a conversation to which you don't feel you can contribute or you don't feel you are learning. The law asks that you go find another conversation that will suit you. No one is to take offense because everyone has that same responsibility. If it were applied to all meetings always, we'd never have to sit through another boring meeting, wasting our time. Meeting productivity would soar.

The Law of Mobility is a lynchpin of OST structure in the way it supports engagement. People stay fired up if they are only involved in meaningful conversations from which they gain or give. Either way, it's progress. No more feeling hostage to a meeting!

An analogy based on bumblebees and butterflies is used to explain that participants are not obliged to attend any conversations at all. If you'd rather hang out at the coffee station or go for a walk during an OST event, go ahead! These centers of inaction sometimes attract very interesting conversations anyway. Or you can flutter about or jump between groups, cross-pollinating ideas. You can re-engage more deeply later, if you wish, or not. In other words, do what you want to do. (Note: There are few formal breaks in OST. People are expected to take care of their own needs as needed. Usually a snack table remains well stocked in a central location.)

- **The givens.** Extremely important when it comes to establishing parameters, the givens are the meeting's non-negotiables. These are solid parameters that participants need to know to decide which ideas, solutions and actions might be appropriate. For example, if all ideas for action need funding within existing budgets, people need to know this. Or if all ideas presented and prioritized during the meeting require board approval, people need to know that too.

Givens establish shared expectations and simply become part of the thinking. Sometimes people find surprisingly creative ways to fund projects about which they feel passionate. Or, they take more care to think through the business case if they know an idea must go before a board. Whatever your givens, ensure they are determined before the meeting by the organizing committee or sponsor and are read and posted during the opening.

- **The wall agenda.** This is a focal point in OST. It has a familiar-looking format—a time/place matrix that allows people who want to have the same conversation to find each other. The wall agenda is always open and, as the primary communication tool, must be kept up to date.

People can add new topics at any time. They can change the time and place of a conversation if something else comes up. They can post a non-topic if they feel the group needs something.

At one session I attended, a participant offered to do five-minute shoulder massages. At another, someone offered to facilitate energizers—brief, easy exercises—since people had been sitting for a particularly long and intense session. If a hot topic emerges, new sessions can be added to continue important discussions. These offers are made by posting them on the main agenda. It's how everyone talks to each other once things are underway.

- **Evening and morning news.** During a multiple-day event, the group gathers in its entirety for logistical announcements, or to ask questions, offer feedback and share thoughts. These bookends help people connect and reconnect to the community, stay focused, capture key learnings and attend to broader group needs.
- **The closing circle.** In a one-day event, and at the end of a multiple-day event, the last spot on the agenda is reserved for the closing circle. This is a very special time, as it signals the end of the meeting and is a time for closure. Everyone in attendance has the opportunity to say a few closing words—or not. Again, it is voluntary.

In my experience, people use this time to offer thanks and appreciation or share what most resonated for them during the meeting. Many times, I have had goose bumps as people spoke their parting words. Taking these last few minutes to share personal feelings and thoughts is a wonderful way to celebrate what everyone has accomplished as a community. In longer OST meetings or retreats, the closing circle as described above is an important ritual to transition back into normal work routines.

Together, these elements provide structure and create the container or the parameters of an OST meeting. When each item is well communicated and reinforced visually on the walls surrounding the meeting spaces, people are constantly reminded about why they are there, what they need to produce and how to go about it.

The OST framework enables openness. It withstands vigorous debate, complex subjects and sensitive topics or conflict. Nevertheless, the goal is to keep structure to a minimum, allowing just enough to foster focus, creativity and forward movement. No more, no less. So the question to ask yourself is: What are the minimum requirements for success?

We tend to overstructure, overcomplicate, overcontrol and overproduce. Less of everything delivers much better results. The trick is to determine which minimal requirements are needed to accomplish the task. What rules or parameters will best support the work? Taking time to consider such questions allows you to lead through collaboration rather than manage by command and control.

Diversify to strategize

I once facilitated an OST session for a legal association on the subject of gender issues in law. Initially, the organizers only thought to invite female lawyers (a common approach to women's issues). I recommended diversifying the group to add different perspectives to the mix and increase the chance of breakthrough thinking. In the end, in addition to female lawyers, we invited male lawyers, managing partners, businesswomen and academics. As soon as the topics were posted, the attendees couldn't wait to get to work tackling the sensitive and complex issues that had been raised.

I observed a range of emotions (and an even wider range of opinions!) during the session. There was laughter as well as raised voices, and throughout the meeting, the air snapped with energy. By the end of the day, everyone shared a deeper and broader understanding of the most pressing issues. More importantly, a number of new strategies emerged to be further researched and implemented by the event host.

Often when we hold meetings or gather people together, we think in terms of a departmental team meeting, a managers' meeting, a project team meeting or an executive meeting. We tend to work in homogenous teams rather than in cross-departmental, internal/external, multilevel ones. We also think of issues or projects in this way: Who are the experts within the company to help us? Is this a front-line issue or a management issue? Is this for the customer-service team to deal with?

During a company-wide OST meeting I facilitated, a call-center expert joined a conversation regarding a business unit's struggle with workload capacity. The business unit had been struggling to keep up with customer inquiries, new initiatives and, in some cases, even their core duties. In the past, they had comfortably handled the volume of work, but something had changed and people were burning out. The call-center expert thought she could help by showing them how to look at their processes differently. The CEO approved a month-long secondment of the call-center expert to the business unit to see if she could indeed make a difference.

In one of my follow-up conversations, I asked the business-unit VP how the experiment had turned out. She was thrilled with the results. Her team had changed a number of practices and eased the workload pressure considerably. The team felt more hopeful and had begun to rejuvenate.

The moral of the story? Diversity pays handsome dividends! Had the meeting not included people with a range of perspectives, skill sets and experiences, such cross-pollination would likely never have occurred. Not all meetings require significant diversity. But all should have enough to maintain a healthy mix and prevent attendees from developing groupthink.

5 Lessons for Everyday Meetings

1. **Create your theme.** At the beginning of any meeting, focus the attendees by stating simply and clearly the purpose or goal of the meeting. Post it on a flip chart or a whiteboard so it remains visible throughout the meeting. Our brains work best when we keep our desired end result at the forefront.
2. **Set the stage.** Spend five minutes setting an optimistic tone and expressing your appreciation of attendees' support of your task, project or goal. Present yourself as a host and think of your attendees as guests. (Think hospitality.) Remind people of any constraints—the givens—as it will likely stimulate creative ideas.
3. **Open it up.** Relinquish the need to always control the agenda, and turn it over to the people you need to execute it for you. Set a clear goal, such as, "How can we achieve X, Y and Z?" and then open the floor to topics. If your group is large enough, invite people to attend the session of most interest to them. Post a different topic at each table, for example. Ask someone to take notes for later distribution.
4. **Eliminate presentations.** Provide slide decks before the meeting that are easy to read and understand. Simplify, simplify, simplify!
5. **Allow choice and flexibility.** Offer as much choice as possible and keep givens to a minimum. People will gravitate to what matters most to them and thereby will invest more of their brain/ heart power.

ACTIVITY

Using the five items above, design an upcoming meeting.

1. Create your theme.

....

2. Set the stage by drafting your opening invitation and remarks.

....

....

3. Open it up by asking others to bring forward ideas. Draft how you might ask this in a way that is relevant to your topic.

....

....

4. Eliminate presentations by sending relevant materials out in advance. Be selective and ensure all documents are as concise as possible. Note the prereading required for your meeting below.

....

....

5. Allow choice and flexibility by providing the least number of givens (parameters).

....

....

PART 3:

FEEDBACK AND FEEDFORWARD

↗ OVERVIEW

I t is important to gain perspective, through feedback and reflection, on past events to better understand our choices, actions and responses. However, this knowledge is pointless if we do not use it to support subsequent actions and endeavours. The past serves to inform the future, hence my emphasis on "feedforward."

As leaders, whatever feedback we offer, either through observation or data collection, should serve current goals and our team's future success. It should never serve to allocate blame or lay guilt. A leader's motivation in offering feedback should be a desire to help generate insight, which in turn is applied strategically to create a wanted result.

This new result moves us forward toward our ultimate destination. Without feedback, we would struggle to situate ourselves; with continuous feedback, we can nimbly adjust to generate fresh ideas and gain further traction.

28 | CREATE FEEDBACK LOOPS

Without the fuel that feedback offers, even the most blazing fire will fizzle. Develop and systematize feedback loops to gather information and make effective decisions. Most importantly, integrate them into all important plans and decisions. With good feedback, your team will flourish: they'll know the extent to which they are on or off track, why it matters, the possible consequences and what actions they should be taking next.

Take a moment to think about all the words or phrases you associate with the word *feedback*. Are the words or phrases that come to mind positive associations or do they lean toward the negative? In my seminars, when I poll my participants, it is more common to hear "negative." People often associate the notion of feedback with criticism or being told how they've messed up and what they need to change to redeem themselves.

ACCURATE.
RELEVANT.
CONNECTED.
MOTIVATING.

Feedback loops are used by economists, engineers, mathematicians, biologists and many other professionals as a way to gather information about a gap between the actual and the system parameter in order to alter the gap in some way. The purpose of feedback is to assist in successfully executing the system's purpose. Organizations need feedback to perform well. Some examples of feedback in organizations:

- financial audit/reporting
- performance appraisals/360 feedback assessments
- employee engagement surveys
- shareholders' meeting
- customer and market research
- union grievances, strikes, lockouts

We would be lost without feedback. We couldn't orientate our organizations, we would not know the current reality, and we would not understand how to move forward toward fulfilling our organizational purpose.

As the chart below shows, leaders create strong feedback systems by collecting raw data (evidence), building on this by providing meaningful context in two areas (relevance and consequence) and finally giving employees the time and space to take appropriate action.

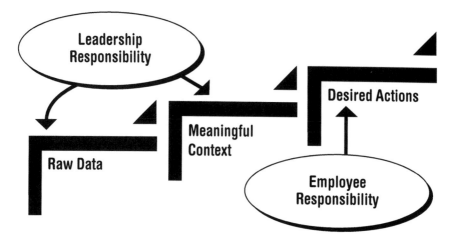

In 2011, *Wired* magazine ran a very interesting article on feedback by Thomas Goetz called "Harnessing the Power of Feedback Loops." *Wired* was reporting on research that used feedback loops (such as positioning a digital sign, which flashed the actual driving speed, next to a sign stating the speed limit) to slow traffic in a school zone with a history of accidents. Below are the four key elements of feedback in relation to the example.

1. **Raw data: evidence.** The radar-equipped sign flashes a car's current speed. First comes the real-time data—quantifying a behaviour and presenting that data back to individuals so they know where they stand. After all, you can't change what you don't measure.

2. **Meaningful context: relevance.** The sign also displays the legal speed limit. Most people don't want to be seen as bad drivers. Data is just digits unless it hits home. Through information design, social context or some other proxy for meaning, the right incentive will transform rational information into an emotional imperative.

3. **Meaningful context: consequences.** People are reminded of the downside of speeding, including traffic tickets and the risk of accidents. Even compelling information is useless unless it ties into some larger goal or purpose. People must have a sense of what to do with the information and any opportunities they will have to act on it.
4. **Action.** Drivers slow an average of 10 percent, usually for several miles. The individual has to engage with all of the above and act, thus closing the loop and allowing that new action to be measured.

The stunning thing about this research was twofold: The drivers already had access to information about their speed (the speedometer), so the digital sign was actually redundant information; and the drivers self-regulated by choice, as there were no real consequences and no police officers were onsite. The following components were found to be key for the success of the feedback loop:

- A consistent, constant, accurate flow of information so people can orientate themselves and know where they stand.
- A relevant context or meaningful North Star so action becomes an emotional imperative.
- A consequence that connects to a larger goal or purpose that is meaningful.
- A forthcoming action, motivated by the above, to close the loop and diminish the gap.

ACTIVITY

Think about your leadership actions and decisions.

- What feedback systems do you currently use in your leadership role?
- What benefits do they provide?

....

....

....

What are the implications for you as a leader regarding the surprising findings of the research described above?

- Redundant information?
- No actual, immediate consequences?

....

....

....

Feedback loops and performance

Leaders who carefully decide what to measure or observe, how to measure or observe and when to feed the information, with context and relevance, to their teams will empower their teams to respond sagaciously with the most appropriate action. Leaders who ignore information management create obstacles for their teams and automatically diminish performance—time to accomplish the task or the quality of the task.

From an employee point of view, without feedback loops, there is greater uncertainty, a greater chance of poor decision-making and less satisfaction because of the increasing probability of barriers stemming from poor information.

Feedback is information to help your team succeed, either collectively or as individuals. In this case, more is better!

ACTIVITY

How is this way of viewing feedback the same or different from how you previously thought about it?

....

....

....

↗ 29 | EMBRACE FEEDBACK

Use feedback to uplift and encourage, even when mistakes need to be addressed. Normalizing feedback takes the sting out and lets people know they don't need to go into protective mode for fear of exposure. Using feedback to learn and build future success invigorates and stimulates new ideas to action. As a leader, walk the talk by embracing personal feedback and demonstrating how to integrate the information to make yourself a stronger leader. Both you and your team will get fired up.

LEADERS LEARN FIRST AND THEN TEACH.

One of the best ways to learn about giving feedback is to learn how to receive it. My view? If you can't take it, don't give it! Take a moment to complete the self-assessment below.

Check (✔) the appropriate box: **1 (Never) 2 (Rarely) 3 (Sometimes) 4 (Often) 5 (Always)**

Receiving Feedback	1	2	3	4	5
1. Do I listen openly to feedback rather than getting defensive?					
2. Do I solicit feedback?					
3. Do I receive feedback easily from my manager?					
4. Do I receive feedback easily from my employees?					
5. Do I receive feedback easily from my peers?					
6. Do I probe for details if the feedback is general?					

7. Do I try to learn from feedback, even if it's not skilfully delivered?					
8. Do I refrain from arguing and focus on the other's perspective?					
9. Do I focus on the future and next steps?					
10. Do I readily accept responsibility rather than blaming others?					

Now that you've taken the self-assessment, sit back and reflect on how you could strengthen your ability to receive feedback. Look at those areas in which you scored low and those that are your strengths. What could you do differently? Think about the benefits of being able to receive feedback fully and easily. Once you have become comfortable with receiving feedback, you will be able to coach your team on how to develop the skill themselves. You will be able to walk the talk in ways that will gain tremendous employee respect.

Why is receiving feedback so difficult for most of us? Mainly because we don't give and get enough of it! That means we're clumsy at giving it (the vast majority of us haven't developed sufficiently strong communication skills to deliver difficult messages with ease and sensitivity) and we're reticent about getting it (because when we do receive feedback, it's largely negative and delivered in a way that is more hurtful than helpful). Positive feedback is rarer than negative feedback, so we know as soon as we hear the word "feedback" that we're not likely to get a pat on the back, a promotion or a pay increase. No wonder we don't look forward to it!

Still, those of us on the receiving end have to take some responsibility for the bad reputation feedback gets. Feedback is really as much about the receiver as the giver. Why do we respond negatively (for the most part) when we're on the receiving end of comments, ideas and observations that could actually help us succeed? Why do we react so strongly to what other people think?

I've reflected on these questions for most of my adult life. If we see feedback as a threat and potentially dangerous to our self-esteem, reputation and position, we trigger our "fight, flight or freeze" mechanism. Once this happens, rational thinking is off the table, and we will have difficulty assessing the validity of the feedback. We go into a reactive mode—action designed to respond to the incoming attack. We are now compelled to defend ourselves. We're trying to protect ourselves from being hurt, and we are also vulnerable to being hijacked. Once in "fight, flight or freeze," we often attempt to

- justify our actions/choices;
- blame circumstances or other people;
- express a sense of unfairness/injustice;
- become argumentative or even aggressive; and
- shut down and become silent.

The masks we like to wear

Sometime in the late 1990s, a friend and coach, Madeline, shared with me a book called *The Undefended Self* (1994) by Susan Thesenga. It's based on the work of Eva Pierrakos and addresses insecurities and unwanted beliefs. The purpose of the book is to help readers face their shadow selves compassionately. Thesenga suggests that in undoing our personal defenses, we redirect and unleash creative energy that enables us to build the lives we most truly desire. Part of the process is to drop the idealized self-image we hold of ourselves and greet the "lower" self.

To be human is to be flawed and imperfect. We all make mistakes, occasionally hurt the people closest to us, and sometimes behave very badly. And yet this simple truth seems very hard for us to accept. . . . Out of fear of our flawed self, we create a masked self, an idealized self, the self we think we ought to be, rather than admitting the imperfect human self that we are. We're all quick to say "I'm fine" when asked, no matter how depressed we may be by our boss's recent criticism, or delighted we are by our recent business success.

These words are grounded in the reality of our humanity, which in turn is deeply connected to the topic of feedback. It speaks to the fact that as humans, we are inherently imperfect.

By not reconciling ourselves to our less attractive side, we doom ourselves to working long and hard to hide it. We tell ourselves, "It's not okay or acceptable to have flaws, so I will simply not acknowledge them." We choose to ignore in ourselves that which is unpleasant to consider or see. So while we try not to see what is truly there, we also pretend with others that this unpleasant aspect is not a part of us. The pretence indicates that we have an inkling of the truth and we work hard to keep it from view. Often this hard work comes in the form of projecting the opposite to ourselves and others, hence the "pretending."

For example, if I suspect I might be somewhat selfish and that some of my choices aren't purely altruistic, I might expend quite a bit of energy demonstrating to others that my motivations are pure. This is my "pretending." I might talk a lot about "the importance of employee engagement," or I might look for ways to express spontaneous generosity (always paying the dinner bill), thereby proving to myself and others that I am not selfish. In reality, I might very well be chiefly concerned with myself: making sure I get my fair share. Rather than acknowledging this part of myself, I deny it. I unconsciously look for opportunities to show it's not true. I volunteer and am generous with my time. I express how important it is to "give back" to the community. But what I really care about deep down is my next contract.

So what are we insecure about? That someone might find out we aren't perfect? That someone might discover we are human? That if I admit to a mistake or a flaw and everyone else keeps pretending, I'm the only one left with a mark against me? We fear others will uncover our imperfections and this will cause problems: we might miss an opportunity, we might lose relationships or be alone, we might not thrive—worst of all, we might not even survive!

Suzie's helpful insecurity

Suzie was known for being extremely helpful. She would go out of her way to add value, even when she wasn't asked. Sometimes this involved a great deal of time and energy on her part. She would offer to organize events or stay late to help meet someone else's deadline. Suzie became the go-to person for anything and everything in her department. People appreciated Suzie and usually told her so. But her manager had concerns: while she helped everyone else, Suzie's own projects languished, and she often failed to meet her deadlines.

When Suzie's manager initially gave her his feedback—"I think the help you give to others is preventing you from meeting your own deadlines; I need you to focus on your own projects to ensure they stay on track"—she became defensive and focused on justifying her actions. She was hurt that her "good works" weren't appreciated and valued. Instead, they were being used against her! She was always there to support her peers, and she worked hard to make sure everyone got the answers they needed to move their work forward. It was unfair that her boss didn't appreciate all of this! After the feedback session, Suzie withdrew and became quite miserable, which subsequently led to a series of coaching sessions with me.

In our work together, Suzie and I peeled back the layers of thinking around her "helpfulness." I suggested to Suzie that she ask herself some tough questions:

- "What is true about this feedback/situation?" (*I do miss some of my deadlines and I often think more about what I can do for others than how can I make my work more effective and be more proactive in related issues.*)
- "Why does this happen? What causes me to be so focused on others' business rather than my own?" (*I want people to appreciate me and value me so I do things for them that will hopefully create a positive response.*)
- "What is my underlying motive for always wanting to help people? What do I get out of it?" (*If people value me then I will be well positioned for new opportunities and people will say lots of good things about me and I will become indispensable!*)
- "What does this tell me about myself—about, in *Star Wars* speak, my dark side?" (*Underneath all of this I am mostly concerned with my own success, and I am trying to ensure people see me in a certain way.*)

When Suzie walked herself through these questions, she was surprised to find that the root of her behaviour was not a true desire to help people but rather a way of acting that quelled her fears and that she hoped would ultimately secure her success. It became clear that being helpful was her way of pretending. Her focus was really on her own success, and she was mostly concerned about herself. She felt unsure about whether people would value her enough to support her, so she looked for opportunities to prove she could add value. However, she did not want to see that her underlying motivations were to make herself look good and thus increase her chance of success. Instead, she told herself and others that teamwork was extremely important to her.

Insecurities like Suzie's stem from a desire to protect ourselves from seeing our imperfections because we think it would be horrible to acknowledge that we are not all good and goodness. What if someone discovers our faults? We'd be in trouble!

What happens if my boss suggests I might need to improve something or address a behaviour that interferes with our team's overall success? Might this trigger a reaction within me? Might it threaten to reveal that I am not perfect and that I make mistakes? Might I then respond in a way that would reject even the possibility that the observation might hold some truth?

We must learn not to be afraid of the fears that lurk in the shadows. Leaving our underlying motivations in the dark only means we have more difficulty aligning ourselves to what matters most to us: our values, our true aspirations, our healthy relationships. It also makes us defensive to feedback that touches on these sensitive areas, especially if the person giving the feedback is onto something.

Suzie discovered that she was afraid she wouldn't succeed and that she believed if she stopped helping people her chances of success would be jeopardized even further. No wonder she resisted the feedback! A lot was at stake for her, in her mind anyway.

ACTIVITY

Think about feedback you have recently received and answer the same questions as Suzie did:

- What is true about this feedback/situation?
- Why does this happen?
- What is my underlying motive? What do I get out of it?
- What does this tell me about myself? The good, bad and the ugly!

....

....

....

Merriam-Webster.com defines *insecure* as "deficient in assurance: beset by fear and anxiety" or "not highly stable or well-adjusted." Ignoring insecurities doesn't remove the fear or create more stability. On the contrary, pretending they don't exist actually gives them more power.

Until we see insecurities for what they really are—fears that are rarely grounded in reality—they will always hold us hostage.

We can't be free of our insecurities if we don't first shine a light on them. They're like an invisible chain that stops us from moving toward our goals, whatever those goals might happen to be. They may never go away completely, but once we set them on a table and look them straight in the eye, we gain a perspective that is simply not possible when we keep them hidden in a closet. Once outed, insecurities invariably become far less powerful.

When we give feedback, if we remember that many people have constructed an idealized self that they have a strong inclination to defend, we may choose to frame the conversation so the listener will receive it as information in support of higher goals. For example, in conducting a coaching session recently with a successful executive, I sensed defensiveness in her comments. I stepped back and said, "You obviously have many strengths. You would not have achieved this position in the company without being very good at what you do. The feedback I am now sharing with you is not about judging the past; it's to help you look forward. This is the area that others have identified as a way to help you take your team to the next level."

When we receive feedback, whether praise or criticism, if we remember it is information offered from a particular perspective that we can use to inform future decisions, we will see it as valuable rather than threatening. If we take the approach that there is always something to learn, we will listen rather than defend.

A second quotation from Thesenga (1994), which is perhaps my favourite from her book, builds on these concepts. She writes: "If you do not pretend to be more than you are, you will dare to be all that you are."

For me, this phrase quintessentially represents "being alive" and underpins authentic leadership. If we can all learn to be a little more like this, we will learn and grow together to create true synergy—as well as more fun! Feedback, if we welcome it, can be an extraordinarily powerful tool in our journey toward more meaningful life and career goals.

Q-TIP

Years ago, when I was dating my future spouse, Evan, he would share stories from his elementary classroom with me. Although I am completely biased, I think Evan is a superb teacher. One of his practices at the beginning of the school year was to post a list of "Five Rules" in the top right corner of the black board for his students. The rules were unconventional, my favourite one being "Q-TIP," otherwise known as "Quit Taking It Personally."

In grade 6, hormones and emotions can run high. Students are often quite sensitive to casual comments and pointed remarks. Evan's rule was designed to help students self-regulate and self-manage. He would explain to his students, with humour, "You are not the center of the universe. Others say and do things for reasons sometimes only known to them. Do not interpret others' actions as if you are the audience, even if the words or deeds are directed at you."

Only yesterday, I spoke to someone in the hallway. He barely paid attention and seemed completely disinterested in speaking with me. When we speak to someone, we expect feedback in the form of a response, and we often interpret how the person responds as an indication of the quality of the relationship. In that moment, I could have taken it personally, but I decided to Q-TIP it instead. Likely, the person I was talking to was deep in thought about another matter and preferred to keep it that way. Fair enough!

So, make it a habit to Q-TIP it. Otherwise, you may run up the Stairway to Conclusions and react to some invalid assumption.

"Dismissive Don" and "Single-Minded Molly"

Take Don, for example. He really wanted to move to another department because he was interested in more challenging work. His manager gave him straightforward feedback about how his interactions with others put them on the defensive. Rather than adjusting his own behaviour, Don told himself it was "their problem," as they were so sensitive. Needless to say, he never got the promotion he wanted.

Molly, on the other hand, was repeatedly encouraged by her boss to support the company expansion because it was the future direction of the organization. Molly appeared to listen, but she stayed focused on her day-to-day operational work, saying she was too busy to take on anything else. She would get to it one day, she said. Three years later, when the company reorganized, Molly was no longer on the radar and was not considered for any of the newly created positions, even though one of them was ideally suited to her expertise.

We often shoot ourselves in the foot by failing to integrate useful feedback. We compromise our own aspirations by not listening. Don ticked off all the right boxes by working accurately and efficiently; however, he destroyed rather than built collegial relationships. Don thought he was on path for a promotion, but in reality, he had drifted miles off-course. Molly also refused to adjust her orientation. She told herself that operations had always been important, and so she was safe. Rather than choosing to inform herself about the company's emerging reality, she buried her head in the sand and became irrelevant.

When people give you feedback you might not want to hear, listen anyway. Even poorly delivered feedback can lead to an exceedingly useful insight. Welcome feedback—rejecting it may put you at risk. Let go of your defensiveness, take a deep breath and try to understand what's being said. You can decide how best to apply the knowledge you gain.

Remember, even difficult-to-hear feedback can help you attain both short- and long-term goals. When we summarily reject corrective feedback, we limit possibility and risk failure that might otherwise have been averted.

Tips for receiving feedback

A leader has to both develop a feedback process and help team members receive feedback, so the tips below can first be applied and then shared. Once team members are used to receiving and giving feedback within these parameters, they'll feel empowered and fired up.

Ask for as much detail as possible. Make sure you understand the context of the feedback and all the relevant facts, especially when a conclusion has been reached. Your manager might say, "You're disorganized and unfocused" or "I think you procrastinate." In this case, you need to understand both the context and what facts have led to this conclusion. Ask: "In what ways am I disorganized?" "Why does it appear I am unfocused?" "What tasks do I seem to be putting off?"

Paraphrase your understanding of the situation. After the other person has stopped speaking, summarize what you've heard: "So you've noticed that I spend a significant portion of my time helping others when I don't seem to be moving my own work forward. Is that it in a nutshell?"

Acknowledge your behaviour, choices or role. Say: "It's true I do like to help my teammates. It's important to me to demonstrate my value. If I don't, I'm not sure I'd get the recognition I feel I have earned, and so I might miss out on opportunities."

Offer or seek suggestions for the future. Say: "Moving forward, I will make sure I take care of my daily priorities before helping others, unless there is an urgent need. Then perhaps it would be good to check in with you as well, just for the time being, until you feel comfortable I can meet my deadlines consistently."

Thank the person for the information. Say: "I am glad you shared your concerns with me. I'd rather know what you are thinking than be surprised come appraisal time!"

ACTIVITY

Ask yourself these provocative questions: *When I resist feedback, is it because . . .*

- I fear that my "shadow side" will be exposed?
- I fear that I might not have chosen in favour of my highest values?
- I fear what the answers above say about me as a person?
- I feel it will hurt my future success if people see that I sometimes don't make the most honourable choice?

....

....

....

30 | APPLY "THE 10 TYPES OF FEEDBACK TO FEEDFORWARD"

Give feedback daily to get your team fired up and keep them all aflame. Every interaction is an opportunity to coach. Keeping feedback (in its many different forms) flowing will ensure that your team as well as its individual members orientate themselves to be productive and progressive. Feedback becomes an activity that feeds forward, helping people grow and learn to build future success.

Feedback, in its essence, is information. And that information, when shared, should support the team or the individual's performance through a wide variety of situations. It will at times appeal to our intellect; at other times, to our emotional well-being. Making full use of all types of feedback will enable you to engage fully the hearts and minds of those on your team.

Management books have focused over the years on the type of feedback designed to close the gap between desired performance and actual performance. Many management programs have been designed to help managers deliver difficult messages, often in the context of performance appraisals. Although this is an important form of feedback, there are many other ways to provide your team and team members with valuable information that will assist them in achieving their goals and objectives.

> **TRADITIONAL FEEDBACK FOCUSES ON THE PAST AND SEES SHORTFALLS; TODAY'S LEADERS FOCUS FORWARD AND SEE GROWTH AND OPPORTUNITY.**

I have developed "The 10 Types of Feedback to Feedforward" over the course of many years of working with teams. Traditionally, feedback has been restricted to pointing out gaps. However, if you think of feedback as information you need to help you succeed, then it is easy to see all of the missed opportunities for feedback that help build a culture of achievement. Below is my top-10 list:

1. Encourage the Heart
2. Align to Meaningful Goals
3. Track for Impact
4. Revisit Plans
5. Assert Standards
6. Correct to Stay the Course
7. Value Effort and Commitment
8. Build on Strengths
9. Develop for Career Progress
10. Celebrate to Uplift and Reward

I'll explain these types in more detail in the chapters ahead.

ACTIVITY

Think about this past week. Place a checkmark next to the types of feedback above that you consciously practice on a daily or at least weekly basis. Circle the ones that require more of your attention. What does this tell you?

....

....

....

31 | ENCOURAGE THE HEART

We are emotional beings. We get discouraged. We sometimes suffer from self-doubt. We thrive on hope. When the flame has been dampened because of difficult times or a tough challenge, encouragement will help rekindle the spark by letting your team members know they are on track and should persevere.

My cousin Dian participates in an annual two-day walk to fundraise for breast-cancer research and care. After her first walk, she eagerly told me about the experience. She described amazing scenes of people lining the route as she and her fellow participants passed by. People clapped, cheered and yelled words of encouragement; they held up signs that said, "You're walking for me. Thank you." "You're walking for my sister." "Thank you for caring!" She related how these supportive words and messages spoke to her heart and infused her with energy, which she definitely needed as the miles and miles of walking produced blisters, dehydration and a variety of other aches and pains.

Encouraging the heart allows managers to uplift people, fortify them for the long haul, and/or instil in them the confidence they need to overcome obstacles on the journey. Sometimes journeys are short but difficult, like walking up a steep incline; sometimes they are long and require endurance, like Dian's two-day walk. Whatever the length or type of journey, encouraging travelers with supportive feedback helps enable their success.

EVERYONE CAN USE A CHEERLEADER.

During my years at a large service organization, I faced many barriers. When my team, peers or senior executives encouraged me to persevere, it gave me the strength I needed to continue when I felt like giving up. But their support conveyed other important messages to me. Their encouragement told me there was meaning in my work and that it was worth pursuing. It showed me that they saw progress (when I sometimes did not) and that they believed I would achieve even more if I kept at it. These were vital messages for me.

I now know, from years of consulting experience, that this same kind of support is equally vital and in some cases critical to the success of people everywhere. It keeps the work meaningful and helps people see their efforts produce results that matter.

One of my clients, Yi Ling, could have used similar encouragement from her leadership team. She felt deflated when they did not seem to value and support a complex piece of work she had undertaken. I suggested she remind herself of why she believed in the work and why she felt it was right for the team. Then she needed to be a little patient and to persevere. As her strategy unfolded, her team and superiors would begin to see its benefits. I reminded her that people adopt new ways at different speeds, and some might even need proof before jumping on board.

Later, Yi Ling told me that if she had not been encouraged, she likely would have given up. Yi Ling's work led to greater productivity and fulfillment for her and her team. It would have been a loss for everyone involved, including the organization, if she had not completed it.

When people close to you struggle to be supportive because your work is difficult to understand or because it impacts them, find external people to support you. On longer, more arduous journeys, we need cheerleaders to help us remember why we took on the challenge in the first place and why we should persevere.

Encouragement nurtures hope. It helps people believe there is a light at the end of the tunnel. Encouraging words say, "I see movement. Keep at it! You'll get there soon. The finish line is just around the corner." Unfortunately, instead of encouraging people, we may dishearten them (unintentionally and unconsciously, to be sure) with ill-considered comments based in our own negative thinking: "Ah, I wouldn't bother if I were you. I don't think you'll get anywhere!" "Yeah, we tried that a million times before, and it didn't work." "Wow. Aren't *you* the brave one to take *that* on."

We have the best intentions and the best interests of the listener in mind and we think we're being realistic. Maybe we even believe we're doing the listener a favour if we try to ground them in reality. Indeed, there may well be the need for a reality-check. But the question is: How do we help people see the truth and encourage them at the same time?

A comment like this might be useful: "I tried a similar approach a couple of years ago and I didn't see results; however, I also didn't work closely with the key influencers. You might want to broaden your stakeholder group." Or it might be helpful to suggest the individual seek alternate paths: "Your work is important to this organization. Why don't you explore other ways of achieving the same thing? There's got to be more than one way to crack a tough nut!" At the end of the day, the current path might work equally effectively. Our encouragement simply re-focuses and re-energizes.

Recently, my eight-year-old daughter, Taylor, was testing for her blue belt in Tae Kwon Do. Unbeknownst to me, at the end of the test, she was to break a three-quarter-inch board with her foot. I knew she had never done this before but had been trained in the technique. As an instructor held the board for her, she did the pattern, kicked and hit the board . . . hard . . . but it didn't break. She resumed her stance and kicked again. The board remained intact. Her third attempt created the same result. Video-taping from the sidelines, I found I had stopped breathing and had become anxious. Then, Master Power spoke, directing his comments at the audience. "Let's give Taylor encouragement." Everyone started clapping and shouting. Taylor stood for a moment, focused on the board and then crack! It broke into two pieces. The audience roared!

Later, when Taylor and I were alone, I asked her, "You knew the technique. How did the audience help you?" She looked at me and simply said, "They gave me power." Never underestimate the value of encouragement.

ACTIVITY

Think about a time you were encouraged. What impact did it have on you?

....

....

....

ACTIVITY

Pick a person on your team who needs encouragement. Why does that individual need to be encouraged? What do you want to say to him or her?

....

....

....

32 | ALIGN TO MEANINGFUL GOALS

Passion begins with meaning. Feedback that helps focus on the goal helps people understand why it's meaningful. Aligning each person and the team to meaningful organizational values, mission and core objectives will keep their drive alive and make their fire thrive.

Many years ago, I led a highly dedicated team. They worked hard and had to navigate a large, complex environment. Sometimes I would see people looking a little lost. This was always a sign that the organizational quagmire had become an obstacle. The inherent complexity of the work often required great attention to detail, so it wasn't unusual for people to lose sight of the forest as they became focused on all the individual trees, saplings, undergrowth, roots and more.

Lost in the woods

Nikki, who reported to me, sometimes didn't wait for me to notice when she began to feel a little overwhelmed by all the various and seemingly disconnected parts needing attention. As a matter of fact, she would announce her frustration in no uncertain terms. "Why are we doing this again?" she would ask, both seriously and a little desperately. It was (and still is) *such* a brilliant question! Nikki was able to identify when her sense of purpose and meaning were compromised. What a tremendous level of awareness to cultivate!

> **OUR VALUES, MISSION AND OBJECTIVES GIVE US A SENSE OF PURPOSE AT WORK, AND PURPOSEFUL WORK UPLIFTS THE SOUL.**

How many of us are afraid to reveal that we've lost the plot, fearing that to appear out of control might be the proverbial kiss of death? One of Nikki's great strengths was a combination of humility and confidence. She was secure enough to say "I don't see the point anymore" when she felt adrift or overwhelmed.

This was a wonderful invitation for me, as the team leader, to re-examine the purpose of her work, validate it and refocus her on what was meaningful about what she did. Occasionally these examinations revealed a flaw in the plan, which either meant we needed a new plan or modifications to the existing one. Either way, the conversation was inevitably useful in affirming the value of the work or redirecting efforts in ways that were more productive.

Upping the challenge, adding great value

Recently, one of my clients, Pamela, shared a story of how she connected her people to meaning. One of her direct reports is the company receptionist. Over time, Pamela noticed that the receptionist, Sally, didn't seem as engaged in her work as she had been in her early days with the company. Sally knew her job well and did all the tasks she was required to do well enough, but there was a lack of energy and a shortage of value-added activity.

Pamela decided to speak with Sally about how Sally saw her role and her work. When Pamela got to this point in the story, I expected her to recount how she had fed Sally the usual clichés, such as "You are the first impression customers have of our company" or "You are the face and voice of the organization." These are both true, of course. However, to truly connect someone with the importance of their role and goals, speaking in specific terms is often far more powerful than regurgitating the same old tired truisms.

I was thrilled when Pamela shared that she had taken a much different route. Instead of the predicable pap, she had said, "Sally, you're good at your job, and I believe you're ready to take it to the next level. I want you to think about how your work connects to our core sales team. How do you think what you do supports them and, through them, the goals of the business overall? I also wonder, how could you support them even more and, by doing so, make the company more successful? I think you can contribute to the business in even more meaningful ways than you do now, and I want to explore how we can make that happen."

Pamela told me that she followed up about a week later with a second conversation to see what had emerged for Sally. Here's how Pamela described the meeting to me: "As she came into the meeting, Sally was obviously energized. She said that she had really thought about it, and she saw how she was not only the first point of contact for the company, but she could facilitate external calls further. Then she said she would take it upon herself to learn more about each salesperson's line of business, as well as who would typically call them and for what reasons. This, she said, would equip her to ask better questions and to ensure the caller got to the right person efficiently. She also said she was ready to take on some of her manager's project work. She had periods of downtime and could be of help, as long as she could work from the main desk."

Pamela was completely blown away by Sally's initiative and told her so right then and there. Over the weeks that followed, Pamela noticed a real shift in Sally's performance. She finessed her routine responsibilities and focused on implementing her new ideas. Not only was Sally excelling in her work, she looked happier and more energized too.

Pamela wasn't the only one to be blown away—I was too! I was proud of Pamela for giving feedback that strengthened Sally's alignment to the core purpose of her role and doing so in a way that inspired Sally and enhanced her ability to do her job well. When Pamela invited Sally to look more closely at the goal of her role, how she fit into the organization and how she could make her work more meaningful, Sally stepped up to the plate and hit a home run. She truly wowed Pamela with her winning response.

When leaders align people to meaningful goals, people, teams and organizations will notice possibilities for action previously unseen. So it makes infinite sense to help people focus (or refocus) on how their work and their goals do (or could) make a difference. Generating greater purpose leads to better results across the board of human-resources performance metrics, from productivity to personal fulfillment.

Activity

How could you create greater alignment on your team?

- For example, do people see how the corporate values translate into their day-to-day work and behaviours? If not, look for opportunities to reinforce this connection.
- Do people see how they are contributing to the mission of the organization, in a way that is meaningful to them versus trite or vague?
- Do people have clear, prioritized goals? If you ask them, you might discover it's not as clear as you thought.

....

....

....

33 | TRACK FOR IMPACT

To keep the fires burning, make sure you track the impact of your actions. When you see forward movement toward your goal, you know you are getting traction. If you are disappointed with the results of your action, reassess and adapt to get back on track. Don't let the team flounder by expending energy without gaining ground. Make the progress visible or find new ways forward to keep momentum strong.

Tracking progress allows managers and employees to confirm that existing action plans will produce the expected results, thereby keeping projects on track. The astounding pace, complexity and competitiveness of the global marketplace can mean initial action plans quickly become irrelevant and newer action plans must surface rapidly to address the emerging realities. Leaders and teams beware: ignore lack of impact at your peril!

After decades of coaching leaders whose projects or initiatives decelerate, dissipate or even disintegrate, I'm still amazed to discover the plethora of warning flags these leaders chose to ignore in favour of sticking to their initial course of action. Denial is tricky business! When I ask, "When did you know the project was in jeopardy?" or "When did it first occur to you that the project was not on track?" I frequently find people know things are going pear-shaped far earlier than their too-little-too-late actions would indicate.

It sounds crazy, I know, but entire organizations often turn a blind eye to what in hindsight are billboard-sized signs clearly marked "This is doomed to fail." They go into some kind of deer-in-the-headlights

> **PROACTIVE APPROACHES TO MANAGING PROGRESS INFUSE TEAMS WITH ENERGY.**

denial in which they persuade themselves they can still make it work, despite overwhelming evidence to the contrary.

Tracking progress also generates momentum. It highlights the impact of completed tasks and actions, helps you see how to adjust or adapt and keeps next steps at the forefront. Tracking progress is just as important for small projects and daily work as for larger long-term initiatives.

A long-time coaching client who has become masterful at progress engagement summarizes the benefits this way: "It gives me a chance to make my own observations and to ask them for theirs in an informal, non-threatening kind of way. I really listen to where they're coming from and pay careful attention in particular to signs of discouragement. I make sure they are able to see the real progress they're making, if indeed they are. And I ensure their expectations for progress are realistic. I'm amazed at how often people set themselves up for failure by expecting too much of themselves and others. I have a good team, and mostly I find they move projects forward well. But equally important, if they're not making the kind of progress they should be, I can help them redirect their activities in ways that will increase the impact of what they're doing."

When a leader keeps an eye on progress and gives or solicits continuous feedback, he is better able to stay on track, expedite the tasks at hand and identify potential opportunities to maximize positive outcomes.

How often you meet with your team depends on what you are monitoring. Quarterly is best for performance-management meetings. Monthly is more of a general guideline when you don't have regular contact with people. Weekly is often for when you want to create a ritual and have a team meeting. Daily dialogue gives opportunities for feedback as well as ways to proactively manage obstacles and factors that could derail initiatives. There are various ways to give feedback on progress and the value of the current path:

- Hold check-ins to ascertain whether people see the impact of their actions or take the right actions to get full impact.
- When a leader asks a team member a question like "How do you feel your project is going?" he may get a wide variety of answers: a vague "It's going okay" or an enthusiastic "I'm very pleased!" or a disillusioned "I feel like I'm spinning my wheels." These conversation-starters open the door to exploring expectations for progress as well as how it's being measured.
- Conduct environmental scans with your team and stakeholders to make sure your action plan is aligned to current situations and circumstances.

- Ask for feedback from stakeholders as well as from those with unique perspectives to ensure the progress you see is real and not just smoke and mirrors. Ask project leads to do the same.
- Meet quarterly with your project leads to review actions to date, assess outcomes and impacts and identify emerging opportunities.
- When a leader creates feedback loops and shares his own personal observations, he infuses his team with energy. By paying attention, he says to them, "Your work matters, and I want you to get the best value from the time and energy you put into it." A good leader wants his team members to be as effective as possible so they can enjoy their progress and achievements. Are you that kind of leader?

Daily dialogue and discussion: Just do it!

You don't have to wait for a specific time frame to make observations about progress with your team. Take the opportunity on a daily (or at least weekly) basis. There's nothing better than ending a day or week on the upswing with a high five. It makes people feel like what they do makes a difference. There are many fast, easy and personal ways to do this. Here are three specific examples.

1. **Progress Pit Stops:** Each day, drop by someone's desk, perhaps later in the afternoon, and say something along the lines of, "I noticed you managed to move your top priority forward today. Good work!" or "I think you were able to influence your key stakeholder today with that well-written e-mail. I'm sure they'll see the benefits more clearly now. Well done!"
2. **Show and Tell:** Take fifteen minutes on Fridays (or whichever is the last day of the week for your team) to celebrate the forward motion of the week. Ask team members to bring one example of tangible progress and share why it mattered to them. As each person takes a turn, everyone else's job is to listen and applaud. It's a great way to end the week on a positive note. In my experience, people will make a big effort to bring something meaningful to the table, as they want to leave the workplace feeling good about themselves and their job.

3. **VVVIPS (Visual, Visible and Very Important Progress Stories/ Statements):** Progress reports don't have to be boring documents. Creating visually interesting stories or statements that team members can see helps maintain focus, track input and give direct quantitative feedback, particularly if the task is onerous or routine or both. Progress stories or statements can take many visual forms—including photos, testimonials, anecdotes, line graphs, bar charts, Lego towers, totems, posters, pinboards— and can be used to track anything from sales targets to action plans to key performance indicators. Making physical signs of progress simultaneously keeps the work top of mind and reinforces important goals.

ACTIVITY

What important individual or team task/project would benefit from making progress more visible? Brainstorm ways to do this below.

....

....

....

A real-life VVVIPS

A client of mine, Tim, had a dreadfully boring project that needed doing: A backlog of documents (boxes and boxes of them) had to be scanned and filed in a particular way as part of a risk-management and compliance strategy. Progress was extremely slow, and no one really wanted to do the work because it was *so* tedious.

Tim, who was the department manager, decided to lead the project himself with two goals in mind: to motivate his team to get the job done and to demonstrate that once the backlog was eliminated, the scanning would be everyone's responsibility and it was everyone's job to attend to it.

He started by counting all the boxes of files that had to be scanned. He drew a huge thermometer on an even bigger poster board (it took up most of one wall of the team's workspace) and marked it off with a line for each box, spaced an inch apart. Each team member was asked to spend one hour a week on scanning. After each hour, they coloured in the thermometer based on the number of boxes they had completed during their scanning session. People really embraced this idea, and everyone pitched in. They enjoyed the feeling of accomplishment at the end of the hour and celebrated, as a team, as they got closer and closer to their goal of getting all the documents scanned.

This is a great example of how one can easily create a system for ongoing feedback, track it visually and visibly, infuse it with importance and do it in a way that adds an element of fun for the team.

Keep the Progress Pit Stops going!

I recommend that regular check-in conversations take place at least weekly. As a leader, you want your people to feel they get a good ROI (return on investment) for their time and effort. People are usually willing to work hard and focus on a task; however, if they feel their time and effort have not produced some tangible result that is valued by someone, it's demotivating and the focused attention will fade.

Informal individual conversations allow leaders to keep their finger on the pulse of their team's energy, effort and excitement levels so timely adjustments can be made. For example, perhaps there is a better way to tackle a task so the person can work faster (less time/effort) with the same result. Or perhaps by adding a step, the value-add increases substantially (better result).

Rectifying a time-effort imbalance

One of my clients, an accounting team, needed to create a special document if they noticed a discrepancy in the data. The document kick-started a series of checks that may involve four or more people and sometimes took months to resolve before the case could close. One team member, on her own initiative, started doing something different. Here's how she described it to me: "When I notice one of these data issues, I don't automatically create an exception document. I just get up from my desk, walk over to the other department and ask a member of that team to take a quick look at the file. If the problem is an obvious fix, we deal with it on the spot."

Instant resolution! Simple cases no longer burdened the system, thus saving time and hassle for both teams. The new procedure was shared with both teams after it was discovered during a regular check-in between the team member and her team leader.

ACTIVITY

Reflect on your team's existing work.

- What current task/project is off-track?
- How do you know?
- When did you first know?
- What can you do about it now?

....

....

....

What to measure

Often it isn't the number of measures but the right measures that count. This is even more important for less-tangible projects, such as culture-change initiatives. For example, when a company that organizes itself around products and the technical aspects of product development moves to a client-centric philosophy and operation, the shift will surely result in major challenges. Such a change requires substantially different ways of measuring progress. Instead of tracking the number of contracts sold, for example, measure the customer experience, such as the length of time needed to answer a client's question; the client's ability to understand the contract with ease; or the variety of ways the client can access people and information.

What does the team notice? Do they measure things that truly reflect progress, or do they track so many aspects that data abounds but no one knows what it means or what to do with it? If we say we want to make life easier for clients because we know they are short on time and value convenience, but we don't measure the quality of their interactions with us, how will we know if we are making progress toward this goal? If we only measure the number of contracts gained, retained or lost, how can we possibly understand what makes it easy or hard for clients to interact with us?

Such initiatives require leaders to sharply tune in to the environment. A leader may certainly plan and execute a strategy and the tactics that go along with it, but in my experience, this is rarely sufficient to guarantee success. She must also solicit and give feedback confirming that she, the project and the team are all on target, or that she needs to redirect efforts to a more fruitful approach. To be honest, I've yet to come across a project or even day-to-day work that didn't need at least *some* tweaking along the way. Have you?

Knowing what to track is critical. Ask yourself these questions:

What do you want to formally measure? What activities can be planned, executed and evaluated (communications, learning events, employee and client engagements, research and development)? How will they be evaluated? What will be your key performance indicators (KPIs) or outcome measures, and why do they matter in relation to your goal?

What meaningful signposts of progress might you track informally? Consider water-cooler or lunchroom conversations (What do people really say about the project? What do they complain about that might represent a roadblock or lack of progress?); the level of explicit support through the offering of ideas or aligned actions (What do people say and do to be helpful versus compliant?); and anecdotes like success stories (What small or big wins do people brag about?).

ACTIVITY

Know what to track. What significant or meaningful task/project could you be tracking that you're not? How could you track it?

....

....

....

Both formal and informal methods are needed to track progress and confirm all is well. There is nothing worse than sticking to an agreed-upon action plan only to discover that certain actions have backfired and people are quietly resisting or even sabotaging the project, initiative or change—or that another complementary initiative was launched and no one thought to incorporate the existing action plan into it, thus missing a golden opportunity for both strategies to advance more efficiently through obvious synergies.

ACTIVITY

Which of the above suggestions might work for you? What new ones could you add to the list?

....

....

....

Project/Key Task	How Are You Measuring Progress?	What Tool Could Help Make Progress More Visible?

34 | REVISIT PLANS

Fire up your team by taking a breath to reassess. Sometimes we need to stop, go back or take a less direct route to make more significant forward gains. Learn when and how to revisit set plans rather than allowing a doomed plan to de-energize your team. Further investment of time and effort is often well worth it.

I have already touched on the need to adjust action plans in the previous chapter, but adjusting deserves a separate discussion partly because it's often overlooked or undervalued. I've noticed that most organizations deal with their strategic plans in one of three ways:

REGRESS FOR THE SAKE OF PROGRESS.

1. Write plans and put them on the shelf—never to be consulted again—and instead "go with the flow."
2. Marry them for better or for worse and become dysfunctionally attached to them until the marriage ends in a messy and costly divorce.
3. Revisit, reassess and adjust them on a regular basis to meet the challenges of changing conditions.

Can you guess into which two categories the majority of organizations fall? In my experience, some organizations become exceedingly attached to existing strategies, goals and plans, whether or not those plans remain relevant moving forward. In others, it seems that once people work through a business challenge, a specific problem or a burning issue, they resist revisiting their decisions and/or solutions—sometimes to their own detriment, as well as that of their team and organization.

Regress for the sake of progress

My dear friend Dave described the following to me one day: When climbing a new mountain, it's exciting to trek straight up. It's new terrain with new views and new challenges. With each step, the distance to the top decreases. However, if a hiker reaches a point in his climb that is impassable or too dangerous, he must backtrack to find a better route—not a prospect to be relished! Even the word *backtrack* says *regress*. We're not moving forward anymore; we're going backward, over old ground. Not only that, but we're now increasing instead of decreasing the distance to the top.

Perhaps we view revisiting previously made decisions in the same way, as *regress* rather than *progress*. Maybe we don't see the value in redoing something that has already been "done and dusted." Elena, a colleague of mine, couldn't bring herself to rewrite a paper she had been asked to revisit. She felt she had already invested enough time and effort in the piece and saw little value in putting more into it. Elena may have been right. On the other hand, she may have missed a good opportunity to take her thoughts and ideas to a whole new level by viewing what she had written with fresh eyes.

Like Elena, most of us resist revisiting work we've already completed. It doesn't feel like forward movement. Perhaps it feels a little bit like watching a rerun and so forms a psychological barrier. In contrast, when we watch a TV show for the first time, we don't know what's coming next. It's fresh and, hopefully, entertaining. We engage more easily because we don't know the episode. Not knowing heightens our anticipation; it holds the possibility of surprise and invites us to focus to avoid missing important clues and plot elements. Watching a rerun is a different experience because it doesn't create a sense of progress in the same way a new episode does. We don't learn a new story line, we are not introduced to new actors or characters, and we are not as delighted by the humour or surprised by the plot twists.

Even our language creates barriers. For example, in the text above, I have used the words *revisit*, *reassess*, *regress* and *rewrite*. We employ countless others every day: *relaunch*, *redo*, *reorganize*, *reimagine* and *rework* among them. Even *rehearse*, which is what we do to prepare in advance, is often not something we joyfully anticipate. The prefix *re* itself is somehow discouraging. Once we get a taste of progress from achieving an initial milestone, we naturally resist activities that make us feel we are going backward instead of forward.

It makes perfect sense. And who can blame us? Who wants to be told, after she has poured her heart and soul (not to mention her blood, sweat and tears) into a piece of work, that it must be redone? (I bet you can almost hear the voice in that poor woman's head: *What? Redone? You must be kidding! It took everything I had to get that done once. And now you want me to go it again?*)

Leaders have to learn to recognize this resistance in their teams. It becomes an issue when evidence indicates a second pass would produce a more impactful result, or a revisited action plan might generate better outputs given changing circumstances. The thought that we have already done something causes many people to "persist in the resist."

We don't adjust. We don't want to redo the report or revise the action plan. We choose to ignore the feedback and push on, even when it's to our disadvantage in the long term. Instead, we focus on the short term: the paper is "good enough" to use with our existing audience, so we don't reframe it to fit potential new stakeholders. Maybe we say we'll work it out later and steam ahead with a new system, despite emerging information regarding problematic support.

Leaders can help their teams see the value in adjusting by giving feedback on how emerging circumstances might impact the current course of action, reflecting back to teams the real results and truths surrounding what has occurred to date and helping teams reprocess by asking important questions like these:

- "Will you reach your goals effectively and efficiently if you continue to follow the current course of action?"
- "What has changed in your environment that might compromise your action plan?"
- "What opportunities are emerging that we didn't foresee and might want to leverage?"
- "What new ideas have you had while managing your project/ tasks that are not currently in your action plan?"

Use the above list of questions to support a team member now.

....

....

....

Slow down before you spin out

Leaders understand the advantages in slowing the course of action. We have been taught to dial it up, ramp it up or turbocharge it, but rarely are we advised to take a deep breath and slow it down. To assess properly and adjust, we sometimes need to take time to examine, reflect and consider. In our fast-paced world, this may be counterintuitive; it may even be viewed as counterproductive. Nevertheless, it can be crucial to slow down in order to get to the right answer or the best result for ourselves and the organization.

Good leaders encourage their team members to make time to think and reassess. A CFO I worked with once remarked to me, "I don't have time to think. That's not good in my job!" And she was right. It wasn't good. It is crucial to get off the runaway train and take time out to look at issues and opportunities from various perspectives.

To be effective, leaders must think through the implications of current courses of action and adjust when required. Furthermore, in our frenzied, action-packed, multimedia world, natural downtime is rare. So we need to create space for ourselves to see what is there to see. Then and only then can we truly give situations and circumstances appropriate consideration.

ACTIVITY

Close your eyes. Take three deep, long breaths. Breathe in and out deeply and slowly. What did you notice?

....

....

....

Another way to slow things down is to take the "scenic route" rather than a more direct path to our destination. I find scenic routes to be particularly effective within change projects, where the most direct course of action may not always be the best course of action.

A classic example of this is when executive teams decide—after great deliberation—to implement a strategic change in direction. They spring it on their organization without warning, expect their staff to start executing it immediately and are taken aback when the troops don't all instantly jump on the new bandwagon. I sometimes can't help being surprised when the executives are surprised that there is resistance.

In these moments, I remind the senior team that they have considered the issue for many months or at least weeks. As decision-makers, they have had an opportunity to process the vision, assess the current state of affairs, evaluate options and choose what they believe to be the best way forward. Their teams have not. Their teams need a chance to digest it all and feel their way forward. That takes time.

I have seen good projects that had to be abandoned because the company executive tried to push them forward too quickly and directly. It's practically impossible for a senior team to force employees forward when they have dug in their heels. If there is movement, it will be slow, laborious and generally unpleasant. A relatively leisurely, more circuitous route may actually be more efficient and beneficial in the long run. Speed and agility have their place, but they don't always win the race—remember the fable of the tortoise and the hare?

The bottom line is that leaders can greatly support their teams when they provide feedback to encourage people to invest further time and energy on a project or objective by revisiting plans and reassessing actions taken to ensure true progress. It's easy to follow a checklist of actions; it's another thing to analyze impact and adjust to make greater gains more efficiently. At times, backtracking and slowing down to review progress is better than ploughing ahead with the wrong ideas.

ACTIVITY

What current project or task would benefit from a more scenic route—that is, slowing it down?

....

....

....

35 | ASSERT STANDARDS

When a team has clear, prioritized goals and a shared understanding of teamwork, they are empowered to make the right choices and decisions. Empowerment is the fuel of engagement. Performance standards support this, as they provide parameters within which the team can create, deliver and excel. When a sports team knows the rules of the game, they can focus on creating plays that avoid violations and enable exceptional performance.

It's not unusual for performance issues to emerge when there's a lack of clarity around deliverables and/or performance standards. In my experience, performance standards are more difficult to describe and therefore assert when they relate to behaviours. It's relatively straightforward to discuss objective measures like being on time and on budget—you either are or you aren't. Perhaps because many managers find behavioural standards subjective, they are more reluctant to assert them and discuss situations when those standards are not met. While I completely appreciate this challenge, more subjective behaviours and tasks can be addressed with clear thinking and practice.

Let's take a look at two concrete workplace examples: producing quality submissions and/or proposals and ensuring positive and productive peer interactions. Both have subjective elements that, if not properly described and asserted, can rapidly generate issues ranging from lost business to lower productivity.

BE EXPLICIT AND LAVISH.

With submissions and proposals, leaders must be clear—with themselves, first and foremost—as to their standards of measure. They must also be specific. In the case of quality submissions, for example, here are the kinds of questions a team leader needs to answer:

- How would you describe a top-notch submission?
- What are the elements that make it such?

- Can you provide a template and/or sample that will clearly establish the benchmark?
- Looking at past submissions, what worked well and what didn't?

When you provide feedback to your team, be prepared to paint a sharply focused picture of what you want. Improvement depends on your clarity and ability to demonstrate your ideas. If you're unable to articulate what you want done differently, you are highly unlikely to get different results.

With respect to peer interactions and teamwork, it is vital to give immediate and specific feedback that asserts your standards. After years of consulting, I know everyone has a different opinion regarding what is acceptable in the workplace. It is a leader's job to protect the culture and uphold corporate values and professional standards. When a leader sees one of his team members being disrespectful, confrontational or engaging in any unwanted behaviour, the onus is on him to assert what is and is not acceptable. If you're a leader, that's your responsibility.

For example, as a leader, you might say to someone who tends to show up late to meetings, "I know you have many projects on your plate. However, I expect you to be on time for meetings. It demonstrates respect for your colleagues. If need be, give yourself more buffer between meetings to ensure you can be on time."

If you are copied on an e-mail exchange that is generating conflict between colleagues, you will want to act immediately, saying something like, "E-mail can be a challenging way to communicate, especially when there is a difference of opinion. In such instances, I don't want you using e-mail. Instead, I want you to ask to meet with the person face-to-face and discuss the matter in a constructive way. E-mail often escalates situations and can damage relationships. Your goal in any peer interaction should be to ensure you preserve the relationship while you address the matter at hand."

Asserting such standards preserves exceptional performance. Both high-quality results *and* high-quality processes are required for sustained achievement and fulfillment at work.

Mismatched meaning

Early in my career as a consultant, I coached Denise, a manager who had received a poor performance rating for project management from her boss, Carole. Denise was proud of her achievements, but Carole was critical of her performance. Denise thought she had done a good job of completing the project in question; Carole saw significant shortfalls. There was an obvious disconnect, which we needed to clarify.

Carole felt Denise had mismanaged the fiscal aspects of the project, overusing consultants and allowing the project to run over budget. Denise, however, had concentrated on scheduling and operational results, and because of her work the project was completed on time and had a clear impact on the business. Denise knew about the budget overrun but thought the explainable variance was reasonable.

Lack of clarity around the key success measures led Carole to rate Denise poorly overall on project management while ignoring her strengths and accomplishments. Both Denise and Carole were disappointed as a result. They did not have the same understanding of how success was defined for this project.

It's hard to overemphasize the importance of explicitly describing end results as well as expectations for how work should be done. Leaders often mistakenly assume that what is clear to them is equally clear to their team members. They forget that none of us is a mind-reader.

Communicating ideas is easier said than done. Expressing what is clear in our mind's eye so that it is crystal clear to someone else is a challenge. What gets in the way? Most often assumptions do: assumptions about the meaning of terms and concepts (in the case above, "project management"), assumptions that everyone has the same values and focus (that, say, financial management is most important) and assumptions about what constitutes success and failure (for example, getting the project done in time versus the key performance indicators)

Developing shared meaning

I recently had a conversation with a new client, Yves, about team dynamics. Yves is clear about the value he places on teamwork. He told me he regularly speaks to his team about its importance, and his energy around the subject is quite intense. He emphasized to me, for example, that getting to the right answer is not enough. He feels the team has failed if it achieves a goal with the input of only one or two people at the expense of true collaboration, which is central to his department's overall success as their roles are ultimately interdependent.

Yves believes, as I do, that the quality of the long-term results is only as good as the teamwork that supported their achievement—both, not one alone, are important measures of a team's success. He has a clear idea of what teamwork looks like, but if he wants his team to behave in the same way, he need to express that definition and help his team understand how to translate it into expected behaviours. When that occurs, both Yves and his team will have a shared meaning for teamwork.

Views on what teamwork looks like differ from one person to the next; it will be crucial for Yves to assert his expectations through clear, concise feedback. If, for example, the team alienates one of its members in the process of producing a high-quality report, Yves will have to see it, flag it and give clear, concise feedback about the issue. His performance standard requires an inclusive approach in which it is unacceptable to remove a team member from the process. When such a standard isn't met, the team will need to be told. This is not always an easy task.

ACTIVITY

Pick three behaviours you see your team members doing that lack professionalism or are undesirable in some way. Now think about the standard you would like to inspire people to achieve. Write notes below.

....

....

....

36 | CORRECT TO STAY THE COURSE

Sailors know there is no point staying the current course if it is taking you off track and pointing you in the wrong direction. Employees want to be successful. Give them feedback that helps them track their progress toward a goal that matters and adjust their trajectory when needed, and you are bound to fuel your team's fire.

We frequently learn crucial feedback for the first time during performance appraisals, when it can also be punitive—for example, no bonus this year because we have a "meets" instead of an "exceeds" on our appraisal. Most managers do not manage feedback well in general and have an even tougher time sharing observations that might be taken as negative. There is definitely an art to corrective feedback; this section explores that art.

To begin, here's a useful definition of *feedback* from businessdictionary.com: "In an organizational context, feedback is the information sent to an entity (individual or a group) about its prior behaviour so that the entity may adjust its current and future behaviour to achieve the desired result." If this definition represented the nature of feedback in reality, everyone would be dying to get it.

> **AS A LEADER, MAKE IT YOUR GOAL TO TRANSFORM CORRECTIVE FEEDBACK INTO A POSITIVE, INVIGORATING AND INSPIRING EXPERIENCE.**

Imagine your boss approaching you and saying, "Do you have a minute? I'd like to offer some feedback." With the definition of feedback above, you would think: "Excellent! I can learn more about my present course of action and better understand if I am achieving the impact I need to reach my goal!" Not only would you welcome the feedback, you would actively seek it out. You would solicit it and tease out all the information available to support your aspirations.

As a leader, you have the power to create this type of excitement around feedback. You have the opportunity to build a team culture in which feedback is embraced and used to build future success. Sceptical? Don't be. It can be done, believe me. I'm 100 percent sure, because I've done it myself and I've helped others do it too.

I recommend working with your team so they learn to see and experience feedback positively instead of negatively. Encourage them to find ways to access meaningful data, information or knowledge to inform future decisions or actions, so they can achieve their objectives more effectively.

ACTIVITY

Brainstorm ways to bring more data into your team's discussions.

....

....

....

Will I be blindsided?

Use feedback to check in on how things are progressing with yourself and your team, and do it often enough so that people become accustomed to it. There are many types of feedback, including feedback that tells you what you do well. When feedback is not offered often enough or is only offered as criticism, people can feel blindsided and won't welcome it when they need it most.

Feedback is a gift. People (and sometimes systems) offer facts, impressions or perspectives that allow us to evaluate our present course of action. After listening to and assessing the feedback, we can choose to stick with our current route if we still believe it's the best way forward; or we can adjust the route to enable us to get to our destination faster, more easily, without collateral damage or with greater impact/return on investment. We never give people that chance if feedback about how the goal is being met is not correctly given in the first place.

Four critical steps to giving effective corrective feedback

Over the decades of working with leaders, I have discovered there are four critical components of delivering corrective feedback so it is effective:

Step 1: Suspend your conclusions

It is very important that you enter the conversation free of the negative emotional baggage that often comes from concluding something about the other person that is unflattering and perhaps even irritating. You need to enter each conversation with a clean slate. Better yet, generate within yourself positive emotions like appreciation, caring, empathy and love. The recipient will feel your support and be much better able to hear your words.

Often, when receiving feedback, your employee's limbic system is in a heightened state and is looking for signals that will tell it whether it is safe or in danger. Ensuring that your listener feels supported and safe will prevent the limbic system from triggering its "fight or flight" mechanism. People will stay relaxed and will engage in a healthy, productive conversation. Before you give feedback, check in with yourself:

- Ask yourself, *How am I feeling? Is the emotion positive or negative? Will it support or hinder the conversation?*
- Remind yourself of the other's positive attributes.
- Remember that we are all imperfect beings trying to do our best but needing support.
- Think about someone who helped and cared about you at some point in your past when it really mattered. Choose to be that person for your employee now.

Step 2: Know and articulate the goal

To deliver corrective feedback meaningfully, whether in writing or verbally, you must first know the answer to two important questions:

- What is the long-term end result the person desires?
- How will your feedback support the pursuit of this goal?

The receiver should understand that your feedback is intended to help him or her achieve results—that's why you must know and understand the goals and aspirations.

As your team's leader, you work for them. You want to serve them well and make them look good. One way of doing this is to offer meaningful corrective feedback. You care about how they approach their work and you want to save them time, to maximize their resources, to build their network of positive relationships and to support their passion and fulfillment at work.

Begin with a reminder of your mutual goal with a message like one of these:

- "Hiroto, I know you are concerned about how your project is unfolding. May I share some observations with you that might help you move your work forward?"
- "Samuel, given that monthly reports are a big part of your role, can we take some time to sit back and look at how well the current process is working? I have noticed a couple of interdepartmental challenges I think we need to address to ensure you meet your commitments in the most efficient and effective way possible."
- "Jenna, having healthy, positive internal relationships is really key to your operations role. The better your relationships, the easier your work flows. I've noticed tension in our broader team meetings between you and two of your colleagues. I'd like to learn more about what's happening and figure out a way to support those relationships."

The feedback you offer should be tied to a meaningful goal or purpose. Don't assume this is obvious. Even if it is, saying it aloud reminds others of the goal, thus ensuring it remains the focus of the discussion. Otherwise, corrective feedback may feel more like criticism than support. This is so important, it's worth repeating: For corrective feedback to be successful, the recipient must feel supported, *not* criticized, by the feedback.

Before you begin a corrective feedback conversation, make sure you can clearly and easily articulate the goal the feedback serves. This is your North Star. It will help you assess the current course of action and generate ideas to correct it, if needed. Focusing on the target depersonalizes the feedback and makes it about results instead of the individual.

Step 3: Step back to move forward

Too often, we enter feedback sessions having already decided what the employee needs to do differently. While we might have great ideas, we need to validate them through proper information gathering and analysis. We also need to give employees a chance to think challenges through for themselves. People learn more if they come up with answers (such as potential new directions, behaviours and tasks) themselves than if they are spoon-fed solutions.

Information gathering starts with questions like "Luke, can you give me an overview of the project from your perspective?" "What input have you had from your key stakeholders?" "What has been working very well?" "What challenges have you encountered?"

Once you have a clear picture of the situation, you can offer your observations, which either support or contradict what Luke has said. Either way is fine. When there is an apparent discrepancy or contradiction, it simply means there is more to explore. Thus: "I have noticed that one of your stakeholders has been advocating for another project, which may compromise yours by competing for resources. Are you aware of this?"

You may also need to ask supporting questions to help Luke think it through. If Luke says yes to the question above, you may then follow with: "Have you discussed it with the stakeholder to explore synergies?" or "Have you clarified which project will provide the best return on investment in the event we have to choose a priority?"

How the conversation flows depends on what the other person says. Remain clear on your objective: sharing your observations and asking questions to create a clear picture of the situation and jointly explore the best possible solutions.

When we step back and assess a situation, our brains see the big picture and all its moving parts more clearly. We are then better equipped to see relationships and potential connections (or disconnections) that may have previously gone unnoticed. As the situation comes into sharper focus, the required corrections may be obvious. If the path is not crystal clear, we can unleash our creative thinking and problem-solving skills in service of the desired end result. Either way, stepping back gives us the perspective we need to move forward more effectively.

Step 4: Decide the new course of action

Sometimes a minor change in direction will suffice; other times, your employee may need a whole new game plan. It depends on what happens as a result of steps 2 and 3 above. Regardless of the size of the correction, step 4 is where you clarify and agree on what will be done differently. You might say things like:

"Now that we've had a chance to think this through, how would you like to proceed?"

- "What do you think needs to happen to get the outcome you want?"
- "What corrections do you need to make?"
- "What support will you need from me?"

If Luke cannot see an alternative course of action, be prepared to offer suggestions and talk through them so they are understood and deemed appropriate. At the end of the conversation, Luke must have ownership of the plan—he should see himself as the captain of the boat, charting and directing a new course. It's worth pausing here for a cautionary reminder: do not take the monkey onto your back. (See "Who's Got the Monkey?" by William Oncken, a *Harvard Business Review* article written and reprinted in 1999, for more on this.) It is Luke's project, not yours. You are there to help Luke develop his own skill set through clear feedback and healthy discussions, not to rescue his project.

Once you agree on a corrected course of action, ask Luke to update you in a week's time (or whatever might be appropriate) so you can evaluate his progress. Make corrective feedback part of how you work, not an event that happens during the company's mandated performance management meetings.

Activity

Use the above four-step approach to prepare and deliver a piece of feedback.

1. Suspend your conclusions.

   - Ask yourself, *How am I feeling? Is the emotion positive or negative? Will it support or hinder the conversation?*
   - Remind yourself of the other person's positive attributes.
   - Remember that we are all imperfect beings simply doing our best but needing occasional support.
   - Think about someone who helped and cared about you at some point in your past when it really mattered. Choose to be that person for your employee now.

2. Know and articulate the goal.

   - What is the long-term end result the person desires?
   - How will your feedback support the pursuit of this goal?
   - Tie the feedback to a meaningful goal or purpose.
   - Begin with a reminder about the goal you both (or all) support.

3. Step back to move forward.

   - Clear your mind of what you think has to be done.
   - Park your good ideas until later.
   - Focus on asking questions to help the other person think it through for himself or herself. Begin with information-seeking questions.
   - Probe to truly understand how the other person is thinking about the situation.

4. Decide the new course of action.

   - "Now that we've had a chance to think this through, how would you like to proceed?"
   - "What do you think needs to happen to get the outcome you want?"
   - "What corrections do you need to make?"
   - "What support will you need from me?"

Notes

....

....

....

....

....

....

....

....

....

37 | VALUE EFFORT AND COMMITMENT

Delivering results requires time, energy and resources. People must invest personally in their work. That's why it's important to show gratitude and recognize effort when a task or project is completed. It replenishes some of the energy consumed by the work. To get and keep your team fired up, be generous with your appreciation.

It is important to value others' contributions. Often I hear managers say, "I don't need it, so I find it difficult to remember to do it for others" or "We're paid to do the work. Why do we need to keep thanking people for doing their job?" Taking another for granted or withholding compliments does not serve your team well. No one wants to be anonymous and superfluous.

Thirsty for thanks

While working with early-childhood educators recently, I was reminded of the importance of complimenting, valuing and appreciating as forms of feedback.

> RECOGNITION COMES IN MANY FORMS. DEVELOP A FULL REPERTOIRE.

The educators work as a team in a very large day-care center. During a preliminary visit to the center, the high level of activity struck me immediately—the place was buzzing with energy from children and teachers alike. The latter were focused on the individual tasks at hand: one read to a group of toddlers who sat captivated in a semicircle on the floor at her feet, another cooed to a baby as she bottle-fed her in a rocking chair, a third completed paperwork at a desk in the corner, and several more attended to a variety of other tasks. It was an impressive, if overwhelming, sight!

Later, during an off-site team-building session for the center staff (about 25 teachers in total), we ended the day by brainstorming ways in which they could support each other's engagement at work. I was astonished by the number of times the teachers expressed the idea of giving feedback in the form of compliments, praise, appreciation or recognition. This theme emerged strongly in each of the five working groups we had formed for this exercise. When a trend emerges with such prominence, it indicates a real desire. Apparently, this form of feedback was not abundant in the center's current environment.

Valuing someone through genuine compliments and appreciation tells people that you see them, you recognize the impact of their work and you notice their progress. There are powerful reasons to invest in this form of feedback, not the least of which is the ease with which it can be given. Such feedback does a number of other things as well:

- generates goodwill
- shows you care
- builds resiliency
- supports self-confidence, enabling people to take risks
- reinforces things meaningful to the work or the culture
- gives people a signal of progress
- generates a feeling of well-being by releasing endorphins in the giver and the receiver
- feels good to give and even better to receive
- hones the giver's observation skills in a positive way (for example, by practicing the art of seeing rights instead of wrongs)
- creates positive rather than negative energy
- surprises and delights recipients
- is resource efficient (i.e., costs nothing and takes little time)
- forges stronger personal workplace bonds
- makes work more fun
- has no downside (or none I can think of)

Appreciation as a leadership practice

As a leader, how appreciative or grateful are you for your team? How often do you express your gratitude in sincere and meaningful ways? I challenge you as a leader to vocalize your appreciation to a different person on your team every day.

Appreciation and gratitude are powerful. They create reciprocity: when you demonstrate your caring in authentic ways, people respond in equally generous ways. When you give, you will be surprised by what you receive in return. But please do not misunderstand—getting something in return should not be your motivation for offering compliments or saying why you value someone's work.

If you are unaccustomed to expressing appreciation, start by looking for positives, however humble they may seem. We often focus so much on what needs improving that we forget to identify and articulate what works well. Take time to notice what's right with a situation. When something strikes you as worthy of mention, make the effort to share your observations with your employee or team. Here are five examples of simple phrases of appreciation that are based on observations:

1. "You handled the meeting well today. You kept everyone engaged."
2. "Archiving can be routine work, but I want you to know that you make my life a lot easier. I'm amazed at how quickly I can find things now. I really appreciate that."
3. "I want to say I really appreciate how you stay so positive even when your work isn't going as you had planned. Your positive attitude helps all of us."
4. "I truly value the time you take on your reports. It means I never need to do a close copy-edit, and it presents the department in a very professional manner to the senior team."
5. "I noticed you quickly implemented the action we agreed in the meeting the other day, and I see it's already had an impact on the project. Thanks for the quick work."

When you take the time to notice what works well and, more importantly, to share your observations, you keep people connected to purpose, fuel their passion and highlight progress—all of which are vital leadership functions. Remember this facet of feedback. Be generous with your appreciation. Create a culture of appreciation.

ACTIVITY

List each person's name in the chart below. Write three things you value or appreciate them for. Make a plan to tell them.

Name	What I Value and Wish to Recognize	When and How I Will Do So

⬀ 38 | BUILD ON STRENGTHS

Identifying strengths and using them helps build bigger and better successes. When your team knows you are looking for what's right rather than what's wrong, they will be inspired to produce more and more rights. Find what's right to light the fire and keep it burning strong.

Building on what works follows naturally from some of the ideas outlined in the previous chapter. Because we are so accustomed to focusing on what *isn't* working, we overlook chances to build on success. When things work well, we often don't look at *why* they work and thus miss opportunities to build on strengths and incorporate them into other facets of our work.

What do you notice about the following?

$$1 + 5 = 6$$
$$4 + 9 = 12$$
$$7 + 4 = 11$$

CREATE VIRTUOUS CYCLES.

The vast majority of people will say that the second one is wrong. Rarely does someone say, "Two are right and one is wrong." Why is this? We are trained very well to notice mistakes. We have been conditioned by years of education and practice. It is so entrenched in how we think that it seems only natural to focus on what is wrong. In fact, most of us have a hard time noticing what is right and what is working well.

We take all that is right with the world for granted and bring our attention to bear on what needs fixing. In doing so, we deprive ourselves of the opportunity to build on our strengths and gain traction by creating virtuous cycles. When we identify and focus on strengths, we can use them to continue creating success, which reinforces both the strength and the achievement. We can create these by reinforcing positive results, consciously building on success.

The virtuous cycle

All leaders have seen how something negative can cycle to something even more negative and more destructive. You can use the same principle to cycle strength. To recognize, celebrate and share performance excellence is a highly meaningful form of positive feedback that also increases the likelihood that success will continue and perhaps even spread to other endeavours. This is a virtuous cycle, in contrast to a vicious one. As a leader, in focusing on strengths you increase your team members' awareness of their capabilities so that they can leverage those strengths to create additional success.

This can also be done at the collective level. You can support the excellence of one of your team members and provide an opportunity for other team members to benefit by learning and growing. Similarly, the practices and experiences of successful, high-functioning teams can be shared and spread to enhance overall organizational performance.

When leaders establish an environment within which team members build on each other's success (in support of the team's overall success), they create a true learning environment. Taking the time to see and understand what works produces extremely positive action: it ensures people feel valued and safeguards a company's best interests by supporting improved performance and results.

Leveraging strengths

Take Connie. Connie was not great with managing details, and her leader, Jeremy, could always find a mistake in her report or an oversight in her plan. However, he noticed that Connie was able to think strategically and never missed connecting the dots between tasks and overall goals. She was also very good at stakeholder management, as she was intuitively able to see the project from all perspectives and to identify potential synergies and conflicts.

One day, Jeremy spoke to Connie about her strengths. He shared with her his specific observations. She was surprised he had noticed and even more surprised that he did not mention an error she'd made in her last report, since another colleague had already pointed it out to her. Instead, Jeremy suggested they revisit her role within the team, add responsibilities that played to her strengths and delegate some of the work that required intensive attention to detail.

Connie was thrilled! In the months that followed, Connie was able to increase stakeholder engagement around the team's highest-level goals, clearing the way for additional funding. Connie's strengths, once leveraged, created more success for her and for her team as a whole.

Cloning your stars

A vice president, Lama, recently shared with me her intention to leverage the success of one of her employees as one of her continuous improvement strategies for the year. This employee achieved excellence under trying conditions and outperformed her colleagues in significant ways. Rather than create a competitive environment, Lama intends to use this team member's success to help others on the team attain equal or greater success.

She has already begun to analyze the employee's workflow processes and other habits to see if her way of working will transfer to the rest of the team. Assuming it can, Lama will create a peer coaching system so that all can benefit from the insight of one team member. I've seen this kind of strategy bear tangible results in a diversity of situations, from the shop floor to the C-suite.

Reinforcing company values

Zach, a client-service representative, got more positive client feedback than anyone else on his team. Zach's team leader asked himself why. What did Zach do differently with his clients that caused them to feel so good about dealing with him? Customer care was a corporate value, and so it was important to Zach's team leader to understand what was different about Zach.

A few follow-up calls to his clients as well as a few questions to Zach himself showed that Zach always ensured his customers got the help they needed, even when it was outside his area of expertise. He took care of the client until each had a satisfactory or complete answer to a question or a workable solution to a problem. Even when Zach had to work through other departments to get the job done, he always followed up internally to ensure the client's need has been met.

Once the leader and the rest of the team clearly understood what worked well, they decided to make Zach's follow-through approach a team approach to delivering exceptional value and care to each customer.

Making talent scalable

CEO Mohamed noticed that Yasmine, one of his senior managers, was an amazing troubleshooter. She consistently turned around teams or projects in crisis, somehow transforming them into success stories. Instead of moving Yasmine every 18 months to address a new problem area, Mohamed set out to discover exactly how she worked magic to achieve such stellar results. Once he understood what she did, he used her to train others in her effective turnaround competencies.

Mohamed's goal was to equip all managers to handle similar challenges within their own teams. The result of the training was a group of highly skilled managers who operated as a SWAT team for some of the company's greatest challenges or important opportunities.

A note of caution: Once you start the process of sharing success and learning from it, it's important to find success *everywhere*. If you focus on one or two individuals, you risk alienating the rest of the team by making them feel undervalued or underappreciated. Find something worth sharing in each individual's work. If there's nothing to find, step back, look at the individual's overall performance with an eye to their development needs and ask yourself what needs to be done to lay a foundation for true success.

ACTIVITY

What's working well on your team? How can you build on these?

What's Working Well?	Who Is Responsible?	How Do I Build on This?

39 | DEVELOP FOR CAREER PROGRESS

To sustain your team's passion, pay attention to career paths. The work at hand is important, but most people also want to advance their longer-term goals. When your team members know you will provide relevant feedback to help them stretch and grow, they will continue to see how their current work serves their aspirations. This connection functions as an intrinsic motivator to keep their energy aflame.

Developmental feedback is intended to help prepare people for promotions or other opportunities, such as project work or management or a specialist's role. I often encounter leaders who are wholly satisfied with their teams, and because their people exceed expectations, they sometimes feel feedback is no longer necessary, except to encourage and appreciate. Although these forms of feedback are important, even at this stage, a good leader will also ask herself what type of feedback could help take her team members to the next level. She might ask herself, for example, "Given what I know about the department, the company or the industry, what area of focus would benefit this person's development?"

> **THE RIGHT AMOUNT OF CHALLENGE ALLOWS US TO STRENGTHEN EXISTING SKILLS AND BUILD NEW ONES, OPENING DOORS FOR FUTURE OPPORTUNITY.**

Personal growth and learning are important to most of us. You don't have to be ambitious (eager to climb the corporate ladder, for example) to want lifelong learning. In fact, human beings thrive on challenge and growth. We want to use our existing talents and develop new ones—that's what mastery is all about.

Peter Senge, in *The Fifth Discipline* (1990), writes, "Personal mastery goes beyond competency and skills . . . it means approaching one's life as a creative work, living life from a creative as opposed to a reactive viewpoint." Senge's work, co-developed with Robert Fritz, references how vital it is to be connected to our aspirations. When we know our desired end results, we will develop to achieve them. Development is not something we do as an extra or on the side. It is an action we take to create the things that are most important to us.

Mihaly Csikszentmihalyi, professor and former chairman of the Department of Psychology at the University of Chicago, is yet another proponent of development. He has written extensively—in books including *Finding Flow* (1998) and *Good Business* (2003)—about the relationship between challenge and our ability to meet a challenge. When the two match, a state emerges that he calls "flow."

To create these flow states, Csikszentmihalyi writes, we need to bring our skills to bear on a meaningful challenge. This does not mean being challenged into a state of anxiety. Quite the opposite. Flow is the sweet spot in which our evolving talents meet an appropriate challenge.

Good leaders support their employees with feedback that helps them grow and develop beyond their current level, whatever level that may be. Development is essential to maintain engagement and passion in one's work and in life. As human beings, we want to evolve. It is natural for us to do so. When we don't, we become sluggish, uninterested and bored.

Three examples from real life

The examples below typify the kind of situation in which developmental feedback might come into play:

- A stellar employee executes brilliantly and exceeds all your expectations. However, when you sit back and think about the entire organization, you see he does not have as much support within his peer group as he does with his direct reports and senior managers. You share this observation and together discuss how to validate the observation, why it matters in the long term and what might be done to improve his peer-group relationships.
- One of your best and most reliable employees is a specialist. She is a great asset to the team because of her expertise, but there really isn't another position for her in your region. You consider other possibilities and realize she might be a good candidate for a role in the parent company. She needs to develop skills like strategic

thinking and acquire some global experience. You think about ways to support her development in these areas and discuss her long-term interests with her.

- You have a particularly astute HR manager who is also interested in the commercial side of the company. Based on her current management skills, her ability to quickly understand the business and her capacity to learn, you would like to move her into a business unit. You meet with her to explore this and decide to support her in gaining the necessary certifications.

Your knowledge of your team members, their aspirations and the environment in which you operate equip you to assist in making the most of their talents. Given some thought, I am certain you will discover ways to provide meaningful developmental feedback for the individuals on your team. Observe and trust yourself. However, if you are uncertain how to support your direct reports, remember it's your responsibility as a leader to help them find others, such as mentors and coaches, who can.

Tips

1. Immediately following the completion of an objective or project, conduct a "lessons learned" debrief. Answer the following questions and end by creating a focus for development for the next project or major objective:

   - What went well? Why did it go well? Which of your skills contributed the most to these successes?
   - What didn't go smoothly? Where were their mistakes or hiccups? Which could have been avoided? What skill, if applied, could have prevented the misstep?
   - Given the above answers, what might be a development area for future projects or major objectives?

2. During performance appraisal time, for each employee who has met your requirements, sit back and reflect upon their successes and where they have struggled. List their strengths. List their challenges. Think about what development area would serve them well in future work.

Answer the following questions to isolate important development areas:

- What skill would they need to develop to move from "meets expectations" to "exceeds expectations"?
- What skill would they need to develop before you could recommend them for a promotion?
- What skill would they need to develop before you would be comfortable having them represent the department on a high-profile project?

3. Before succession planning meetings, for each employee currently exceeding your expectations, ask yourself the following questions, and meet with each of them to propose a development challenge:

- Is this person ready to replace me in some of my duties so he or she can develop further? If so, which of my activities would be suitable to give this employee an opportunity to demonstrate abilities, be exposed to new knowledge or broaden the scope of their current work?
- Is this person an expert in his or her field but needs to learn about other areas of the organization before advancing? If so, what lateral moves might be appropriate to help this employee gain a better overview of the organization? What projects would have him or her work cross-functionally and learn about other departments? Is there an opportunity for a secondment so he or she can experience another area intimately?
- Is this person ready for a larger role in this organization? If so, what might that role look like and what might be a next step in positioning the individual for this—what training might be needed? If not, what's holding him or her back and how can that be addressed?

Answering the questions above will help you surface important development goals and provide employees with excellent information and ideas for advancing their careers. This type of feedback is often neglected, in part because it might create inconvenient vacancies in your department. Often, though, it's simply not on leaders' radar as they focus on managing the work at hand. Be aware, however, that progressing in one's career is often as important as progressing in the current job and meeting the goals and objectives of your position.

Feedback, in all its forms, is the backbone of performance. Giving it (when it's done properly) builds exceptional relationships between leaders, followers and peers. It has the potential to strengthen both individuals and teams and, through them, entire organizations. A leader never goes wrong by investing time in this vital area of engagement. As Ken Blanchard, coauthor of *The One-Minute Manager* (1982), says, "Feedback is the breakfast of champions."

ACTIVITY

Everyone on your team needs a development goal. We all need to challenge ourselves and stretch beyond our day-to-day work, even if it is modest.

Name	Developmental Goal	Suggested Actions

40 | CELEBRATE TO UPLIFT AND REWARD

Your team works hard and, in today's world, often under a lot of pressure. Letting off a little steam and acknowledging progress can go a long way in sustaining momentum and rejuvenating energy levels. When completing a task, rather than racing to the next task or project, hang out at the finish line and bask a little in your achievement. Take a moment to acknowledge and enjoy the fruits of your labour. It will replenish and reinspire your team for the next lap.

Celebration is a type of feedback loop and another way to create a virtuous cycle. Your team achieves a milestone—real progress—so you host a celebration to acknowledge that. This positive event encourages further progress and further celebration.

FUN, LAUGHTER AND CELEBRATION ARE KEY DRIVERS OF EMPLOYEE ENGAGEMENT— AND PERHAPS THE MOST IGNORED.

ACTIVITY

Think about the last one to three months.

- When have you celebrated a work achievement?
- What did you celebrate? With whom?
- Why was it important to do so? Were there any missed opportunities?

....

....

....

Most of us don't take time to celebrate at work. As leaders, we continually miss opportunities to add fun and uplift spirits in the workplace. Once we achieve a goal or complete a project, we immediately move to the next thing rather than take the time to appreciate our hard work and enjoy the resulting success. We don't make time to celebrate and rejuvenate.

Why is this feedback? Because when you celebrate, you clearly demonstrate to the person (or group) that their accomplishment matters, their efforts have not gone unnoticed and they have contributed in a significant way.

Years ago, I was working with a team in conflict. One team member said, "Let me just say that the last 12 months have been stressful. As the in-house carpenter, I led the renovation of one of our key properties. I did a lot of the work myself. It was a ton of work and very challenging! I practically killed myself to get it done and no one—not my manager, not the CEO, no senior person—has ever said thank you or admired the result. I don't know why I bothered."

Generally, this team did not feel appreciated by the manager. There are many ways to express appreciation. Sometimes it's important to celebrate a small but significant milestone (a team member has worked hard to get a project approved and you want to celebrate his tenacity) or ongoing excellence (a team member has retained an important client and you want to celebrate her commitment to service) or a major contribution or event.

As leaders, it's our job to integrate celebrating into the team and corporate culture. *Celebration* is a big word, but it need not necessarily entail a big event. Yes, a celebration may be large and boisterous; equally, it may be quiet and subtle. Celebrations might relate to specific goals and objectives, like these:

- Create your own team awards and give out a goofy gift or trophy, such as a stuffed frog for the person who "leapfrogged" their numbers for the quarter, or a 120-watt bulb for the team member who came up with a great idea or took a step out of the box this month, or a Lego knight in shining armour for the person who helped save a team member or retain a key client that week.
- When a team member finishes a big project that took a great deal of blood, sweat and tears to complete—system implementation, new product launch, office renovation or move—celebrate them and with them! Invite the CEO to attend.

- Celebrate the end of busy times or seasonal work: contract renewal season if you are in insurance, Christmas and other such holidays if you are in retail, the end of the main building season if you are in construction, the end of tax season if you are in accounting. Whatever your business cycle, make a point of marking the end of a particularly busy or strenuous period with your team.

Sometimes, celebrating can be simply about recognizing relationships and/or milestones, that may or may not relate to work. Here are a few suggestions drawn from my clients:

- Acknowledge each other's birthdays (or engagements, marriages and additions to the family) in fun ways—a cake in the boardroom, a luncheon or an after-work gathering.
- Support each other in non-work passions. Attend a team member's road race or support a charity event in which a teammate participates.
- Create energizing annual team events: a day outside the office dedicated to helping a non-profit with a project; an out-of-town team retreat focused on a learning and development need; or everyone attending, helping with or participating in a corporately sponsored event, such as a 10-kilometre walk or a career fair.
- Find unique ways of celebrating events or honouring special days from all cultures, from Lunar New Year to the Holy Month of Ramadan, from Kwanzaa to Thanksgiving.
- Throw a party for someone who has achieved a designation or attained a certification.
- Call a team meeting with sparkling non-alcoholic beverages served in champagne glasses when someone receives external or internal recognition, like a prize or an award.

Ask your team how they would like to celebrate, and find something unique and/or fun to do. Recently, a small HR team I know decided to have a spa day to celebrate the end of a highly stressful quarter. Do whatever makes sense for you and your team, but do *something*!

ACTIVITY

Think about other ways to celebrate. How could you celebrate recent wins, improvements or milestones?

....

....

....

41 | SET A FOUNDATION SO FEEDBACK DOESN'T FAIL

Your mindset impacts how you present your message and the environment you create when delivering feedback. Use the four building blocks of feedback to help you provide meaningful feedback. When you take care and show respect, you preserve the spirit and dignity of each team member, maintaining the foundation upon which the team can engage and thrive. Will it fire them up? You bet!

I often hear managers say that feedback is not something they need, so it's not natural for them to provide it to their own teams. Or they are so busy they don't really have the time for anything extra. Others admit that they often avoid it when they fear it will be emotional or confrontational. It's no secret that feedback often goes wrong. But why? Let's take a look.

CREATING A POSITIVE SPACE HELPS YOUR MESSAGE GET THROUGH.

Why feedback goes wrong

Even when managers give feedback, they don't always understand why it fails. In my experience, feedback fails for because managers

- tell and talk when they should ask and explore to understand;
- run up the Stairway to Conclusions, making assumptions and interpretations rather than staying grounded in facts;
- focus almost solely on what needs to be fixed or improved and miss commenting on all the good stuff, neglecting the majority of the 10 types of feedback;
- reprimand rather than improve employee self-awareness; and/or
- don't know how to receive upward feedback.

As a result, employees feel judged, defensive, undervalued, silenced and scolded like children.

Delivering feedback well

Hosting productive, uplifting feedback sessions challenges even the most skilled leader. It is possible to deliver feedback well, but it takes practice, awareness and flexibility. Leaders need to want to pursue excellence in this area, as it takes ongoing attention and a good deal of time and effort. I've found it productive (and so have my clients) to focus on four main building blocks: language, tone, empathy and informality. Let's take a closer look at each of them.

Language

During graduate school, I became interested in the power of language, in particular how our choice of specific words changes the meaning (and often the impact) of what we want to communicate. My fascination with word choice emerged through gender studies, in which I examined the connotations of *girl* and *chick* compared to *woman* and *guy*.

Later, I became intrigued by the energy held by different words. Have you ever noticed that some e-mail messages elicit emotional responses from recipients? That's because word choice creates a subtext to the overall message. Some words hold positive energy, some neutral and some negative (for example, *appreciate*, *house* and *problem* respectively).

Our word choice may make a message painless to hear and thus more likely to generate a positive responses or difficult to accept, perhaps even causing an emotional hijacking. Consider these two examples:

> "We made some progress today, but we still have a long way to go. Can we book another meeting next week to see if we can *finally* resolve this problem?"
>
> "Thank you for taking the time to meet with me today. Our conversation was productive, and I now understand your group's needs more fully. I look forward to pursuing a solution that will benefit both of our teams. May we meet next week to keep our momentum going?"

When giving feedback, it is important that we think about language. We want to give clear messages, but we also want to let the other person know we want to help and support. The goal? Create a win-win framework.

What words or phrases do we sometimes use or hear that can create defensiveness or an emotional reaction?

....

....

....

Tone

A dear colleague of mine, Ken, taught me a welcome lesson about the value of toning things down when speaking from a position of power. It's often better to be tentative than assertive or direct. I watched him many times skilfully address sensitive topics in a manner that opened up a conversation instead of closing it down. When you are tentative, you present yourself with humility—not as an all-knowing omnipotent leader—which puts the listener in the role of a partner, not the fool.

A tentative approach also infers that your perspective may not be 100 percent correct and you are open to other views. For example: "I am wondering how you think we might approach this challenging situation?" as opposed to "I want you to go see the project lead and don't let him walk all over you this time. Stand up for yourself. Make sure you tell him we need at least two weeks' notice before we make such changes!"

I acknowledge context is everything, and we must use the full range of communication techniques and devices available to us in leadership roles. However, using a tentative tone can help create a dialogue instead of a debate. Tone establishes the baseline. If the tone is positive, you increase the likelihood of a pleasant conversation; if the tone is edgy, you may set yourself up for a tense, difficult conversation. Your listener will react to your tone, and the tone you choose may reflect your internal attitudes and beliefs.

If you've concluded a person is argumentative, you may begin the conversation with a defensive or forceful posture to protect yourself from a possible assault or prevent a strike by flexing your muscles first. Either way, the conversation is not off to a good start.

When confronted with such a situation myself, I suspended my conclusions about my employee. Instead, I thought about what might give rise to the argumentative behaviour. I thought about the person's personal preferences and reminded myself that the person was more receptive when given a chance to present his perspective upfront. Then, when he felt I had listened and understood his point of view, he was more receptive.

So I presented the issue in question and asked him to tell me about his experience. I very briefly summarized what I had heard, so he knew I understood. Then I asked questions and made observations to help him see other points of view.

In the same way, if you feel irritated when you speak to your employee (maybe because you've had to correct the same error for the third time), your tone may reflect your irritation. Even if it is not an angry tone, it may express impatience or frustration or simply be very direct: "May we speak again about your recurring error on the monthly report?"

When I was faced with a similar situation, I knew I had to move myself out of feeling irritated to feeling more balanced about the person's abilities. I sat for a couple of minutes and reflected on all the things I valued about the person. Doing so instantly put the recurring mistake in perspective and enabled me to establish a friendly, caring, appreciative tone rather than a judgmental one when I approached the person to find a solution to the issue in question.

People often react to tone more than to words. It's worth taking a few seconds to adjust your mindset before opening your mouth. A caring, helpful tone will go a long way in facilitating a challenging conversation.

ACTIVITY

Think about one of your team members. Think about feedback you need to give that individual.

- What judgments have you already made? Note them below.
- What negative thoughts or feelings do you currently hold in the back of your mind? Note them below.
- Step back and suspend judgment. Detach yourself from your emotions. Replace these thoughts and feelings with positive ones to set a supportive/helpful/positive tone. Note them below.

....

....

....

Empathy

The third building block for delivering feedback well is empathy. Empathy, the ability to imagine how it might be to experience a situation from another's perspective, is underutilized and often misunderstood. When you can truly imagine the thoughts and feelings of another, you create a bond that says "I can identify with you." You affirm the other person as a human being, not just as a workmate. I can't overemphasize how important empathy is within the arena of human relationships:

- It reduces stress and defensiveness in those with whom you empathize, because they feel understood.
- It builds trust because others feel they can rely on you because you "get" them.
- It enhances the quality of conversations so you can delve into underlying causes and generate true solutions.

These key benefits will help you deliver feedback well, because effective feedback happens within a context, and context is as much about relationships as it is about the tasks or projects at hand. Great leaders would do well to listen to relationship expert Dr. James Dobson, who writes in his book *What Wives Wish Their Husbands Knew About Women* (1997):

> The right to criticize must be earned, even if the advice is constructive in nature. Before you are entitled to tinker with another person's self-esteem, you are obligated first to demonstrate your respect for him/her as a person. When a relationship of confidence has been carefully constructed, you will have earned the right to discuss a potentially threatening topic. Your motives will have been thereby clarified.

Many leaders with whom I work don't want to talk about empathy in the workplace—they feel it's too touchy-feely and often, in their view, inappropriate. This is only true if you divorce work from life. And of course, we can't. Work is a part of life.

Work relationships are some of the most important relationships we create. We typically spend about half of our waking day at work. Many people see their coworkers much more than their family members and friends. Depending on work and sleeping schedules, maybe more often than their spouse or children too. These relationships can make a huge difference in our lives and by their nature contribute to or detract from the quality of our lives. When we diminish their importance, we do others and ourselves a disservice.

On employee engagement surveys (including my own), it's not uncommon for people to site their colleagues as the main reason they would recommend their organization as a place to work. They appreciate the friendliness, caring and support their coworkers offer. That's why coworker relationships are a key factor in employee retention.

Other relationships are also primary. For example, some research indicates a difficult relationship with a manager is a more common reason than salary for people to leave an organization. Sure, most people would jump ship if offered oodles more money to do the same work elsewhere. But much more commonly, employees defect because of a poor relationship with the person they report to.

So how does this relate to empathy? Empathy is one of the cornerstones of relationships, and the quality of your work relationships makes a difference in your ability to lead and manage. It is particularly important when offering corrective feedback.

For example, you may think Tudor made a poor choice by becoming emotional in a meeting. However, you can empathize with the fact that

Renee made derogatory insinuations about him, and Tudor perceived the stakes to be high, so he felt the need to respond. It doesn't mean you agree with Tudor's choices or you won't address his behaviour. But it does mean you can provide the requisite feedback from a place of appreciating the challenges of the moment.

When long-serving Lara struggles with a change in her job responsibilities, you can think how it must feel to have been doing the same job every day for 15 years and then to be thrust into the unknown. You could imagine Lara might resist and be uncooperative because she wants to do her job well, is concerned about her ability to learn and fears she might fail at the new task. Being empathetic may help you acknowledge the significance of the change for Lara and offer your support, while addressing the unhelpful behaviour.

Empathy and respect foster confidence and trust. Employees need to know you care about them as people, not as corporate assets. Empathy creates strong relationships that enable people to receive feedback more easily. It's at the heart of supportive, growth-oriented, challenging work environments, and ultimately, it improves performance.

ACTIVITY

For whom do I lack empathy? How might I alter my views so I can appreciate their experience? How might this help me speak to them in a supportive rather than a judgmental way?

....

....

....

Informality

The fourth and final entry in my quartet of building blocks is informality, specifically with respect to a conversational style and environment. A feedback session is not the time for a leader to stand on a soapbox or give a mini-lecture. It's about exchanging ideas and information. It's a two-way conversation in which the leader asks lots of questions and engages the other person in a discussion. You might set the stage by speaking for a minute or so at the outset, but from then on, it should be an exchange where both (or all) conversants participate equally.

Your speaking style and the setting should relax the other person, not make them anxious. Formality tends to make people feel a little tense and ill at ease. Informality, on the other hand, helps us feel less threatened and thus more receptive. Everything, including the seating, should contribute to a relaxed, informal atmosphere.

Avoid sitting on opposite sides of a table, for example. It creates a barrier and physical tension before you even start. Sitting side by side has the opposite effect—it helps create an atmosphere of cooperation and collaboration in which the parties are literally "on the same side." How you place the chairs may seem like an insignificant detail, but the nature of the physical space makes a big difference in how people feel. It's why I don't use tables in many workshops. Tables create barriers.

I learned just how critical a role physical environment plays when I worked in collective bargaining. Early in my career, I led a large retail operation. My workforce comprised seven collective agreements, encompassing front-line staff, team leaders and supervisors. When meetings between management and unions were required, an adversarial atmosphere existed from the outset, with the union invariably on one side of the table and management on the other. This established an us vs. them dynamic.

I recall walking into the room on so many occasions and feeling the tension at the negotiating table before the negotiations even started! Meetings would quickly disintegrate into arguments, sometimes even shouting matches. It seemed inevitable.

When a new CEO, George, took over, he refused to use tables! He insisted that the collective bargaining take place in a space set up like a living room or lounge, with only low tables for drinks and papers, plus comfortable chairs for the long hours of discussion. Colleagues who attended the meetings told me the new environment initially felt strange, and people weren't sure how to act. However, once they got down to business, the tone and characteristics of the conversation took on a different quality and resulted in a new agreement in record time.

Sadly, the practice didn't continue in the long term. But it offered me a true and long-lasting insight into the power of shifting from a formal, structured approach to an informal, casual approach during potentially challenging conversations.

During my years of leading teams and providing various forms of feedback, I committed to paying attention to three elements to establish informality and set the stage for success. I use them to this day, and I'm confident you can employ them to great advantage as well.

1. **Me:** First and foremost, I relax. I don't start a feedback session unless I am focused (not distracted) and unperturbed (not concerned about how the conversation will go).

2. **Setting:** Next, I focus on ensuring the other person is comfortable. When I worked in the corporate world, instead of as a consultant as I do now, I often held feedback sessions at the local coffee shop instead of at the office. Or I chose a small, intimate meeting room equipped with a flip chart for brainstorming and analysis—since interactivity fosters informality. These days, I use the same principles in coaching sessions, client meetings (if appropriate) and collegial feedback opportunities.

3. **Style:** Finally, I ensure the discussion is conversational, with an opening something like this: "Susan, I want to talk about your current project. I feel a little out of the loop and I want to make sure we're on track. Can you tell me where you're at and how you think it's going?" Or "Another department has approached me about ways we might keep each other better informed. Let's chat about what you're currently doing as project manager and what else you might do. I'm sure we can come up with some possible solutions."

ACTIVITY

What new habits do I want to adopt around informality?

....

....

....

To support positive and helpful feedback sessions, I encourage you to take the time to set a strong foundation. Orientate your mind and heart so the words you speak, the tone you use, the understanding you gain and the ambiance you create will help you guide your team to even more success.

I had a first-hand experience years ago that underlined for me the potential impact of a manager-employee relationship. I had taken over a new and quite small department in a recent business start-up. After about three months, an employee's spouse dropped by to see her husband on her way to an appointment. I had not yet met her, so she came to my office to introduce herself. She then proceeded to thank me profusely for helping her family. I honestly didn't know what she was talking about until she said, "Douglas comes home at night a different person. We have our old Douglas back!"

I didn't know what to say. I had no idea Douglas' previous situation had troubled him, and I didn't know that how we worked together served him so well. I certainly knew we had a good rapport, and we worked more as coworkers than as boss-employee. But I had no idea of the impact I'd had on Douglas—and equally important, on Douglas' family—when I made a conscious choice to collaborate with him and treat him as the professional he was while we shared laughs and had fun at the office.

To this day, I thank Douglas's spouse for teaching me such an important lesson early in my career: What you do and say as a leader, and how you lead, matters a lot.

PART 4:

PROGRESS AND FEARLESSNESS

↗ OVERVIEW

Moving forward is sometimes easy—our action plans seem to fall into place and all the stars align. Things unfold in ways that exceed all our expectations. Other times, though, gaining momentum can be elusive and fraught with obstacles and ambiguity, demanding hard work, persistence and courage.

Success is never guaranteed. However, we can make the journey as fulfilling as possible by appreciating and recognizing our progress along the way. To maintain and build our energy and enthusiasm for our goals, it is important to pay as much attention to our gains as it is to the merit of the goal.

Leaders, who are results-oriented, often skim over milestones or small but significant advancements and instead foster a sense of ongoing urgency to drive their teams forward. This winds up being energy-depleting. Leaders need to learn to pause, even briefly, to celebrate or at least notice and mark progress so the team feels uplifted and energized for the next milestone.

Even when obstacles emerge and mistakes occur, leaders need to mine the gold in these situations so the team continues to learn and apply any new knowledge. This learning can be framed as progress, as the acquired insight strengthens the foundation for future success. Obstacles also present opportunities to think in a different way, build new skills and test old boundaries. This kind of fresh and creative thinking often requires courage on the leader's part. Tackling roadblocks and forging new paths means taking risks, such as breaking from tradition, challenging the status quo, impinging on other's "territory" and dismantling bureaucracy.

Fearless leadership inevitably supports forward movement and, as a result, a sense of progress.

42 | PEG YOUR PROGRESS

To fire up your team, bring the conscious and unconscious signals of progress each team member possesses to the surface. Your team will not sustain energy without experiencing hits of progress. Even when facing disappointments, frame for progress by seeing what's been gained, no matter how modest. Then focus on this positive change to rebuild momentum and keep the team's energy flowing.

In Part 3, I discussed the notion of tracking actions to ensure team efforts are effective in moving the team toward its goals. Now I would like to focus more on the concept of progress—and how critical it is for people to feel a high degree of progress if you want them to be passionate about their work. I discovered the importance of progress over 10 years ago, and my ongoing research continues to bear out its essential role in generating a passionate workforce.

The defining event for me came when Dave (my now business partner) and I were discussing the key components of being fully engaged in work. He had spent a lot of time thinking about the importance of meaning and the need to see your work as meaning-filled. He had also reflected a lot on the need for action. In fact, he had created a model that defined passion at work as high meaning supported by high action. Brilliant!

WE NEED OUR OWN GPS SYSTEM.

We discussed for hours this insight and observed that when we act to support the things that are most meaningful to us, we feel congruent and aligned to our values, our purpose and our goals. During our conversation, I began to feel the model wasn't quite complete. Later that night, I reflected on my seven years as a corporate manager in a large organization and on the main reason I had resigned.

The years I invested working for that company bore much fruit for me personally. The job itself was fulfilling: I worked on many exciting projects with some amazing people, and I honed my leadership skills through many lessons learned. I enjoyed dedicating myself to realizing the potential of my teams and fulfilling our mandates. We all worked hard, cared a great deal about our work and took many action steps to ensure our mutual success.

Naturally, there were also many frustrations. This particular company was extremely bureaucratic. In addition, it was permeated with politics. When bureaucracy and politics are combined, it can create an environment in which people feel they must trudge through heavy, sticky, gooey mud as they try to execute the actions they believe are key to advance their meaningful goals and objectives.

The longer I worked for the company, the more this environment weighed on me. Taking action required significant energy in this culture. I began to notice that full engagement in my work was more difficult to achieve. I began to complain to my boss that "change around here is too slow and fraught with political landmines." I complained that "our leaders don't have the courage to do the things that will bring their stated end results into reality more quickly."

We all worked so hard, did what we believed were the right things, and certainly we had some impact, but we wanted more and we felt unsupported by our environment. We knew we could achieve our goals and realize our vision, but the effort required to navigate the bureaucratic, political culture was exhausting, and advancement—at least to us—seemed excruciatingly slow.

As I reflected on this experience, I discovered what was missing from our discussion. Action alone is not enough. Action needs to produce a sense of *progress*!

I thought about my teams and other caring, conscientious people who'd worked with me over the years. When people care a great deal about something and take action in support of it, they expect their efforts to move them closer to achieving their goals in a timely manner. Plus, there is an expectation and hope that this forward movement will hold significance. In other words, the outcome the action produces will represent something meaningful in and of itself. To experience a true sense of progress, actions must create meaningful results and become building blocks for further action so that, over time, goals are achieved.

When this happens, we feel like we're making progress. It's not enough to just "do stuff." We must feel our actions are moving us onward, closer to our goals and objectives. It is key to see our results unfold in ways that feel substantive. No one wants to invest of themselves, their time and their energy without seeing a return on their investment. This return shows up in the feeling of progress—and that progress must be at a pace that uplifts us and encourages us to persevere. Without a sense of progress, people cannot fully invest or engage in their work.

But there's a catch: what feels like progress to me may not seem so to you. I may be thrilled with the results of our actions; to you, they may seem miniscule, even meaningless. I may feel the pace of progress is appropriate—it may even exceed my expectations—while you may feel disappointed by what you perceive as a diabolically slow rate of change. Our sense of pace and progress comes from a subjective place. While one person may feel uplifted by an accomplishment, another may feel quite flat.

As we journey toward our purpose and the goals about which we care deeply, we scan our environment for signals of progress. Sometimes we do this quite subconsciously, such as when we anticipate feedback. When we receive positive feedback in the form of recognition or sometimes a simple word of appreciation, we experience a "hit" of progress. This hit of progress is like an energy booster. It encourages the heart and often rejuvenates us, even if it's just a little. Conversely, when we feel our action does not produce anticipated results, we do not get a hit of progress. We are de-energized, sometimes a lot, sometimes only a little.

Making progress possible

As individuals, it is essential that we monitor our individual signals of progress. For leaders, it is a core leadership practice to create the conditions under which people can experience progress. When our team sees its work as meaningful and everyone also experiences high progress, we have passionate teams. We can do this in many different ways. Three ways to start are thinking about it, digging deeper and paying attention.

Think about it
To fire up your team, you need to be able to walk the talk and be fully engaged yourself—so begin any exploration of progress with yourself first. Spend some time reflecting on what drives your sense of progress. What tells you that you are advancing in meaningful ways? Is it exceeding your sales targets? Receiving formal recognition? Seeing an idea come to fruition? Solving a tough problem? What (specifically) makes you feel like you're getting somewhere?

Usually, there is a pattern. Regardless of the job, the project or the type of work, our individual progress-drivers remain fairly consistent. If it's recognition, for example, it's important we feel acknowledged for all key tasks or projects regardless of where we work and with whom. Some drivers may change over the course of our careers, but for the most part there are clear trends.

It's important to figure out what represents progress to you. Without a sense of progress, you will struggle to help your team engage and find fulfillment in their work. Once you have figured it out for yourself, guide your team through the same questions and discovery process so you can share your individual signals of progress with each other. Once we are conscious of our teammates' signals of progress, we can look for opportunities to highlight them in support of our colleagues' engagement.

Dig deeper

Uncover the signals of progress that sit beneath the surface and bring them into the light so that you can manage them, either for yourself or to support one of your team members. All of us possess subconscious signals of progress of which we are unaware until we mine them. Though hidden, they are important, so it is key to bring them to consciousness.

An excellent way to do so is to think of situations, circumstances or events you or others have complained about. Even better, think about a complaint you have today. Chances are, the complaint stems from an unfulfilled signal of progress of which you are not conscious. Ask yourself: *What is it I want, and what signal of progress would tell me I am on my way to succeeding?*

A number of years ago, I was asked to work with a team in which accusations of favouritism had been levelled—particularly by one employee, Monique—against a team leader (Serge) who had only been in place for three or four months. Serge's boss wanted to ensure the issue was nipped in the bud.

When I met with Monique, she was extremely emotional about the situation and obviously cared a great deal about it. She told me Serge only took certain people out to lunch and an inner circle had formed. She knew business was discussed during these lunches, so those who were invited knew more about what was going on than those who were not. The overall result of this favouritism, according to Monique, was a divided team.

The more Monique talked about these lunches, the more emotional she became. When her initial anger gave way to tears, I shifted the discussion away from the team to explore the personal side.

> *Me:* How is this favouritism impacting you personally?
>
> *Monique:* I'm left out and I don't know what's going on.
>
> *Me:* How would you not feel left out?
>
> *Monique:* (looking at me as if I'd just asked the stupidest question in the world) Well, I'd be asked to lunch too!
>
> *Me:* So being included in the lunch date would make you feel part of the club?
>
> *Monique:* Yeah, but it's more about knowing that my boss likes me enough or values me enough to include me.
>
> *Me:* Oh, so you're not really concerned about going to lunch; you're concerned about how your manager feels about you. Is that it?
>
> *Monique:* (a little surprised) Yeah. It is.
>
> *Me:* Okay, so the invitation to lunch signals to you that your manager respects you and wants to include you in the business conversations you think he is having during these lunches?
>
> *Monique:* Yes, and I also want him to like me as a person.
>
> *Me:* All right. So a good relationship with your manager is important to you, and you are feeling uncertain about how your relationship is developing because you aren't included in the luncheons. The lunch invite is simply a signal to you that the relationship is on track. Is that it?
>
> *Monique:* (after a pause, looking intently at me) Yes.

The next phase of this conversation has to do with choosing signals of progress that are substantive and within your control.

> *Me:* If the relationship is important to you and you are not clear about where it stands, what actions could you take to either check in or further develop the relationship?
>
> *Monique:* (a little embarrassed) I could talk to him about it and ask him for feedback.
>
> *Me:* Yes, and let him know the relationship is important to you and that you want to build trust and confidence. Don't be

shy about saying what's important to you. And yes, it's a great idea to ask for feedback and talk about ways you could work on your relationship.

Monique: Okay.

Me: But how will you track your progress? What will be your signals of progress?

Monique: Hmm . . . I'm not sure. I guess if I see we're building a rapport. You know, that conversation is easy. And I could always invite *him* to lunch!

Me: Absolutely! And what else? What about the trust and confidence?

Monique: I could check in with him and ensure I am meeting all his expectations just to make sure we're communicating enough.

Me: Good! And that ongoing feedback will be an excellent way to track progress.

The issue wasn't favouritism or lunches. The issue was that Monique did not see the progress she hoped for in this new relationship. Monique had fallen victim to a subconscious signal of progress, which was leading her down the garden path. She was so focused on the lunches she did not take the time to clarify her true desires. Because she had not clarified her true desires, she could not take positive, constructive actions to support them or find healthy signals of progress.

With a little bit of coaching, Monique's whole approach to the lunch problem changed. She was able to identify the underlying issue (feeling she wasn't on track with respect to the relationship with her boss) and take concrete steps to address it.

As leaders, we need to understand our team members both individually and collectively so that we can help create conditions that will give them a fulfilling work experience. Helping identify the unconscious signals of progress held by individuals or your team collectively will give you the information you need to influence how they experience progress. Remember, the greater the sense of progress, the more likely your team will be fired up.

Pay attention

There are signals of progress around us that simply do not register in our brains. We somehow disregard them and filter them out. Your environment may contain many signals you simply miss. Watch out for them. Every step forward, every bit of progress that is appreciated encourages the heart and marks our advancement, thus building confidence for further achievement. Learning how to frame for progress is an important leadership skill.

Editing this book is a case in point. As a fellow author, Lynn, once said to me, "Who would have thought drafting would be the *easy* part?" Drafting is often fast-paced, and progress is clearly visible. Editing, on the other hand, can be slow and tedious. It requires reflection, further consideration and discussions with your editor. Although the results are fruitful, the pace is much slower, so appreciating what seem like minor changes (like catchier titles) that will add up to big things (more reader engagement) is important.

I was also reminded during the editing process that it's useful, when in the trees, to take a step back and look at the forest to gain perspective on progress. For example, we had been editing many small chapters in soft copy for what seemed like a long time. Editing in small chunks, while helpful from a content-management perspective, was troublesome (at least for me) from a progress point of view. It felt too slow.

I decided to pull all the pieces together and print a hard copy so I could review "where we were at." To my surprise, a good chunk of the book was already finished! When I stepped back and gained a broader perspective, I saw much more had been accomplished than I had thought. By staying in the trees too long, I missed seeing the forest of progress we had made.

This could be happening right now to people on your team—perhaps to you as well. Stop, step back and take stock. I guarantee you'll see progress that previously escaped your view.

A metaphor for understanding

Imagine this: You've decided to go on a cross-continent holiday. You love to travel and you've always fantasized about taking a road trip. You apply for a sabbatical from work (call it an early midlife crisis), you trade in your car for a Volkswagen Type 2 (officially known as "hippie van"), you invite your best friend along for the ride (any road trip worth its salt includes a partner in crime) and the adventure begins!

You decide to take secondary highways so you can see interesting scenery and visit smaller communities. You haven't spent much time with your best friend lately—you've been super busy at work—so there's lots of catching up to do. You stop when you want to explore all the new and interesting places you've always wanted to see.

Some days you drive 500 or 600 kilometres, other days you stay put and enjoy yourselves. You're bursting with new experiences, gaining lots of new knowledge about people and places and, in some cases, making new friends. Life is good . . . for a while.

But the continent is huge, and driving isn't everything it's cracked up to be. Soon, the quaint little communities start to look more and more the same, you're running out of things to say to your buddy—in fact, he's starting to bug you a little—and pulling off to hang out at a scenic lookout has lost some of its appeal. To make things worse, you've come to a long stretch of desert that will take you a few days to cross. You're beginning to wonder if this road trip was such a good idea after all. The early excitement of "Where shall we go next?" gives way to "Are we there yet?"

Work is a lot like going on a road trip. Sometimes it feels like a fresh adventure, and signs of progress are easy to spot. Sometimes work is more like a desert crossing—everywhere you look, there's just sand and scrub, not a sign or signal of progress to be found. Worse, your goal appears as a distant mirage.

Yet it doesn't mean progress isn't there. It is. Often, seeing it can be accomplished simply by looking at the world differently. Maybe you track your progress more carefully on a map, or set driving goals for the day, or learn about desert terrain and develop a trained eye—one that notices subtle changes you had previously missed. Maybe you stop and take interesting photographs of boring things. Maybe you seize the opportunity to have deeper conversations with your friend. Once you challenge yourself to notice and appreciate the possibilities for progress (and the signs thereof) that exist around you, you'll be surprised at how much you've been missing.

Reframe for progress

Fern, an HR manager in a large multinational company, received a well-deserved promotion and moved into a global role. Her primary mandate was leadership development. However, Fern also had her own goal: she wanted to change the complexion of the organization (literally) so that people at all levels of the company reflected the demographics of the populations the company served.

Fern undertook her new role with terrific passion and gusto. She had big plans. Over the next few months, I heard a lot about Fern's initiatives from her colleagues:

- She had started a women's network so senior women could help mentor younger or less-experienced women in the company. Women were attending the network events with great enthusiasm.
- She had partnered with a national university to connect her company's leaders with relevant and powerful research around diversity, inclusiveness and culture. High-potential leaders were raving about the new program.
- She had the ear of the CEO, who met with her regularly for updates on her various projects.

When I next saw Fern, about 12 months after her new posting, she was quick to express her frustrations. She said she felt dejected. Not much had changed; the company still looked the same. As I listened, I became more and more confused. Her colleagues had told me about so many wonderful Fern-led changes and initiatives, yet Fern herself sounded depressed. Where was the disconnect?

Then it hit me. Fern was so focused on her end result that she did not see or appreciate the progress she had made toward her goal. She was missing the opportunity to celebrate the success of the women's network as an important building block. She was deaf to the positive feedback offered by leaders on the collaboration with the university. She was definitely not appreciating her access to the CEO, who had the power to effect transformational change!

So I asked Fern a pointed question: "When you took on the new job, where did you expect to be in 12 months?"

Fern considered for a moment and then replied, "I don't exactly know, but I thought more would have changed."

In my mind's eye, I had a vivid flashback to my days with a Crown corporation, and I knew Fern had become blind, as I had, to important signals of progress. Her impatience for transformation stopped her from seeing and enjoying the significant gains of her first year. As the old adage says, Fern needed to "take time to smell the flowers."

She had planted many seeds. She had nurtured them into healthy green shoots that were beginning to mature. But her expectations for progress were disproportionate to the time frame. A multiyear project cannot be completed in 12 months, at least not under normal circumstances.

I pointed this out to Fern, and she instantly recognized that her expectations for progress—the speed at which she wanted the company to transform—had derailed her normally positive attitude. We talked about how she could pay more attention to feedback and notice modest but significant changes, to ensure she remained energized and passionate about her long-term goal rather than becoming cynical and depressed about the organization. We both left our coffee date feeling excited about the possibilities for year two!

When we frame or reframe for progress, we feel encouraged (which helps build endurance for "long-haul" projects or goals), we nurture a sense of self-worth (because we recognize the impact of our actions), and we build muscle strength for more complex, challenging projects. As leaders, we need to first know how to do this for ourselves. Then we need to help our teams and colleagues do the same.

Progress-ive tips

As a leader, there are many things you can do to help yourself and your team keep a high sense of progress. Through years of research and a coaching practice, I've developed the following tips to help leaders sustain progress for their teams.

1. **Communicate expectations.** Progress is relative. You need a meaningful goal to gain a sense of progress, so make sure everyone knows the deliverables and why they matter. Often this means clarifying objectives and providing clear performance standards. Don't leave this to chance or leave your intentions vague. Precisely articulating your expectations is a discipline that will serve you well.
2. **Set the pace.** Let your team know what you believe is a steady, healthy pace. You don't want them burning out with frantically intense action (especially if there's no urgency). Nor do you want them to move so slowly that people get frustrated with a snail-like rate of change. Think this through. Talk to your team about

it. Set a pace that makes sense for your team in the context of your environment. The right pace for your team will help you sustain a healthy sense of progress.

3. **Manage perceptions.** Since progress is subjective, you need to help people see what is there to be seen. For those who think nothing's moving forward, take the time to point out what has changed in a factual and pragmatic way. This is about grounding them in reality. A leader is often the only person on the team who has the vantage point to appreciate seemingly small changes from a broader point of view. It is your duty to make sure you communicate them. Otherwise, your team may become disillusioned.

4. **Highlight value.** Your team may see progress but not value. For example, they may know they have successfully implemented a new back-end system, but since they don't talk to clients directly, they have no sense of the difference it has made to simplify business transactions. As a leader, connect them to meaningful client feedback. Make sure you highlight the progress in such a way that they can see they have contributed to an enhanced client experience. Make it visible by posting client feedback by the water cooler or having the service manager come in to thank your team—or, better yet, ask a high-profile client to provide feedback in person.

5. **Cheerlead.** When you know a task or project requires a great deal of time and effort for modest progress, it is crucial to encourage your team. Do not stand silently on the sidelines as they labour. At regular intervals, tell them you appreciate their efforts, let them know that the incremental changes they are making are needed and valued and assure them the small wins are building the foundation for bigger ones. (Note: What you say must be true. Cheerleading must be authentic and grounded in reality.)

ACTIVITY

Pick a project or a current objective. Make a plan based on the above five tips. Make notes below.

....

....

....

....

....

....

43 | MAKE BAD POTS

Fire up by encouraging yourself and your team to play and experiment. Celebrate the effort and risk-taking, and always look for the learning so that future actions can be informed by past experimentation. When you or your team succeed, reinforce the role of playful discovery and keep encouraging more and more of it. You and your team will remain fresh, creative and inspired.

A dear friend of mine, Ric, who lives in the UK, collects unusual and beautiful ceramic pots. Among his collection are several created by Tim Andrews (http://www.timandrewsceramics.co.uk/), a ceramicist who lives and works not far from Ric's home in Exeter. Ric often visits Tim, whose work has become popular and highly sought after over the years. The once unknown artist now sells his pieces at handsome prices.

During a visit to Tim's studio, after his work had become well known, Ric noticed that Tim was not in his usual fine form. Having developed a certain rapport with the artist, Ric felt comfortable sharing this observation. Tim's response was simple, straightforward and profound: "I don't have time to make bad pots," he sighed.

> **MISTAKES MOVE US FORWARD IN INTERESTING WAYS.**

On the surface, this might seem like an odd statement. "Who needs more time to mess up?" you may well ask. Most of us feel we screw things up enough just going about our daily business! But I don't think the artist's complaint referred to commonplace errors like those we make every day. I believe he was frustrated by the fact that he was so busy he no longer had time to experiment, to develop his craft, to push himself beyond his comfort zone, to create new innovative designs, to try something different—something that might turn out to be unusual, even remarkable.

The initial results of experimentation are not always stellar. Playing with an idea or forging into unknown territory more often than not results in failure until one discovers what does and does not work. The creative process is often iterative; it requires time, reflection and often many false starts to realize an artistic vision. (The same applies to most processes of discovery. Consider the famous quote by inventor Thomas Edison: "I have not failed. I've just found 10,000 ways that won't work.") But the artist cares enough about his idea, concept or vision to keep making bad pots until he produces one with which he is satisfied.

Do you have time to make bad pots? Do you *take the time* to make bad pots? Or do you fill each available minute with tasks from your to-do list? Do you take on so many projects you are rushed off your feet? Do you ever say "stop" to a boss who thinks all is well and you still have capacity? Do your team members say no to you? Are they stretched too thin? Do they have time to make bad pots, or is their workload such that their creativity and problem-solving skills are dulled? As a leader, you need to ensure your team has time to make bad pots so they can take your group's performance to the next level.

Do you value downtime, silence, play and experimentation sufficiently to build it into your work time? Do you insist that your team does as well? Most of us feel making space for creating is a luxury. Many of us—including our organizations—have developed the habit of busy-ness. One of the most common challenges in the modern workplace is "action-itis"–there's simply too much going on!

When my colleagues and I conduct employee-engagement surveys on behalf of clients, we measure various emotional states. Of the emotional states we measure, *rushing* and *obsessing* are two of the most common experiences. Both involve high action levels. People try to do too much. They push themselves, not as an exception but as a rule, to get it all done. The results, as everyone well knows, are ill health, lackluster performance and burnout.

Lack of reflection enables unhealthy states. No downtime means no time to assess the importance and relative value of tasks. We don't triage our tasks; instead, we try to do them all. Like Ric's friend Tim, we don't have time to make bad pots. We're too busy trying to get our to-do list done. This is truly unfortunate, as making bad pots is essential in this age of innovation. Our workplaces need to support reflection, experimentation and play. Our intuitive, creative right brains are starving for time to help us be successful.

Eight tips to create more creative space

Here are some suggestions to help you and your team think about time as your most valuable asset and select how you use it carefully.

1. **Know why you should meet.** Many managers and team members tell me they are booked from the time they walk into the office until close of day, which means they need to work on their own commitments after hours. This is neither healthy nor sustainable. When invited to attend a meeting, be clear on why you should attend—or not! Do not automatically accept all invitations. Clarify meeting objectives and your role, and then decide whether or not to attend.

2. **Consider alternatives.** Perhaps you can send one of your team members or colleagues to a meeting instead of attending in person. Maybe you can read the minutes rather than attending or secure the objective by means other than meeting.

3. **Meet efficiently and effectively.** If there are no other alternatives to meeting, make sure you make the most of the time spent doing so. Consider employing facilitation processes to make the best use of the time spent.

4. **Identify your personal peak times.** Determine when during the day you are most productive and work intensely at that time. For example, if you are a morning person, carve out two hours early in the day for your thinking/creative time. Perhaps even do your first two hours from home if necessary to ensure you do not get interrupted. Help your team members figure this out as well.

5. **Schedule time to reflect.** Block your calendar for two hours each day for personal work, just as you would for meetings. Protect that sacred time. Ensure your team does the same.

6. **Take on your top three.** Each morning, list the three most important things you need to accomplish that day. No "should-do" or "others want me to do" or "insignificant to-do," even if they've been hanging around for a while. Instead, choose three things that will make the most difference to your overall goals and objectives. Write them down. Don't post them on your calendar as a task. Book three different time slots in your calendar when you will work on these three items. Make them earlier in the day so you can't bump them for urgent last-minute items. Once you have nailed down this technique, teach it to your team and insist they use it or adapt it to suit their own style.

7. **Let go of the little stuff.** Do not get obsessed with keeping your e-mail folders clean, for example. With the rate of e-mail, this is almost an impossible task. One could easily spend hours on end filing items from inboxes and sent folders. File only the important stuff and delete the rest. I know many people who spend significant time sorting through e-mails when they could be investing in team development, strategic planning or tackling the frustrating obstacles. Check in with your team on this as well. E-mail is the biggest time-sucker in today's workplace.

8. **Assemble think tanks.** If an existing problem requires a cross-functional remedy, offer to host a discussion to facilitate a solution. Teach your team members to do this as well. For example, Phong's department constantly missed deadlines because the progress of its work depended on other departments, which had different priorities. Phong and his team developed workarounds, but they were inefficient and demoralizing. Finally, Phong invited his peers and some of their team members to join his own team in finding interdepartmental solutions to the issue. They held a think-tank session, unleashed people's creative problem-solving skills and removed the obstacles.

ACTIVITY

Which of the above suggestions could you begin implementing right now? All of them are habits. Select one and decide how to make it a practice. For example, "Beginning today, I will ensure I am clear about the objective of each meeting I accept and understand how I will add value before I confirm my attendance."

Suggestion I want to work with: ....

How I will convert it to a habit (what I will say or do differently moving forward):

....

....

....

44 | TURN OBSTACLES INTO PROGRESS

Roadblocks are inevitable. How we view and approach them is what makes all the difference. Say, "yes, and . . ." to every obstacle so it can become a building block for change, an innovation, a clever strategy or a new direction. When your team has purpose, removing or reconceiving obstacles will get your team back into the groove and fired up to keep moving forward.

A s a leader, you want to keep your team momentum strong. It takes effort to kick off a project or a new initiative or even to execute a relatively simple change in workflow processes. Once the ball gets rolling, momentum builds and things can get pretty exciting. Your team is in flow, or to use a sports analogy, "in the zone."

Eventually, however, even the best-laid plans run into bumps in the road and slow down; sometimes they even come to a grinding halt. The obstacles may be relatively easy to overcome (a little creative thinking does the trick), they may be more substantial (a lot of brainstorming and many resources are required to resolve the issue) or they may seem insurmountable (the road has been closed for major repairs and there are no obvious detours in sight).

> *OBSTACLES CAN STOP YOU OR KICK-START YOU.*

A leader's job is to help his team identify and remove obstacles. The leader's involvement may range from a little support in the form of some advice, perhaps, to hands-on assistance, such as marshalling additional resources. If the leader does not help remove the obstacles, she puts her team's engagement and passion at risk.

Three leadership skills I recommend to help deal with obstacles are checking in, seeking alternatives and creating options. Let's take a closer look at each with some case studies.

Check in

One of the trickier aspects of road-clearing is knowing when a team needs help. A surprising number of teams and individuals are silent about their challenges. People often want to sort things out on their own for a variety of reasons. They may underestimate the problem, want to demonstrate their competence, not want to bother the boss or others or be fearful of reprisal.

It's the leader's responsibility to check in with the team, ask questions and monitor progress to ensure things are moving at the expected pace. How to check in? Simply sit down and ask your team about their challenges and how they feel they are progressing. Here are some questions you can ask:

- "How is the task/project progressing?"
- "What signs of progress are you making? How do you feel about them?"
- "What other signs are you looking for that you aren't yet getting?"
- "Is progress happening as quickly as you would like?"
- "Is the task/project moving along efficiently?"
- "What obstacles are you facing? What actions can you take to overcome them?"
- "What obstacles have you overcome to date? How did you manage them? What can you control? What can't you control? How can you stay focused on what you can control and take the rest as a given?"
- "What milestones have you hit? Which ones might you miss? How can you mitigate this? How can you create new ways of working to meet the milestones?"

I once worked with a team that sold various products and services to consumers. For a certain payment type, they had to issue manual receipts. The client received a copy to confirm payment, the business kept a copy for their files, and accounts needed a copy to ensure the finances were accurate. The existing process dictated that the receipts were to be handwritten using carbon paper to make duplicates. The process was time-consuming, antiquated, cumbersome and frustrating, and the team was keen to automate it.

They had made a request to their manager, but nothing seemed to be happening. Months had passed with no forward movement on the automation. Worst of all, the challenge of writing hard enough to ensure everything was legible through all three copies many times per day had caused a number of employees to develop carpal tunnel syndrome!

When I raised the issue with the manager, he was surprised. He had been aware of the need to automate but had not realized the process was resulting in health issues. When I asked about the automation timeline, the manager scoured his inbox looking for the information. Eventually, he retrieved an e-mail, dated some eight months earlier, stating that the automation would happen as soon as all bugs had been worked out with the IT department. The manager had not made any further inquiries. Over the course of the next few hours, he re-established contact with the IT department and reactivated the initiative.

The manager was understandably embarrassed he had neglected to keep abreast of the situation and thus inadvertently dropped the ball. Plus, he had not understood the serious impact of the manual receipt system on his team. When I followed up with the team, I asked them why they had not been more vocal with their manager to ensure the project remained a priority. They said they knew their manager was overwhelmingly busy, and they didn't want to add to his workload.

Inaction on both sides grew a small obstacle into a much more substantial one. Had the manager been attentive and probed his team for further information, or had the team spoken up regularly and emphatically, the obstacle would have been removed months earlier. In the end, the team was thrilled to have an automated system. Needless to say, the hit of progress resulting from its implementation, combined with the ongoing efficiencies it produced, rekindled the team's engagement.

Seek alternatives

One of my greatest frustrations when I worked in a very hierarchical organization was the numerous levels of approval required for what seemed like the simplest things. And when a project had real substance? Watch out! It could take weeks or months to move it forward, particularly if someone with authority was not convinced of its merit. When seeking approvals, I generally barraged those involved with e-mails, presentations, meetings, endless follow-up and the like in an effort to push through my projects.

It wasn't until many years later, when I was consulting, that one of my clients unknowingly gave me an excellent alternative for managing similar situations. As I watched her work over a period of time, I noticed she approached things quite differently than I had. If one of her projects was stonewalled, she would find—through her network of internal contacts— who within the company influenced the stonewaller. She would eventually discover and employ to her advantage the links between herself, the influencer and the blocker. Through her professional network, she was often able to advance her initiatives via key influencers. I wished I had thought of that instead of exhausting and frustrating myself as I had done.

As creatures of habit, we tend to approach workplace challenges the same way time after time. We use tried and true strategies because they have been effective for us at some point. The problem is, they may be ill-suited or ineffective in the current circumstance. Eventually, we all encounter obstacles that are more difficult to get out of our way. When that happens, it is easy to become frustrated, even disillusioned, perhaps to the point of giving up. To make progress, we sometimes need help finding new avenues, new strategies and new tools.

Where we only see a dead end, others may see possibility. This is the time to reach out and seek others' perspectives. Share your problem with wise counsellors to see if they have come up against similar roadblocks. Ask lots of questions. You may be surprised at the number of options that suddenly open up for you to pursue.

Create options

There's nothing worse than being on a roll and getting stopped dead in your tracks. You're working on an important goal, you have a solid action plan, and you're seeing good results with your preliminary work. Then, all of a sudden, a new CEO is appointed, and she wants to review all key initiatives to ensure each significant project has a solid business case behind it. You must persuade the new CEO your project deserves continued funding. Your project—which had been moving along quite nicely, thank you very much—comes to a standstill, and the progress you've made to date looks like it may go down the drain. What do you do?

A CEO client of mine found himself in exactly this situation. The new group CEO decided to review market conditions before investing further in certain lines of business. Sam, my client, found this exceedingly difficult. He didn't know how to keep his team motivated and engaged. Worst of all, he was concerned that if the market review took too long, he might lose some of his best people to his competitors. His team was full of young, bright people who were amazing at getting stuff done and poor at twiddling their thumbs.

Sam and I considered various possibilities. Clearly, he viewed the situation in a negative light. He felt the wind had been taken out of his sails, and he was completely deflated. I understood. Yet to move through it, he needed to appreciate that how he chose to manage the situation would determine whether or not his team regained a level of engagement. So I pushed him to think about how his current reality could be an opportunity. "Could something positive emerge from this?" I asked.

We began to brainstorm. It was slow going at first, but asking good questions soon got our creative juices flowing: "How could we use our time to further other interests?" "How could we use this time to support our own personal professional development?" "How could we help the new CEO with his review, if not of our own business line, perhaps in another?" "How could we support other teams that are maintaining the day-to-day business?"

We soon had a long list of great ideas and actions Sam and his team could implement while their project was under review. In the end, they managed to maintain meaningful progress during the hiatus by helping other departments who were under-resourced.

You can always act on your own behalf to remove obstacles in your path. You don't need to stand by helplessly. Checking in, seeking alternatives and creating options will help you find your next steps forward. Know you can influence your work in profound ways.

ACTIVITY

Remember: As a leader, promote progress by removing obstacles that can't be controlled by team members. In the rare occasions they can't be removed, you should explain why. You must also take on obstacles that the team or individual members do not have the skill, power, authority or political savvy to tackle. (Note: It's important that leaders share their approaches with team members so everyone's skill in this area develops.) Facilitate overcoming obstacles by checking in regularly with team members, seeing alternatives and creating options. Start by writing your answers to these questions below:

- What obstacles do your team members currently face? List them.
- What actions are the team taking to address them?
- If these actions are not effective, how could you help your team discover other possibilities for action?
- Are there actions only you can take? If so, ensure you execute these in support of your team.

45 | TAKE SEVEN STEPS TO "YES WE CAN"

When a team is infused with optimism, it will find the energy to tackle even the most daunting task. When your team believes it can figure things out, it will tap into its innermost creative center and produce amazing results. Saying yes to circumstances and seeing team talents prevail will set your team alight with vitality and power.

"How can we...?" questions are key to overcoming obstacles. As a leader, you can facilitate productive, even powerful sessions using them as your springboard into creative thinking with your team. Often, leaders hesitate to surface blockers and barriers, especially if they already have a heavy workload. However, you can work with your team to find a solution and in the process make it enjoyable instead of onerous.

Helping your team remove hindrances and free themselves to focus on value-added activities will boost their engagement in multiple ways. They will feel more confident in their ability to effect change, less frustrated by challenging situations and more able to engage in meaningful work. A little time and effort upfront, from you as the leader, will have a huge pay-off on the backend. Below is a seven-step process to help you work on obstacles collaboratively.

> STOP FOCUSING ON WHAT YOU CAN'T DO AND START FOCUSING ON WHAT'S POSSIBLE.

Step 1: Identify obstacles

Pose the following question: "What obstacle, if addressed, would improve our progress?" Sometimes many obstacles will come immediately to mind; sometimes there will be few or none.

Step 2: Do an environmental scan

To stimulate people's thinking, think about your current workplace and consider the following questions:

- "What needs our attention?"
- "Where can we make a difference?"
- "What business challenges excite us?"
- "What changes would make our (or our customer's) life much easier?"

As you answer the above questions, consider the following:

- clients
- resources
- problems
- weaknesses
- products
- services
- systems

Step 3: List "how can we?" questions

Based on your work above, create a list of "how can we?" questions that describe what you would like to improve. Try to be as specific as possible in the language you use. For example:

- "How can we improve our response rates?"
- "How can we improve our core processes?"
- "How can we build stronger support?"

Step 4: Select your "how can we?" challenge

Examine your list and consider the following evaluation criteria:

- If accomplished, how much impact will it have?
- How easy will this be to achieve?

Select the item that has the most potential for impact and will require the least amount of effort. You want to pick something that can be done in a reasonable amount of time and that will make a noticeably positive difference.

Step 5: Brainstorm courses of action

Brainstorm a list of possible actions that you could take to make your "how can I?" challenge a reality. Remember to follow key brainstorming rules: work fast, quantity not quality matters, no debating, build on other's ideas.

Step 6: Select actions

Select the actions from your brainstorm list that you believe have the best chance of leading to your success. Then plan how you will get the time and resources you will need to accomplish these actions.

Step 7: Implement plan

- Commit to taking these actions.
- Set a timeline for each action and stick to it.
- Track your progress along the way.
- Adjust action plans as needed.
- Celebrate your successes and failures.
- Document your lessons learned.
- Involve others in your actions and results.

Facilitate a "how can we?" meeting.

Put your collective brain to work and find innovative solutions by focusing everyone on possibilities vs. obstacles. The single most powerful question for moving from a current state to a future desired state is to ask, "How can we?" Ask this question to your team to help them overcome real or perceived obstacles. Here's how:

1. At the top of a flip chart, write the "How can we?" question, filling in the specific goal that you are having difficulty with.
2. Take two minutes to brainstorm all possibilities for action.
3. Create a list of at least 10 items.
4. Discuss each idea to explore its potential. In other words, build each one into the best it can be.
5. As a group, decide on your best idea. You can vote or use a consensus model. It's up to you.
6. Generate some next steps and create your progress plan.

When circumstances are tough, the "How can we?" question is even more important. In particularly challenging situations, it's helpful to add a precursor to the question: "Given this set of circumstances, how can we _____?" The brain is our most powerful tool. If we set it to work on a problem, it will generate innovative solutions through creative and original thinking. Follow the same process as above, only this time, describe your given.

For example, "Given the new CEO has frozen our project, how can we make use of our time in meaningful and productive ways?" Ask: "Given _____, how can we _____?" Be prepared to be surprised by your brain's performance!

ACTIVITY

Pose yourself a "how can I?" question and use the process described above. See what results you get. You may be surprised by the results you get when you tell your mind there must be a way. Although this question can work when reflecting alone, it's best used when working with others.

How can I ....?

My Ideas:

1.
2.
3.
4.
5.
6.
7.

8.

9.

10

Think about each idea more deeply to explore its potential. Build each idea into the best it can be. For each idea, ask yourself, how could I make this idea feasible? Notes:

....

....

....

Decide on your best idea, generate some next steps, and create your progress plan. Next steps:

....

....

....

46 | SEE PROGRESS AS ITS OWN REWARD

Rewards and recognition are short-term motivators. Intrinsic motivation comes from caring deeply. When your team really wants to achieve its goal, reaching milestones and seeing the team get closer and closer to its desired end result will spark a sense of progress and gratification. That spark will in turn light the fire of energy and enthusiasm.

We care. We devote time. We invest energy. We want to see forward movement! When we do, we experience a sense of progress that gives us a hit of satisfaction. Progress functions as a reward for having invested of ourselves.

We have taken action and seen its impact. Achieving progress confirms our ability to create the things that matter to us. It tells us we can act on our own behalf in ways that are productive, useful and helpful to us and others as we journey to even more important end results.

When we care about what we are creating—our goals, objectives, desired end results—we are motivated more by intrinsic rewards than by extrinsic ones. We may appreciate rewards like financial gains and public recognition; however, we need to satisfy our intrinsic drivers to sustain our self-motivation and sense of well-being at work.

> **INTRINSIC MOTIVATORS CREATE A SENSE OF WELL-BEING.**

Writing this book is a perfect example of this. Once it was completed, it gave me an immense hit of progress. I didn't need any external validation. Bringing the idea of the book to fruition was its own reward. External rewards (or "carrots") did not come into play.

In my workshops, many people tell me that their fulfillment at work comes from a job well done and they, not others, are the audience for this performance. It's great when a manager or colleague gives positive feedback, but that's not what's fundamental. Others appreciating the work is supportive and boosts confidence, perhaps, but what matters more is that they know they did their best and that they find the result pleasing.

When we are motivated by intrinsic drivers, we possess a form of autonomy that is extremely valuable. Our emotional state at work is not dependent on other people or organizational reward and recognition systems. These are secondary. What is primary is how we experience and appreciate the output of our caring, time and effort.

If we are grounded in this, external forces will not throw us off our game. We will be less vulnerable to what other people think and systems that are often flawed. We will discover that we are genuinely more fulfilled in our work, wherever we work.

Suelyn was an early-childhood educator. She taught in the two-to-three-year-old room at her day care. Compared to other education professionals, early-childhood education is underfunded, and as a result, the teachers are substantially underpaid. When she thought about this inequality, Suelyn would become upset and irritated by the injustice of how little society valued this key stage of developmental. How was it possible that, despite the research clearly showing the preschool years as the most important years of development, it was the most neglected facet of our education system? It just didn't make sense!

Yet Suelyn continued to pursue her career. Why? Her answer was simple: "I love to see children learn and progress. That's my reward."

When you care enough about the goal, extrinsic motivators are secondary to seeing your goal become a reality. People need to pay their bills and look after their families, but they'll sacrifice many discretionary expenses to pursue their deepest aspirations. When they see they are hitting their milestones or receiving meaningful feedback or closing the gap between where they are and their desired end result, this progress is like a hit of endorphins. The sense of well-being that accompanies this experience of progress is its own reward.

This is the key to self-motivation. Once we have attained this orientation at work, we become very grounded in what matters most, and our forward movement fuels more activity, which creates more forward movement. It is a virtuous cycle that is self-sustaining.

ACTIVITY

1. List the life goals that matter most to you.

....

....

....

2. List your career/work goals that matter most.

....

....

....

3. Pay attention to what gives you a sense of progress.

....

....

....

As you learn to pay attention to the progress you are making toward those goals that matter most to you, you will become increasingly conscious of a sense of well-being. You will focus less on external motivators and more on your own aspirations, with progress as its own reward.

Unleash your team's energy by dealing with any inability to work constructively together. Allowing unhealthy behaviours to exist drains your team's oomph and, ultimately, dampens team spirit, depletes resilience and does everything *but* fan the flame of success.

I have seen senior teams struggle with dysfunction throughout my career. As a relatively young senior manager in my early thirties, I was shocked to discover that our executive team was largely at war with one another—with turf wars between operations, retail and/or sales and marketing—and that our collective bargaining process had become so entrenched in petty politics that the top leadership from both sides would not have looked out of place on a school playground.

> **EMOTIONS ARE AT PLAY WHETHER WE WANT TO ADMIT IT OR NOT.**

It was truly disillusioning to know that one could not count on the senior team to live the stated values of the corporation. At the time, I thought such behaviour was unique to the organization for which I then worked. It wasn't until I had been consulting for a while that I accepted the fact that most senior management teams fall considerably short of functioning at peak performance. They battle with localized protectionism based on competition for resources; nepotism, particularly in smaller companies or markets; distrust, linked to a need to maintain position or always look good; cliquishness, which becomes exclusionary and gossipy; and . . . well, my list could go on and on.

Resolving dysfunction requires the team to want truth, at all costs. They must be willing to separate fact from fiction, to admit mistakes, to advocate for the greater good and to analyze reality while examining assumptions and beliefs. This is a tall order. It's challenging and uncomfortable work, until one discovers that being real is much easier than wearing masks and pretending. Dropping pretence and ridding the higher echelons of an organization of dysfunction frees leaders to focus on co-creating an amazing business. What a groundbreaking concept!

It's in our nature to be emotional as well as intellectual. When we try to separate the two, we do so in a vain attempt to persuade ourselves and others that we can, when in fact we cannot. We must bring our multiple intelligences to bear in the workplace—to be all we can be, as individuals and as organizations. Life is too short and too precious to settle for anything else. An exceptional work experience is available to each and every one of us, if we choose to make it happen. But it can only be realized if we embrace the fullness of who we are as human beings.

Misunderstandings with team members are inevitable. We will have challenges adapting to others who hold different preferences, we will make real mistakes communicating, and sometimes we will even hurt others in the process. We are human and imperfect. How we deal with imperfection makes a difference. When we acknowledge the situation, hold honest conversations and forgive each other, we open the door to ongoing functionality instead of disastrous dysfunctionality. Functional teams remain healthy and happy, and they benefit from the positive interactions and collaboration that re-emerges when conflict is well managed. Ensuring functionality is a leadership responsibility. Make it yours!

When we allow our emotions and intellect to be distracted by unproductive and unhelpful issues and behaviours, we have less energy available to fulfill our aspirations. We do others, our organizations and ourselves a disservice when we don't make it real. We hold everyone back, including ourselves, when we operate under the misguided belief that emotions don't belong in the workplace and thus fail to navigate effectively the emotional topography in our organizations.

Humans are emotional beings, wherever and whenever we engage with each other. Suppressed emotion results in dysfunction regardless of the environment; it happens as often in the workplace as it does in the home. Denying the vital role that emotion plays within an organization is counterproductive. And, in my experience, such denial is invariably rooted in fear, not aspiration. As in baseball, there are different leagues of dysfunction:

- **In Little League,** the team meets all its mandated objectives. However, personality differences lead to conflict rather than to taking advantage of diversity to achieve greater things.

- **In the minors,** the team struggles to meet all its objectives. Some are met; some are missed; "explainable variances" deflect accountability. Team members do not support each other to ensure all objectives are met. They are unable to collaborate, recognize needs other than their own or shift resources to areas with greater needs (because they don't see them, or to protect their own position). Team members withhold support to others to conserve their own energy and time.
- **In the majors,** the team cannot communicate without conflict. Most e-mail exchanges trigger negative reactions in recipients, followed by unreasonable responses, which escalate into all-out, tit-for-tat war. One or more team members may monitor other team members for evidence that *they* are to blame for team problems, leading to the formation of divisions and tribes who then recruit outside supporters, thus creating battle lines that may penetrate other layers of the organization. A total breakdown ensues, and the team cannot work together. At best, individual members attend to their own work and try to ignore everyone else.

ACTIVITY

Look at your team objectively.

- What dysfunctional behaviour exists on my team?
- What outcomes result from this dysfunctional behaviour (be concrete and specific)?
- How do I contribute as the leader?
- What can I do about it as the leader?
- How can I explicitly build a healthy team?

....

....

....

48 | FIND THE FIT

Tackling conflict or dysfunction requires you to use many tools in your toolkit. Before you begin, take time to reflect and plan. The case study below is to help you see how you might use this toolkit. Know your efforts will pay off and persevere. Think of yourself as a guide who will help the team navigate through the quagmire and come out on more solid ground. To move the team forward, you need to fearlessly confront the dysfunction.

A few years ago, I worked with a team of four, all of whom had been with the organization for some time. The three employees had worked together for a number of years, while Tamira, their manager, was new to the team and to the role of leadership. The quartet was struggling to work effectively together.

Tamira really wanted to get the team on track and develop her leadership skills, but she was stumbling. The symptoms of an unknown underlying problem were:

> *IT ALWAYS BEGINS WITH A TRUE DESIRE TO MAKE IT WORK AND THE COURAGE TO LEAN IN.*

- The team felt Tamira was a control freak and a micromanager.
- Tamira encountered argumentative behaviour and resistance when she assigned tasks.
- Team members were beginning to complain loudly about Tamira.
- There was gossip about others in the office, especially regarding favouritism.
- The team felt neglected, overlooked and underrecognized.
- Absenteeism and tardiness were the norm.
- Team members did enough to not be fired, but they were definitely coasting.

If you managed this team, how would you handle the situation? How would you coach the new manager? How would you support the team?

I used Open Space Technology (OST) to start the meeting, and then we moved to creating the agenda. Once that was done, we focused on deep discussions and encouraging certain types of thinking. Finally, we reconnected members to their aspirations. Let's look at these topics in depth.

Opening the space

As the facilitator, I kicked off our first session using one of the techniques OST (see chapters 26 and 27). We sat in a circle on comfortable chairs. Luckily, this client had a lounge, so we were able to set up a living-room-like environment.

I asked Tamira to listen and question to build her understanding so she could see things from the employees' perspective. In other words, she was not to worry about defending herself, but instead to develop an empathetic view of how the team experienced their work environment. As part of the process, team members answered my open-ended questions, and based on their answers, we explored the topics they introduced. My role was to host a conversation for the team.

I began a round-robin discussion by asking two questions: "What are your hopes for this working session?" and "What do you fear might happen?" Each person had a moment to reflect before they spoke, first about their hopes, then about their fears. Here are the types of thoughts they shared:

Hopes	Fears
We can learn how to work with our manager.	Nothing will change.
We can improve our relationships.	Being honest will make things worse.
We can be happier at work.	I'll feel caught in the middle.
We can learn to work as a team.	We won't know what to do to make it better.

My job was to create a space in which people could be real—that is, free to say what they truly thought and felt in a non-threatening environment—and then work with that energy to move the group forward. I also asked the group to share what they saw as the key message from the list of hopes.

After I heard from everyone, I summarized: "So, everyone wants to figure it out. People have a true desire to make this work for their own personal health as well as for the good of the group." I did the same for the fears: "Everyone is uncomfortable with the uncertainty of the situation. You all fear a positive outcome is not guaranteed, and how to get to a positive outcome might remain unclear."

The foundation for the session was now laid. Before we moved into content, it was crucial to ensure that each person made a clear choice about her own role moving forward.

I continued: "Before we begin our work in earnest, it's important we each think about our own personal desires and the extent to which we are prepared to act upon those desires. In a moment, I will ask you to share your answer to the following question, stated in various ways to help people think it through: 'Given you each want to make the situation better, are you prepared to personally do things differently? Are you prepared to make personal change? Are you willing to invest intellectually and emotionally in making things better?'"

I gave them all a chance to reflect, and then I heard from each in turn: "Yes." "Yes." "I think so." "Yes."

I asked the "I think so" individual what it would take to move her to a "yes." After a moment of reflection, she said, "I just don't want to be disappointed again."

I responded, "So you are afraid that you will try hard and the outcome won't be what you are hoping for?"

After a bit of silence, she said, "Yes."

I reminded everyone again about choosing in favour of true desires and not avoiding action because of fear. "So, if you really care about making this work, would you rather take action to make it work or would you rather not try, in case you are disappointed in the end, and just see what happens?"

The woman smiled and said, "Okay, I get it. Yes, I want to try, and yes, I am willing to invest in it." And we were off to the races!

Creating the agenda

I moved on to content with a version of, "Tell me a little bit about your work."

One participant offered, "The things we are told to work on don't always makes sense, given what we're supposed to be doing."

I asked a number of follow-up questions: "What are you supposed to be doing? What's an example of what you are told to do? And, why doesn't this make sense?"

During the conversation, Tamira was able to get a picture (empathetically and non-judgmentally) of how her employees moved through their day. Remember, empathy in an organizational leadership context is really about understanding another's thoughts and feelings so you can imagine how they experience their work environment. It is not about agreement; it's about learning how to address the situation through deep understanding.

In the case of this team, many of the issues they voiced revolved around what the manager "should" do; what good management "should" be; why things were not fair; and why they felt disrespected.

Deepening the discussion

Once we were clear about how they saw the work, we explored the situation through the lens of personal accountability. My question back to the group was, "Given each of you is a player in this unfolding drama, what choices have you made that contributed to your frustrations? And, likewise, what choices have you made that contributed to your successes?"

Often, this question is met with stunned silence. As a facilitator, I listen carefully, demonstrate empathy and feel compassion around what people experience as challenging circumstances. No one wants their work to be a miserable, unfulfilling, frustrating daily grind. I totally get that, and when I listen, it's with complete honesty, sincerity and empathy. But it's my job to help them take charge of the situation and change it into something better.

Empathy allows you to understand others' perspectives so you can support them effectively. You can connect with them as another human being who is struggling with a life situation. We all struggle. We all become confused about how to move forward. We all want to be happy.

But empathy alone will not resolve challenging situations, because without a clear understanding of the power of their own choice, they will stay stuck. To properly support others, you must help them see how the choices they have made contributed to the existing situation.

So back to the question at hand: "Given that each of you is a player in the unfolding drama, what choices have you made that contributed to your frustrations, and what choices have contributed to your successes?"

One person, Anne, finally spoke up and said, "Well, I probably should have told the manager off a long time ago!"

I thought, *Well, not ideal, but it's a start!* So I replied, "You are on the right track. Let's look more carefully at what you are saying. But let's take it back to before you were angry. What could you have done when you first felt the work you were being asked to do wasn't making sense?" Again there was silence, and the conversation went on like this:

Anne:	You mean the first time I thought, "Why are we doing this? This isn't what we normally do!"
Me:	Yes.
Anne:	You mean I could have spoken to the manager then?
Me:	Yes.
Anne:	Well, I wanted to see where it was going to go.
Me:	(laughing) So, you decided to make it a game? Reminds me of Blind Man's Bluff. (More shocked silence.) Why wait? Why create a game from something straightforward?
Anne:	I didn't feel comfortable approaching the manager.
Me:	Why?
Anne:	I didn't know how she was going to react.
Me:	Had she given you any cause to fear her?
Anne:	She sometimes gets irritated.
Me:	Do you sometimes get irritated?
Anne:	Well, yes.
Me:	Is that any reason to fear speaking with you?
Anne:	No.
Me:	Okay then.
Anne:	I see what you are saying. You're saying I could have talked to the manager right away when I was first upset about doing that work.
Me:	Yes. (Pause.) What difference would it have made if you had spoken to her about it right away?

Anne:	Well, it might have clarified things. I still might not have liked the answer though.
Me:	True, on both counts. What other difference would it have made?
Anne:	I would have gotten it off my chest and maybe even offered a couple of suggestions.
Me:	Yes, and what might be different today, if this had become your general practice?
Anne:	What do you mean?
Me:	If you had made it a habit to sit and talk with your manager and work to understand more about what you were being asked to do (the whys and wherefores) and had offered your input, if you felt there were better ways of handling it, what might be different today?
Anne:	Oh. Well, I guess we'd be communicating better and probably wouldn't be dealing with so many built up issues.
Me:	So, moving forward, what will you do differently?
Anne:	Talk more.
Me:	My mom always told me you have to talk and talk and talk. She was talking about marriage, but it's as true at work!

One by one, we tackled each issue through the lens of personal accountability. It's always easier to see what the other person could have done differently. It's easy to judge and criticize. For most of us, it's much harder to see what *we* could have done differently. However, when we see how our choices create our reality, we feel the power inherent in choosing, and we can then see how new choices will lead to a different result.

Although the discussion may feel awkward initially, it will lead to positive energy. Why? Because when we understand, we choose consciously, and we feel more empowered. When we feel empowered, we are not victims. I have seen the process of people "getting" this hundreds of times—it is a tremendously liberating awareness.

Encouraging thinking: using the "Improv Rules"

As the session moved to specific topics—such as rejiggering a workflow process, helping someone uncover their true aspiration or addressing an issue—we used the simple and powerful "Improv Rule" of always saying "Yes, and . . ." so the team could have the positive experience of working together without criticism, without rejection and without tension. Instead, they experienced working together in a way that communicated that everything offered was valued.

It is crucial for teams to experience themselves working in a high-functioning manner. Healthy teamwork must be more than a concept in the realm of theory and possibility; it needs to be grounded in reality. Finding opportunities for teams to collaborate while resolving conflict is critical. It's fun to create together. It's fun to build on each other's ideas. It's fun to appreciate each other.

Providing a real challenge—an issue or opportunity upon which to focus—springboards team members into seeing each other in a new light. They will have real evidence that they too can work in fulfilling ways. It is possible, and it is happening! Without this type of experience, people may remain fearful and doubtful.

Reconnecting to personal aspirations

As we explored their work, I discovered each team member was clear about what was frustrating but didn't have much to offer in terms of what was enjoyable about the work. We ended the first session with clarity around a substantial list of what wasn't working and a few things that were, reframed through the lens of personal accountability. In essence, we had a snapshot of current reality.

I began to suspect their frustrations were a symptom of a deeper underlying disconnect with their own career goals and personal aspirations. In the second session, I shifted to a discussion about aspirations to help them connect more deeply with their sense of purpose.

Here's an outline of the sequence in the second session. I began by asking each person to journal for 30 minutes describing their ideal day in detail. This was an activity I did with a colleague, Alex, in 1995; it provided me with great clarity around my long-term plans, and I've used it to great effect with clients throughout my consulting career.

The description was to be written in the present tense and provide a blow-by-blow description of the day: "I wake up in a four-poster bed overlooking the ocean. Beside me is my life partner. I slip out of bed and walk into the kitchen, where I make a pot of my favourite coffee to sip while sitting in my patio garden . . ." And so on.

This kind of written "visioning" affords people who have lost sight of their true aspirations with an opportunity to reconnect. Sometimes I get asked if the day described should be a weekday or a weekend, a question arising from the fact that most people do not love what they do. I always answer a weekday, but discuss, after the activity, why it doesn't need to matter.

On this team, everyone except Tamira wanted a different career, but none of them had done anything about it, mostly because they felt it wasn't realistic, or they were afraid of making the wrong move. Fundamentally, fear prevented each of them for different reasons. Learning to act in service of your true desires takes practice, as does having the courage to set aside your fear so that being afraid doesn't stop the show. The members of this team hadn't flexed their aspirational muscles or conquered their fears.

One by one, we talked about each person's ideal day. We offered encouragement, asked questions and occasionally offered suggestions. Our goal was to align today with tomorrow: How does your current work help you achieve your longer-term goals?

When people see this connection, work is infused with greater purposes and hope is restored. When the connection is not strong, people need to soul-search to discover how best to serve what matters most. When people see their work as supporting their overall progress in life, they rarely worry about the small stuff and are more inclined to tackle the bigger stuff if doing so will support their aspirations.

At the end of our time together, two team members decided to re-engage fully with the team and the organization. Two decided to leave the organization to pursue their entrepreneurial ideas. The latter recognized that, ultimately, the issues within the organization were not the main causes of their discontent. Instead, their own choices were poisoning their attitudes. They needed to say yes to their true desires and trust they could handle whatever happened in the future.

None of these participants has ever looked back. Those who remained with the organization now had a mindset and the communication skills to work together productively. The manager learned she had lacked empathy and had limited others' input. After our session, she removed those barriers and learned to connect authentically with her team.

Remember, as a leader when you refuse to accept dysfunction and confront it fearlessly, you will eliminate this obstacle to progress.

ACTIVITY

Think of your own issue and design a session around solving it. Select two or three tools from the 50 in this book. [Add lines below as per other activities]

....

....

....

49 | UNTHINK UNWANTED BELIEFS

If you want to keep your team fired up, make sure conceptual thinking—including unwanted belief systems—doesn't diffuse energy and distract. When indivudals are unable to create the results they truly desire or sustain their success, chances are conceptual thinking is running interference. To get the juices flowing again, fearlessly dig deep to discover what's holding you and your team back.

K arthik is a professional in a large bank. His goal is to acquire top-level certification in his field. Joseph, Karthik's manager, appreciates his dedication and attention to detail, as well as the fact that he digs deep to understand how things work.

However, Joseph has also observed that Karthik's strengths are liabilities at times, mainly because he uses the same approach and applies the same strengths to every situation. Although Joseph feels Karthik is competent in his current role, he has started to think Karthik doesn't have "what it takes" to attain the higher qualification. Specifically, Karthik's poor time-management skills prevent him from meeting deadlines, creating enough study time and taking on development projects.

BAGGAGE? WHAT BAGGAGE?!

Joseph has spoken to Karthik several times about how he manages his time and has suggested ways Karthik could meet deadlines and study more efficiently. But Joseph feels these recommendations fall on deaf ears, and Karthik's problematic behaviours persist. Though Karthik is initially unaware of it, he holds dear a concept, a personalized ideal, toward which he feels he must strive.

In reality, Karthick has an opinion of himself that he'd rather not have. This unwanted belief causes him to oscillate: he takes action to achieve his true desire (acquiring further credentials), but the closer he gets to attaining it, the more he feels compelled to satisfying this personalized ideal in order to hide from what he really thinks about himself.

I borrow the terms "conceptual thinking" and "unwanted beliefs" (one example of conceptual thinking) from structural dynamics creator and consultant Robert Fritz. Many people hold unwanted beliefs or opinions about themselves that might include things like "I am worthless" or "I am a disappointment" or "I am stupid." These exist in our subconscious. Our conscious mind does not want to see them. After all, who among us wants to see that we think we are stupid or worthless?

Fritz describes how we adopt "compensating strategies" to hide our unwanted beliefs or opinions from ourselves. Why? Because we confuse belief with reality, and we think beliefs about ourselves matter. We bury them in our subconscious, pretend we don't believe them and adopt strategies to protect ourselves from having to see them. The protective strategies are observable actions designed to disprove the unwanted belief. For example:

- We do things like taking on projects or helping people to prove we have value, if we believe we are worthless.
- We seek success to prove we are not a disappointment.
- We present our intelligence—by accumulating degrees or writing articles, for example—to prove we are not stupid.
- Or perhaps, like Karthik, we are painstakingly thorough, obsessing about details and digging deeply to understand, just to prove to ourselves that we know what we're talking about as opposed to pretending to know or being a fraud. (In fact, "I am a fraud" turned out to be Karthik's underlying belief about himself.)

Compensating strategies do not serve our truest desires. Rather, they are created by fear. We are afraid our beliefs might actually be true, and the strategies serve to hide what we really think about ourselves from ourselves. However, what we believe about ourselves doesn't matter unless we let it. An unwanted belief is an opinion, a perspective, a view, an interpretation; it is not reality. Unwanted beliefs have power only if we give them power. We give them power by allowing them to matter. This is always to our own detriment, as they become obstacles to meaningful progress.

Why would we let an opinion (rather than a fact) drive our choices and actions? It makes no sense. Think about it: If today we believe we're worthless because somewhere in our past someone made us feel this way, we relinquish our personal power in the present to our interpretation of a past event we may not even recall. When we take on such opinions about ourselves and give them credence, we put energy into disproving them—taking on projects we don't really want to prove we have value, pursuing high-powered careers to prove we are competent and collecting degrees and awards to prove we are smart.

Compensating strategies like these will distance us from our true desires because, rather than spending time and energy on our aspirations, we spend time and energy trying to disprove beliefs that exist only in our own minds. I know many professionals who burn out trying to prove to themselves and others they "can make a difference" rather than enjoying a career rooted in the creative process, one in which their goals and actions are aligned with their deepest aspirations.

How can we prevent unwanted beliefs from sabotaging the pursuit of our true desires and therefore compromising progress toward that which matters most? One way is to think critically and see unwanted beliefs for what they are: opinions, interpretations, views, perspectives. We cannot change them, but we can befriend them with a humorous "note to self" like: *Gee, isn't that funny? I actually believe I'm a fraud.* When we see the silliness of thinking an unwanted belief matters and how it drives our behaviour as a result, we can laugh and let it be. Most people describe understanding unwanted beliefs and how they work as a huge relief.

So it was with Karthik. Once he identified his unwanted belief about being a fraud—defined as pretending to know more than he did—he let go of always needing to understand every detail and instead focused on the main issues or points. This saved him a lot of time, which in turn enabled him to meet deadlines. This is progress! Ceasing to obsess over every detail also helped him study efficiently, thereby allowing him to take his exams within the year. This in turn qualified him to work on a number of new development projects. More progress!

Once he let go of needing to prove he wasn't a fraud, his performance improved and he got on with creating the results he truly desired. Each one of Karthik's successes built momentum for the next in a virtuous cycle that helped him realize his goals.

Identifying unwanted beliefs

One way to identify unwanted beliefs is to pay particular attention to how we react to certain types of feedback. When we receive feedback that touches on our unwanted beliefs about ourselves, we may react defensively and dispute the information instead of listening and learning from it. If you find yourself reacting defensively to feedback, ask yourself what lies behind the reaction. Is it an attempt to protect yourself from having to acknowledge an unwanted belief?

By leaning into the feedback, we can learn a great deal about how others see and interpret our behaviours, and potentially about our unwanted beliefs as well. We might even see how choices we make hinder us from achieving what we most desire. Whatever happens, we surely gain by listening rather than reacting. Here's a four-step process to get you started:

1. **Think of feedback you have recently received.** Write it down so you can focus more easily. For example, consider this feedback about your use of e-mail: "When you use e-mail to communicate a sensitive topic to me, I find it leads to further misunderstandings rather than resolution. Somehow, in the way you write it, it feels hurtful to me, and I feel I have done something wrong. And then I react to that. I think it would be better to call me or Skype me."

2. **Reflect rather than react.** Think about your actions and possible underlying motivations. Following the above example, ask yourself, *Why did I choose to use e-mail instead of a phone call? What's in it for me?* Remember, our instinct may be to protect ourselves from a perceived threat (such as feedback that might reveal an unwanted belief). This often activates our "fight or flight" mechanism and we get defensive. Instead of justifying why e-mail is necessary or getting defensive about how we write or blaming the other person for being too sensitive by reading things into the note that we didn't intend, we can consciously choose to take on the feedback and really listen and consider how it might relate to our unwanted beliefs.

3. **Articulate your underlying concerns.** For example, "I have a need to keep things moving forward and so often avoid possibly lengthy calls or try to avoid delays caused by scheduling calls, which can take days. In other words, I am worried that I won't deliver, so I am overusing e-mail to help me get things done, even when a telephone conversation might be more appropriate. My sense of urgency and need to deliver is driving my use of e-mail when it may be more sensible to consider other ways to handle

situations. My belief about myself might be that *I'm incompetent* and my compensating strategy is that *I always deliver!* If I view e-mail as a tool to help me deliver, I may overuse it."

4. **Ask yourself, what are the merits of the idea?** What you can do differently next time? With greater awareness of what drives your choices and actions, you are better equipped to take on the feedback and consider how it can help the work and the relationship. Upon reflection, you may see that e-mail is a crutch for you, relieving the pressure you place on yourself to deliver to prove your competence. Next time, you may choose to schedule a call to move things forward, preserve the relationship and achieve better long-term results. A true win-win!

It may take some courage to look deeply within ("under the hood" as the saying goes) but the rewards are worth it. Investing time and energy in compensating strategies designed to keep us from seeing what we truly believe anyway is a waste of time. At best, it keeps our emotional discomfort at bay but this comes at a price: our focus is not on making progress toward our aspirations but on making ourselves feel better. Fearless leadership is about seeing what's there to be seen, facing it and moving beyond it.

ACTIVITY

Make a summary of how to discover your own unwanted beliefs.

1. Summarize the feedback you received by writing it down in a sentence or two.

2. Reflect on your actions and motivations (what was in it for you) instead of reacting by justifying or defending.

3. Write down your underlying concerns and how they link to possible unwanted beliefs.

4. Write down what you'll do differently next time to get a better result.

....

....

....

To explore further conceptual thinking, check out Robert Fritz's collection, especially *Your Life as Art* (2003) and *The Path of Least Resistance* (1989).

50 | TAKE CARE OF YOURSELF AND YOUR TEAM

It is impossible to fire on all cylinders if your gas tank is low or empty. Self-care is not optional for those who want to operate at full strength. We can ignore our health and well-being for a period of time, but there are always consequences. Lead by example; ensure you replenish the energy you spend by taking care of yourself and then help your team do the same. When you choose in favour of health, you and your team will have what it takes to stay fired up and produce your personal bests, fueling sustainable progress.

The most successful CEO I know exercises vigorously every day. But many leaders struggle with self-care; they work long hours, sacrifice their personal lives and neglect their health for the corporate cause. They put their own well-being on the back burner, while, ironically, insisting their team members practice work-life balance.

I have met many leaders, at all levels, who neglect their health in significant ways. A young CEO I once coached would meet me in his office, hunched in his chair, large dark circles under his eyes and a gaunt look on his face. He was exhausted from the challenges associated with leading the company. When I raised the issue of self-care, it brought him to tears.

MAKE HEALTH A FUNDAMENTAL CHOICE.

Similarly, a mid-career executive I know works incredibly long hours, goes home for a couple of hours in the evening to be with her daughter and then, after putting her daughter to bed, spends time on her Blackberry or laptop until the wee hours of the morning. When I check my inbox, it's not unusual for me to find e-mails she has sent at one, two or even three o'clock in the morning. She rarely sees her friends, and her husband has become a roommate. Sadly, I've seen this pattern develop with many female executives over the years.

A plethora of research documents endless examples of the ways in which unhealthy work habits like these reduce life expectancy. Here are just a few:

- Less than six hours sleep per night creates sleep debt. This unequivocally impacts your performance the following day, no matter what type of work you do. Over an extended period it increases your health risks by making you more prone to, for example, diabetes, heart disease and many other ailments. Various studies show that nightshift workers are thought to decrease their lifespan because of disrupted sleep.
- The fact that stress is a killer has been widely known for years. Accumulated stress, without timely relievers, will knock you dead without warning. In *The Blue Zones* (2008), author Dan Buettner writes about his research on centenarians, where they live and more importantly how they live. His work clearly shows that low-stress work is a contributor to longevity; it also describes how those with greater stress can use social connections and relationships to release and recharge. A memorable example of this is something as simple as Blue Zone village women meeting daily after their chores are done to kibitz, share stories or break bread.
- Mindless eating makes you fat and compromises your performance. When we eat mindfully, we experience the taste, smell and texture of the food. This creates a fuller experience and leaves us feeling more satisfied. Mindless eating, on the other hand, often leads to overeating, and we end up consuming more calories than we can burn off. As we gradually gain weight, we tax our bodies, which in turn makes it more difficult to sustain our energy and our performance.

Like Dan Buettner, Dr. Trisha McNair, a UK-based physician, has compiled statistics around longevity. Her book *The Long Life Equation* (2008) includes the following observations:

- Eating breakfast can add one to three years to your life. (See? Your mother was spot on about starting the day the right way.) Health experts say eating a good breakfast infuses you with energy, kick-starts your metabolism and helps you stay a healthy weight.

- Exercise (including daily walking) adds, on average, four years to your life. Walking is also a fabulous way to spark creative thinking; it can put you in a flow state that generates new ideas and insights.
- Having a social circle also adds four years; it reduces stress and increases the likelihood that we will be influenced to make healthier lifestyle choices. Human beings are designed to be social. Our limbic system requires it, even if we are introverts. We are naturally empathetic and able to connect to others in meaningful ways.
- According to Daniel Goleman and other researchers, psychopaths (people unable to experience empathy) constitute less than 1 percent of the population. That means 99 percent of us are "people who relate to people." Suppressing empathy (because it may be perceived to be a sign of weakness) is unhealthy for our spirit. Try nurturing it (and others) instead, and add years to your life in the process.
- Oddly, adding six years is good dental hygiene (including brushing and flossing your teeth). A great deal of research clearly connects gum health with disease. The healthier your gums, the less likely you will encounter problems with heart disease, your respiratory system and diabetes.
- A number of years ago, I attended a conference with a group of dentists who happened to be interested in organizational development for their large practice in California. During our time together, the issue of flossing came up, and the information they provided was fascinating. I was amazed to learn it can help reduce heart disease and diabetes, as well as dementia.
- Next on McNair's list, tied at seven years apiece, are "finding true love" and "having faith." (The latter is also a finding of The Blue Zones.) Love enables us to flourish and thrive. Research with laboratory animals, such as rats, demonstrates the negative effects on mammals of being neglected, ignored and unloved. Faith provides a sense of security and, according to The Blue Zones, reduces anxieties and worries as outcomes are left in God's hands.
- Surprisingly, the habit with the greatest potential to extend your life, adding an average of nine years, is believing the glass is half-full. Yes, being optimistic—seeing what is good in the world and appreciating what exists—can add almost a decade to your

life. In my opinion, optimism is not about a false sense of what is right with the world. It does not mean denying the reality of negative, painful experiences. However, it does mean that when you've had those experiences, you are able to see the good that can come from them. You are able to identify the blessings in everything. Dr. McNair emphasizes that people who see the glass half-full are better able to recover from injury or illness. A friend of mine, Heather, recently shared with me advice she gave her elderly father: "Dad, it's important to focus on what you can still do, not what you can no longer do." Exactly!

As a leader, incorporate health into your work goals and encourage your team to do the same. Help them create and sustain a sense of well-being by doing the following:

1. Do not reward long hours of work. Instead, focus on setting clear priorities and reward people who spend their time on the right things.
2. Help people see the glass as half-full: teach people how to learn from all events, point out what's good about a situation and guide people in gratitude.
3. Take an interest in people's interests outside of work. Encourage everyone to have a hobby or outside work interests.
4. Bring in your organization's wellness coordinator to speak to your group and provide tips and techniques.
5. Ensure each team member has stress-management training.
6. Insist your team members take their breaks and lunch.
7. Organize team-building days that involve physical activity and healthy eating.
8. Advocate for healthy snacks in the vending machines or lunchrooms.
9. Buy pedometers for each team member and set targets together, increasing them as you get more fit.
10. Create a sense of community on your team. Make sure people take time to get to know each other and build trusting relationships.

It's great to have meaningful goals but we need our health to execute our action plans. Looking after our health supports our aspirations. So be good to yourself.

ACTIVITY

Many New Year's resolutions involve a health goal, which is great! The problem is that many resolutions don't make it to the end of January. Why is that? The answer is actually simple: people may make a list of resolutions, but they do not make fundamental choices.

Take a few minutes now to think about the following question: *Do I choose to be healthy?* Really think about it. Sit with the question. Do you really want to be healthy? Do you value health more than other things that are taking your time and energy? Think about the things that are more important to you than health. Think of all the things that are less important to you than health. If you were to make health a primary choice, how would that impact your day and your habits? If you choose to be healthy, what three small things could you do every day that would contribute to your health? Once those have become routine, choose another three things.

....

....

....

↗ A FEW FINAL WORDS

I hope this book has provided you with support as you grow and develop as a leader. My intention has been to share with you the practices I have found most impactful, both as a leader and as a consultant. Since there were many different ideas, tools and techniques presented in the book, I would like to take this final opportunity to reinforce the key overriding messages. To recap:

- In *Part 1: Mindset and Mind Games*, we looked at how our mindsets establish the boundaries for action. When our minds are clear and centered, we act in accordance with our values and keenly respect another's rights and freedom. With this mindset, we lead authentically and courageously and connect in meaningful ways with our team. When our minds are muddled by fear, self-interest or distrust, our actions create barriers to protect us from imaginary danger or loss. With this mindset, we diminish ourselves and others by manipulating or deflecting accountability.
- In *Part 2: Inspiration and Action*, we looked at how inspiration enables followers to act in service of what is most meaningful, regardless of the current set of circumstances. When we believe in our shared purpose and our team's abilities and communicate this clearly and genuinely, we invite team members to collaborate and forge the needed pathways to arrive at shared goals. Leaders with self-motivated, self-organizing teams will see tremendous gains as a result of this self-sustaining energy and enthusiasm.
- In *Part 3: Feedback and Feedforward*, we examined the various facets of feedback and focused on the ten types of feedback that help us feedforward to co-create our desired future. Through complete and comprehensive feedback loops, we create a true learning organization, breeding high performance.
- In *Part 4: Progress and Fearlessness*, we explored the importance of progress in engagement—and how, in order to make significant progress, we sometimes need the courage to take a leap of faith. Sometimes this entails making many mistakes to find a workable

solution or generate a breakthrough idea; sometimes it means bravely confronting obstacles to clear a path forward. At the heart of engagement is a sense of making a difference or a meaningful contribution. As a leader, managing meaning and progress are essential to firing up your team. Time invested here will be well rewarded with high performance and achieving the results we set out to create.

Each day presents new opportunities to learn another leadership lesson. Taking time to pause, observe and reflect will enable you to tap your own knowledge, connect with your core values and listen to your own wisdom to guide you along whatever leadership path you choose. Other people and resources will undoubtedly assist along the way; however, never underestimate the strength and foresight of your own inner leader.

Be mindful.

Be fearless.

Making small changes to get big results

You never know from where leadership lessons will come. Every moment is a gift. Every moment is full of possibility. Just this morning as my spouse and I were getting the kids off to school, I took a pause to appreciate the gift of routine. As a change fanatic, I sometimes undervalue structure and the everyday. But everything has its place. In this case, routine enables us to meet the school bus without stress and with little energy expended, so we are fresh to begin the new challenges of our day at school or at work. Such a small thing, but it sets a solid foundation for the day.

Thinking about this led me to reflect more deeply on the health program I began a year ago. Two doctors had advised I should lose 40 pounds (or 18 kilos) as well as ensure my immune system and other underlying health systems were strong. The task seemed overwhelming. It had taken me years to gain that weight, and I was well-entrenched in a lifestyle—which included a lot of travel for work—that did not easily support this aim.

I started very small: taking supplements thrice daily to support my adrenal system. Once this routine was established and had become a habit, I added another small thing. This time, I changed my approach to breakfast. I found a recipe for very healthy smoothies that were rich in fibre, calcium, probiotics, and vitamin C and D. I loved the taste, so it was easy to make this my new morning habit.

Next, I added walking. I began to schedule 45 minutes in my calendar every day for a walk around our local lake. This was a little harder to do, as it was easy for other things to interfere. However, I decided I would treat it like a meeting, and after that, it was easy to accommodate. Another habit was formed.

Each new habit I added reinforced the other habits, and I started seeing benefits. I lost weight, I slept better and my back didn't ache in the morning. I kept tackling the list my doctor gave me, item by item. And in a relatively short period of time (four months), I had lost most of the weight and was feeling energetic and grounded.

By adding one new small habit at a time, I created a virtuous cycle. At first, the change appeared slow, but as I added more and more new small habits, the change kicked into gear and, in hindsight, happened very quickly. This was a huge lesson for me about establishing small new habits to create transformational change.

So I encourage you to pick one small idea from this book and create a new habit. Don't think about your old habits, just focus on creating a small new habit. Practice this habit until it becomes an easy routine. Then pick another idea and do the same. You will begin to witness changes in yourself as a leader and in your team. It will begin as a subtle, gradual change, but as the days, weeks and months go by, you will experience a meaningful and perhaps transformational change.

Relish the journey. That's half the fun! It will be incredibly empowering for both you and your team. Work will become more fun, and you will see amazing results. Most importantly, you will know that you can be the leader you most want to be—and you will have a team that's fired up to support your shared purpose.

GLOSSARY

accountability: Not about creating a blame game, accountability is about seeing your choice for what it is. A culture of accountability means people understand they create what matters and can always see a way forward.

alignment: Helping people focus on a common goal.

ambiguity: Our complex world defies being known completely. The ambiguity is what we have yet to explore.

archetype: Symbols or patterns of a model where things are representative or copies. An example is *victim, villain* and *hero*.

aspiration: The desire to seek to attain something. The precursor to inspiration and action.

being present: Putting aside distracting thoughts and focusing on the here and now.

catalyst: Something that causes a change or causes something to move forward.

collaboration: A collective created activity best engaged in by those who play.

deep dive: Originally a scuba-diving term, to *deep dive* means to go beyond the surface on something.

diversity: Different beliefs and perspectives. Diversity is an asset when it can push the group's thinking beyond the obvious.

dysfunction: Inability to work constructively together. Dysfunction ultimately dampens team spirit and undermines success

empathy: Understanding another's thoughts and feelings so you can imagine their work environment. It's not agreement, but learning to address the situation.

EQ: Emotional quotient, also known as emotional intelligence, is the measure of one's ability to navigate the emotional terrain of one's life—or, for a leader, to navigate the emotional terrain of the organization.

feedback: Communication in order to successfully execute a purpose. Examples include performance appraisals, auditing and surveys.

feedback loop: Tools used to gather information about a gap between the actual and the parameter in order to change the gap in some way. It is important to decide what to measure, how to measure it and when to feed the information.

feedforward: When feedback becomes an activity that moves people toward future success, it is *feedforward*.

groupthink: A mode of thinking where a desire for harmony overrides any discussion of alternatives.

inspiration: Derived from a compelling purpose, inspiration moves a team toward action.

leadership: Leadership begins with holding a personal value. Leadership is about relationships, and a leader impacts the careers and lives of the people on their teams.

mental models: Assumptions we hold as we reach conclusions. Mental models are shaped by experience, values, ethics, beliefs, biases, assumptions and judgments.

mindset: A mindset is a particular way of thinking about something that's often unseen and unchallenged. A mindset can be either positive or negative.

Open Space Technology: OST is a meeting method that aligns people's passion and willingness to take responsibility. Its four principles are 1. Whoever comes are the right people; 2. Whatever happens is the only thing that could have; 3. Whenever it starts is the right time; and 4. When it's over, it's over.

player and knower: A *player* is someone who is willing to explore—willing to play to find the things that they don't know. Play allows us to begin with not knowing so our experiences aren't clouded by bias or current paradigms. A *knower* is someone who thinks he or she already knows; this individual often relies too much on expertise and often is required to be "right" at the expense of other points of view or facts.

rewards: Extrinsic motivators often related to knowers, because rewards reinforce the idea that you've arrived and the journey is complete.

scarcity and abundance: Two types of mindset that govern business. In a scarcity mindset, there isn't enough of something to go around, so people tend to be closed and unwilling to cooperate with others. In an abundance mindset, people know they have the capacity to create, so there is never a lack.

Stairway to Conclusions: A tool that can be used to show how conclusions are reached. It helps people distance themselves from emotional situations to better analyze and constructively address them. The steps are: observable reality, filtered reality, mental model, assumptions and reaction.

REFERENCES

Blanchard, Kenneth, and Spencer Johnson. 1982. *The One-Minute Manager.* New York: William Morrow and Company.

Bodaken, Bruce, and Robert Fritz. 2011. *The Managerial Moment of Truth.* New York: Free Press.

Buettner, Dan. 2008. *The Blue Zones: Lessons for Living Longer from the People Who've Lived the Longest.* Washington, DC: National Geographic Society.

Carr, Nicholas. 2010. *The Shallows: What the Internet Is Doing to Our Brains.* New York: W. W. Norton and Company, Inc.

Covey, Stephen. 1989. *The 7 Habits of Highly Effective People: Powerful Lessons in Personal Change.* New York: Simon and Schuster.

Coyne, Kevin P., and Shawn T. Coyne. 2011. *Brainsteering: A Better Approach to Breakthrough Ideas.* New York: HarperCollins.

Csikszentmihalyi, Mihaly. 1998. *Finding Flow: The Psychology of Engagement with Everyday Life.* New York: Basic Books.

Csikszentmihalyi, Mihaly. 2003. *Good Business; Leadership, Flow, and the Making of Meaning.* New York: Penguin.

Dobson, Dr. James. 1997. *What Wives Wish Their Husbands Knew about Women.* Carol Stream, Illinois: Tyndale Momentum.

Fallis, Terry. 2010. *The Best Laid Plans.* New York: Random House.

Fallis, Terry. 2010. *The High Road.* Toronto: McClelland & Stewart Ltd.

Fritz, Robert. 1989. *The Path of Least Resistance: Learning to Become the Creative Force in Your Own Life.* New York: Ballantine Books.

Fritz, Robert. 1993. *Creating.* New York: Random House.

Fritz, Robert. 2003. *Your Life as Art.* Newfane, VT: Newfane Press.

Goleman, Daniel. 1995. *Emotional Intelligence: Why It Can Matter More Than IQ.* New York: Bantam Books.

Jung, Carl. 1964. *Man and His Symbols.* New York: Doubleday.

Kim, W. Chan, and Renée Mauborgne. 2005. *Blue Ocean Strategy: How to Create Uncontested Market Space and Make the Competition Irrelevant.* Boston: Harvard Business School Press.

Kohn, Alfie. 1999. *Punished by Rewards: The Trouble with Gold Stars, Incentive Plans, A's, Praise, and Other Bribes.* New York: Houghton Mifflin.

Kohn, Alfie. 2006. *No Contest: The Case Against Competition*. New York: Houghton Mifflin.

Madson, Patricia Ryan. 2005. *Improv Wisdom: Don't Prepare, Just Show Up*. New York: Bell Tower.

McNair, Dr. Trisha. 2008. *The Long Life Equation: 100 Factors That Can Add or Subtract Years from Your Life*. London: New Holland Publishers Ltd.

Owen, Harrison. 1997. *Open Space Technology: A User's Guide*. San Francisco: Berrett-Koehler Publishers, Inc.

Schultz, Howard. 1999. *Pour Your Heart Into It*. New York: Hyperion.

Senge, Peter. 1990. *The Fifth Discipline: The Art and Practice of the Learning Organization*. New York: Doubleday.

Thesenga, Susan. 1994. *The Undefended Self: Living the Pathwork of Spiritual Wholeness*. Madison, Virginia: Pathwork Press.

Tolle, Eckhart. 2004. *The Power of Now: A Guide to Spiritual Enlightenment*. Novato, California: New World Library.

Williamson, Marianne. 1996. *A Return to Love: Reflections on the Principles of a Course in Miracles*. New York: Thorsons.

ABOUT THE AUTHOR

Jacqueline Throop-Robinson is the CEO and cofounder of PassionWorks! Inc. and PassionWorks! Asia, and the cofounder of Breakthrough Learning Inc. and of 360 traction. Over the last 25 years, as a corporate manager, consultant and keynote speaker, Jacqueline has worked with thousands of leaders and employees in more than 20 countries. Her client organizations range from start-ups to universities to government ministries to non-profits and multinational companies. She authors articles on how to create passion in the workplace and the role of leadership in today's complex globalized environment. Recently, she contributed to Business Expert Press' *Designing the Networked Organization* (2011) and *PassionWorks! Your Guide to Passion in the Modern Workplace* (2001). Jacqueline holds a BA, BFA and MA as well as numerous certifications. You can reach her at jacqueline@fireupyourteam.ca.

For a free downloadable assessment to measure how fired up you are, or to sign up for Jacqueline's newsletter, please send Jacqueline an e-mail at the address above.

32821771R00189

Made in the USA
Lexington, KY
03 June 2014